THE SYMBOLIC VISION IN BIBLICAL TRADITION

HARVARD SEMITIC MUSEUM
HARVARD SEMITIC MONOGRAPHS

edited by
Frank Moore Cross

Susan Niditch

THE SYMBOLIC VISION
IN BIBLICAL TRADITION

Scholars Press
Chico, California

THE SYMBOLIC VISION IN BIBLICAL TRADITION

Susan Niditch

© 1980
The President and Fellows of Harvard College

Scholars Press Edition, 1983

Library of Congress Cataloging in Publication Data

Niditch, Susan.
　The symbolic vision in Biblical tradition.

　(Harvard Semitic monographs ; no. 30)
　Bibliography: p.
　1. Visions in the Bible. 2. Bible. O.T. Prophets—
Criticism, interpretation, etc. I. Harvard Semitic Mu-
seum. II. Title. III. Series.
BS1199.V58N5　1983　224'.064　　　　　83–8643
ISBN 0–89130–627–7

Printed in the United States of America

FOR ROBERT

TABLE OF CONTENTS

ACKNOWLEDGEMENTS

This monograph began as a doctoral dissertation under the direction of Frank Moore Cross. I am grateful to him and to Professor Paul D. Hanson for their knowledge, their generous guidance, and their patient teaching. Their suggestions as well as those of Professor John Strugnell have much aided me in revising the work for publication. I also thank Professors Zeph Stewart and William Bossert, Masters of Lowell House, Harvard University, for providing me with housing and financial support in my capacity as Assistant Senior Tutor during three years of research and writing. Amherst College has provided much appreciated funding for the preparation of the manuscript, which was expertly and benevolently typed by Ms. Carolyn Cross. Finally, I thank my husband, Robert Doran, for being, at the same time, my favorite teacher and best fan.

Susan Niditch
September 1979

ABBREVIATIONS

Periodicals, Reference Works, and Serials

AJSL	*American Journal of Semitic Languages and Literature*
ANEP	*The Ancient Near East in Pictures*, ed. James B. Pritchard. Princeton: Princeton University, 1954.
ANET	*Ancient Near Eastern Texts*, ed. James B. Pritchard. Princeton: Princeton University, 1950.
ATD	*Das Alte Testament Deutsch*
BA	*Biblical Archaeologist*
BDB	F. Brown, S. R. Driver, and C. A. Briggs, *A Hebrew and English Lexicon of the Old Testament*. Oxford: Clarendon, 1968.
BKAT	Biblischer Kommentar Altes Testament
BZ	*Biblische Zeitschrift*
CBQ	*Catholic Biblical Quarterly*
CTA	*Corpus des tablettes en cunéiformes alphabétiques*, by A. Herdner. Paris: Imprimerie Nationale, 1963.
Eph. Theo. Lov.	*Ephemerides Theologicae Lovanienses*
Ev. Th.	*Evangelische Theologie*
HAT	Handbuch zum Alten Testament
HSM	Harvard Semitic Monographs
HTR	*Harvard Theological Review*
IDB	*The Interpreter's Dictionary of the Bible*. New York: Abingdon, 1962.
JAOS	*Journal of the American Oriental Society*
JBL	*Journal of Biblical Literature*
Joüon	Paul Joüon, *Grammaire de l'Hébreu Biblique*. Rome: Pontifical Biblical Institute, 1923.
JQR	*Jewish Quarterly Review*
JJS	*Journal of Jewish Studies*
JTS	*Journal of Theological Studies*
KAT	*Kommentar zum Alten Testament*, ed. E. Sellin
Kittel	R. Kittel, *Biblia Hebraica*. Stuttgart: Württembergische Bibelanstalt, 1966.
LCL	Loeb Classical Library
Liddell and Scott	H. G. Liddell and R. B. Scott, *A Greek-English Lexicon*. Ninth Edition. Oxford: Clarendon, 1968.

ABBREVIATIONS

MGWJ	*Monatsschrift für Geschichte und Wissenschaft des Judentums*
Or	*Orientalia*
PEQ	*Palestine Exploration Quarterly*
RB	*Revue Biblique*
TAPA	Transactions of the American Philosophical Society
Th. St. und Kr.	*Theologische Studien und Kritiken*
Th. Z.	*Theologische Zeitschrift*
Ug V	*Ugaritica V*, Bibliothèque Archéologique et Historique 80, ed. C. F. A. Schaeffer. Paris: Geuthner, 1968.
UT	*Ugaritic Textbook*, by C. H. Gordon. Rome: Pontifical Biblical Institute, 1965.
VT	*Vetus Testamentum*
ZAW	*Zeitschrift für die alttestamentliche Wissenschaft*
ZDPV	*Zeitschrift des deutchen Palästina-Vereins*
Ziegler	R. Ziegler, ed., *Septuaginta: Vetus Testamentum Graecum*. Göttingen: Vandenhoeck and Ruprecht, 1943-.

Commentaries and Other Studies

Jeremiah

Bright	John Bright, *Jeremiah*. Anchor Bible 21. Garden City, N.Y.: Doubleday, 1965.
Cornill	C. H. Cornill, *Das Buch Jeremia*. Leipzig: C. H. Tauchnitz, 1905.
Driver	S. R. Driver, *The Book of the Prophet Jeremiah*. London: Hodder and Stoughton, 1906.
Janzen	J. Gerald Janzen, *Studies in the Text of Jeremiah*. HSM 6. Cambridge: Harvard University, 1973.
Rudolph	W. Rudolph, *Jeremia*. HAT 12. Third Ed. Tübingen: Mohr, 1968.
Streane	A. W. Streane, *The Double Text of Jeremiah*. Cambridge: D. Bell and Co., 1896.
Volz	Paul Volz, *Der Prophet Jeremia*. KAT 10. Leipzig: Scholl, 1928.
Weiser	A. Weiser, *Das Buch des Propheten Jeremia*. ATD 20. Göttingen: Vandenhoeck and Ruprecht, 1952.

ABBREVIATIONS

Amos and Zechariah

Chary   Th. Chary, *Aggée-Zacharie Malachie*. Paris: Gabalda,
             1969.

Cripps   R. S. Cripps, *A Critical and Exegetical Commentary on
             the Book of Amos*. Great Britain: SPCK, 1955.

Driver   S. R. Driver, *The Books of Joel and Amos*. Cambridge:
             Cambridge University, 1934.

Edghill   E. A. Edghill, *The Book of Amos*. Westminster Commen-
             tary 27. London: Methuen and Co., 1914.

Elliger   K. Elliger, *Das Buch der zwölf kleinen Propheten*. ATD
             25/2. Göttingen: Vandenhoeck and Ruprecht, 1964.

Hammershaimb E. Hammershaimb, *The Book of Amos: A Commentary*.
             New York: Schocken, 1970.

Harper   William R. Harper, *A Critical and Exegetical Commen-
             tary on Amos and Hosea*. New York: Charles Scribner's
             Sons, 1905.

Horst   F. Horst, *Die zwölf kleinen Propheten, Nahum bis
             Maleachi*. HAT 14. Third Ed. Tübingen: Mohr, 1964.

Jeremias   C. Jeremias, *Die Nachtgesichte des Sacharja*. Got-
             tingen: Vandenhoeck and Ruprecht, 1977.

Köhler   A. Köhler, *Der Weissagungen Sacharjas erste Hälfte
             Cap 1-8. Die nachexilischen Propheten 2*. Erlangen:
             Andreas Deichert, 1861.

McKeating   Henry McKeating, *The Books, of Amos, Hosea, and Micah*.
             Cambridge: Cambridge University, 1971.

Marti   K. Marti, *Das Dodekapropheton erklärt*. Kurzer-
             Kommentar zum A.T. 13. Tübingen: Mohr, 1904.

Mitchell   H. G. Mitchell, *A Commentary on Haggai and Zechariah*.
             International Critical Commentary 25. Edinburgh: T.
             & T. Clark, 1951.

Nowack   W. Nowack, *Die kleinen Propheten übersetzt und er_
             klärt*. Göttingener Handkommentar zum A.T. 3/4. Göt-
             tingen: Vandenhoeck and Ruprecht, 1922.

Rignell   Lars Gösta Rignell, *Die Nachtgesichte des Sacharja*.
             Lund: CWK Gleerup, 1950.

Robinson   T. H. Robinson, *Die zwölf kleinen Propheten, Hosea bis
             Micha*. HAT 14. Third Ed. Tübingen: Mohr, 1964.

Rothstein D. J. W. Rothstein, *Die Nachtgesichte des Sacharja.*
Beiträge zur Wissenschaft vom Alten Testament 8.
Leipzig: J. C. Hinrich, 1910.

Sellin   D. E. Sellin, *Das Zwölfprophetenbuch.* KAT 12. Leipzig: Scholl, 1929.

Weiser   A. Weiser, *Die Prophetie des Amos.* ZAW 53. Geissen:
Töpelmann, 1929.

Wellhausen J. Wellhausen, *Die kleinen Propheten übersetzt und
erklärt.* Berlin: Reimer, 1898.

Wolff   Hans Walter Wolff, *Dodekapropheten, Amos.* BKAT 14.
Neukirchen-Vluyn: Neukirchener, 1969.

Daniel

Bentzen   A. Bentzen, *Daniel.* HAT 19. Tübingen: Mohr, 1937.

Charles   R. H. Charles, *The Book of Daniel.* Oxford: Clarendon,
1929.

Hartman   Louis F. Hartman and Alexander A. Di Lella. *The Book
of Daniel.* Anchor Bible 23. Garden City: Doubleday,
1978.

Montgomery James A. Montgomery, *The Book of Daniel.* New York:
Charles Scribner's Sons, 1927.

Porteous Norman Porteous, *Daniel: A Commentary.* London: SCM,
1965.

The author abbreviation employed without citation of specific pages refers to that author's primary discussion of the
text at hand.

Sigla

G   The Old Greek text, as critically reconstructed.
G^{Zi} The Old Greek text, according to Ziegler. We use this
designation when we wish to contrast Ziegler's choice for
the Old Greek reading with other possibilities.
M   Masoretic text.

Other sigla follow the system of the Göttingen Septuagint.

INTRODUCTION

Many scholars have dealt with the symbolic visions of the OT, but none has approached his topic with enough attention to the relationship between history and form. The developmental, history-of-traditions approach suggested in this study leads to a new understanding of the interrelationships between twelve symbolic visions in OT: Am 7:7-9; 8:1-3; Jer 1:11-12; 1:13-19; 24; Zech 1:7-17; 2:1-4; 4:1-6a, 10b-14; 5:1-4; 6:1-8; Daniel 7; and 8. The study will deal briefly also with four symbolic visions of 2 Baruch and 4 Ezra.

The major difference between the approaches of M. Sister,[1] F. Horst,[2] and B. Long[3] and our approach is one of synchrony vs. diachrony. Each of the above scholars attempts to define the visions which concern this study, as well as a number of other OT visions, in terms of types, forms, or categories of other names. They would sort out the visions into definable groupings of like with like on the basis of content elements, the structure of these elements, theme, or any combination of these criteria of form. Their groupings or categories cross chronological boundaries and are determined on the basis of individual characteristics shared across the board by a selection of visions. The visions of Zechariah which date from the late 6th century B.C. are to be approached in the same manner and with the same expectations as the 8th century visions of Amos. The type is thus a static constant through various historical periods.[4]

---

1. "Die Typen der prophetischen Visionen in der Bibel," *MGWJ* 78 (1934), 399-430.

2. "Die Visionsschilderungen der alttestamentlichen Propheten," *Ev. Th.* 20 (1960), 193-205.

3. "Reports of Visions Among the Prophets," *JBL* 95 (1976), 353-365.

4. See, for example, Long's discussion of "oracle-visions" in Jeremiah. The "form" remains a constant though "literary setting and intention" change ("Reports," 357, 359).

Our assumptions differ. We agree with M. Sister that the
visions which comprise our study from Amos through Daniel do
share a pattern of 1) seeing an image; 2) a question about the
identity of the image; 3) an answer which interprets the image.[5]
It is important to realize, however, that this question/answer
pattern is quite consistently alike in key details of language,
structure, and content in the five visions of Amos and Jeremiah,
whereas these details have been significantly altered in the
symbolic visions of Zechariah. Other important nuances appear
in the visions of Daniel and in the post-Biblical works with
which we will conclude our study. The basic form, defined by
certain core elements which consistently appear in a certain
combination, is nevertheless a flexible phenomenon which can
grow, contract, or evolve to fit changing times and new messages. The contributions of individual authors is also a
factor which should be taken into account.

Previous work

Moses Sister divides a large corpus of vision texts into
three rather inclusive groupings:
1)   Those in which a divine being is present.
2)   Those which contain an image (but not of a divine
     being) whose meaning is self-evident.
3)   Those in which an image appears which must be inter-
     preted to be understood.[6]
On the basis of the above definitions one would expect the five
symbolic vision texts of Amos and Jeremiah, listed above, and
Daniel 7 and 8 to fall into category 3, and so they do. The
most basic problem with Sister's groupings, however, is that
aspects of each group can overlap in any one vision. Sister
makes rather subjective choices as to which aspect of a vision
is the most important determining factor. Why, for example,
should Zechariah's visions of the horsemen (1:7-17) and the
horse-chariot teams (6:1-8) necessarily fall into Sister's

---

5. "Die Typen," 428. Note the similar outline suggested
by C. Jeremias, *Die Nachtgesichte des Sacharja* (Göttingen: Vandenhoeck and Ruprecht, 1977), p. 10.
        6. "Die Typen," 425.

third category? These two visions include the appearance of at
least one self-evident divine being, the interpreting angel.
Sister's typologies are simply not precise.

Sister's lack of precision is further evidenced by the
structure or "Formschema" which he extracts from the visions of
his third category, that of the symbolic images. As mentioned
above, the outline of a core pattern is all well and good, but
Sister tends to explain significant differences between uses of
pattern as minor variations. For example, he notes that in
Zechariah, the "Gottheit is mehr transzendent geworden."[7] For
this reason, the seer asks an angel about the image; God himself does not ask the prophet about the image as in the visions
of Amos and Jeremiah. The basic question/answer pattern is a
constant; it does not really matter who asks the question. In
contrast to Sister, we believe the change in the role of the
questioner to be an important development in the evolution of
the form.

The synchronic approach of F. Horst also leads him to
three categories which he calls "Visionstypen." We quickly can
deal with one of his types, the "Geschenisvision," for it is a
non-symbolic category and does not include any of the visions
of our study. This type corresponds somewhat to Sister's first
and second groups in that the prophet sees a non-symbolic image.
To Horst it is significant that the prophet himself does not
participate in the vision. He simply reports what he has seen.[8]

Horst's category, the "Wortsymbolvision," includes two
sub-groupings: Wortspiel- or Assonanzvisions are represented
by Am 7:7-9, 8:1-3, Jer 1:11-12, and 1:13-19. In these, the
explanation of the symbolic image is achieved via word-play.[9]
In the other variety of Wortsymbolvision, audial play between
the term for the symbol and the interpretation is given up
("verzichtet") so that, "Das Bildwort lediglich für einen

---

7. "Die Typen," 428.

8. "Die Visionsschilderungen," 202-205.

9. Horst forces Am 7:7-9 into this category by an emendation of 'ănāk, which is not supported by text-critical or form-
critical considerations. See our discussion in the study of Am
7:7-9, text-critical note "d."

kundzugebenden Sachverhalt wurde."[10] The image is seen, a
question is asked as to what it is, and an answer is provided.
Jeremiah 24 and Zechariah visions II (2:1-4), III (2:5-9), V
(4:1-6a, 10b-14), and VII (5:5-11) are thus included. Horst,
like Sister, does not consider significant the identity of the
character who inquires about the symbolic image. In fact, he
states that the basic "Schema" can be so varied that "die
Fragen wegfallen, vermehrt oder zerlegt werden konnen."[11] With
that much variation, does one really have a definable form?
Another weakness of Horst's approach emerges in his placement of Zechariah vision II (2:1-4). Should this vision be
placed in the Wortsymbol type along with the others? The relationship between the symbol and its explanation is a key factor
underlying the type.[12] Nevertheless, Horst takes no notice of
the difference in the relationship between symbol and explanation in vision II versus visions VI (Zech 5:1-4) and V (Zech
4:1-6a, 10b-14). In vision II, the symbol of the horns has a
reality within its mythic context. In mythic terms, the horns
actually are horns; they represent themselves. The explanation
merely identifies them more precisely. In visions VI and V,
however, the scroll and lamps are interpreted to mean something
other than they appear. The scroll is a curse, the lamps, the
eyes of the Lord. Vision II thus evidences a subtle but
important nuancing of the relationship between symbol and meaning, a factor which is of formal importance and which should be
taken into account.

Horst's other category is the "Anwesenheitvision," in
which occur "eine Szenerie am Himmelseingang" and "die vision-
ären Teilnahme an einer himmlischen Versammlung."[13] The content elements of this type thus reflect the accoutrements of
heaven as well as the seer's participation in a heavenly assem-
blage. He is not merely an observer, but is addressed by or
speaks to the members of the image. Horst includes Zechariah
visions I (horsemen), VIII (horse-chariot teams), and IV

---

10. "Die Visionsschilderungen," 202.
11. "Die Visionsschilderungen," 202.
12. "Die Visionsschilderungen," 201-202.
13. "Die Visionsschilderungen," 198.

(investiture of Joshua) in this category. Yet why should vision III (Zech 2:5-9), which Horst has considered a Wortsymbolvision, be excluded from this category? The meeting between the two angelic figures should qualify as "eine himmlischen Versammlung," and the seer is included in the scene as one divine being relays the message of the other to him. If one approaches the question of form from the point of view of structure, Horst's category of the Anwesenheitvision looks even less precise. In terms of the ordering of elements of content, vision IV of Zechariah has little in common with visions I and VIII, whereas little actually separates the structure of visions I and VIII from the structure of II. We recall that Horst places Zechariah vision II in his Wortsymbolvision category. The same pattern of motifs is found in Zechariah's visions II (horns), I (horsemen), and III (horsechariot): 1) indication of a vision (employing a form of $r\partial h$); 2) a description (beginning with $hinn\bar{e}h$); 3) question of the seer, "What are these?"; 4) answer and interpretation by angel. In contrast, vision IV (investiture) does not contain the all-important question/answer pattern and is thus formally and typologically quite distinct from visions I and VIII. Strangely, Horst himself notes that the type appears in a formally and contentually distinct (besondere) way in the fourth vision.[14] If form and content separate the investiture vision from the others, where then is the common type? What defines it?

Similar problems emerge in the recent study by Burke O. Long.[15] Long has divided a number of "vision report" texts into "types," taking into account, he writes, not only structure and content but also the intent of the author.[16] Professor Long notes that one type of vision can be used for varying purposes, to present differing messages. In this way, he hopes to pay attention to the history of traditions.

Long's first type, "the oracle vision," includes the works from Amos and Jeremiah which concern this study. He describes them as short reports, simple in content, dominated by a

---

14. "Die Visionsschilderungen," 198.

15. "Reports of Visions."

16. "Reports of Visions," 354-355.

question/answer dialogue pattern. Long notes that the type may be adapted for varying thematic purposes. In Jeremiah 24, for example, the "oracle vision" is a vehicle for propaganda against those who do not participate in the exile.[17] This attention to the changing function of the type is valuable. We disagree with Long's description of the way in which the symbol relates to its meaning in these five visions from Amos and Jeremiah, but we will leave this criticism for later.

Greater difficulties emerge in Long's second category, that of the "dramatic word vision." For Long as for Horst, the major distinguishing characteristic of this type is the presence of "a heavenly scene, or dramatic action, a situation altogether supramundane taken as presaging a future event in a mundane world."[18] Ignoring finer questions of content and structure, Long lumps together visions of such diverse forms as Isaiah 6, an initiation vision, Amos 7:1-6, a vision whose symbols are self-evident and need not be explained, and Zech 1:8-17, one of our examples of the symbolic vision form. Long's pattern, 1) announcement of a vision; 2) transition; 3) vision sequence, is so general that it can apply to any of his varieties of vision report. Long thus has no specific symbolic vision category. His presentation lacks sufficient precision.

Long's third category, "the revelatory-mystery vision," poses similar difficulties. The "intent" of this vision type is "to convey in veiled form, secrets of divine activity and events of the future. Visionary imagery is symbolic, sometimes bizarre, and there is always a pattern of dialogue whose purpose is to decipher its esoteric significance."[19] We appreciate Long's attention to the difference in symbolism between the visions of Amos and Jeremiah versus Zechariah's visions II (horns), V (menorah), and VII (*'êpâ)*, which Long places in the third category. Why, however, does he exclude Zechariah visions I (horsemen) and VIII (horse-chariot teams) from his third category? Long's definition of this category applies equally well to these two visions. More important, we shall

17. "Reports of Visions," 359.
18. "Reports of Visions," 359.
19. "Reports of Visions," 363.

see that the pattern of content and the use of symbols in Zech
1:7-17 and 6:1-8 are identical to the patterning and symbolic
usage of Zechariah's second vision (2:1-4). Visions I and VIII
of Zechariah are simply lengthened versions of the same pattern,
extended with a complex motif which we shall refer to as "the
observation of divine events." (See below.)

The diachronic approach

As an alternative to these less than satisfying synchronic
attempts at categorization,[20] we propose viewing the twelve

20. Among the "synchronic" approaches we should also mention the work of W. A. M. Beuken (*Haggai-Sacharja 1-8* [Assen:
Van Gorcum, 1967]) and of J. Lindblom (*Prophecy in Ancient
Israel* [Philadelphia: Muhlenberg, 1962], pp. 124-148). Beuken
deals primarily with the night-visions of Zechariah. Beuken,
like Horst, senses that Zechariah visions I (horsemen) and VIII
(horse-chariot teams) differ from the other visions in Zechariah. He, however, also includes vision III (Zech 2:5-9) in
the grouping the "Situationsvision." In his view, Zechariah
visions I, III, and VIII are of a type because the word of the
Lord goes forth in each (see pp. 249-250, 258). Thus Beuken,
like Horst, is influenced by considerations of content. Why,
however, is Zechariah vision VI (scrolls) excluded? In Zech
5:3, 4 a judgment against perjurers and thieves goes forth as a
word of the Lord. Beuken's second category, the "Wortsymbolvision," a term borrowed from Horst, seems to be a catch-all
for the visions which do not include specific messengers. In
Beuken's view, this category includes visions in which the
divine action is already in motion; that is, the word has
already gone forth (p. 258). His definition does not do justice to the significant differences in the use of symbols in
vision VI (scroll) as opposed to vision II (horns). The difficulties found in the work of Horst thus reappear.
    J. Lindblom does not claim "type" or "form" status for his
broad groupings of visions. Rather, he attempts to create
large descriptive categories into which visions of a number of
types might fit. He makes a distinction between ecstatic
visions and those which he considers literary, pseudo-visions

symbolic visions listed above as participants in one formal
tradition.[21] We will not deal directly with visions which are

---

(*Prophecy*, pp. 144-145). Zechariah visions I (1:7-17), II
(2:1-4), III (2:5-9), and VIII (6:1-8) are thrown out as non-
ecstatic visions, whereas Zechariah's other visions are considered ecstatic. Lindblom's claims of genuine status for some
but not all of the visions with which he deals are difficult to
support. His distinctions simply are not consistent. (See
Long's criticism of Lindblom in "Reports of Visions," 354.)
Similarly inconsistent are his distinctions between "pictorial"
and "dramatic" visions (*Prophecy*, pp. 124-128). Lindblom considers the initiation vision in Isaiah 6 to be dramatic since
seraphim fly, the prophet is touched, and he talks. Action
takes place. Yet the vision of the flying scroll in Zechariah
2 is not active enough to qualify as a dramatic vision, nor are
the female figures who go forth with wind in their wings in
Zechariah 5:5-11 (see *Prophecy*, p. 145). Lindblom's view of
that which is "dramatic" is a subjective one. His categories
are as unsatisfying as the supposedly narrower types of Beuken,
Long, Horst, and Sister.

21. One should note that the approach of C. Jeremias is
more developmental than those of the scholars discussed above.
He regards the visions of Zechariah as a link between those of
Amos-Jeremiah and Daniel (*Die Nachtgesichte*, pp. 47, 107, 227)
and like us notes that certain key nuances appear in Zechariah's
use of visions (*Die Nachtgesichte*, pp. 92, 94, 227-233). On
the other hand, Jeremias shares with previous scholarship an
emphasis on the content of the visions and a neglect of their
structural form. He really does not approach the symbolic
vision as a literary form and therefore considers the visions
of Ezekiel to be important and integral links on a chain which
leads to Daniel. Jeremias is not concerned with the fact that
none of Ezekiel's visions neatly parallel those of Amos-
Jeremiah, Zechariah, or Daniel in terms of patterning of content.

Jeremias accepts the ideas of a number of the scholars
discussed above. His analysis thus rises or falls with theirs.
For example, relying on Lindblom's definition of dramatic

not in this formal line of development, though Isaiah 6, Ezekiel 1, and other OT visions will be included in the discussion
where relevant. The attempt to deal with too many visions at
once, in fact, may be the cause of the problems discussed above.
Among the twelve symbolic visions, we distinguish three major
stages of development. These stages are not rigidly drawn, and
each flows easily into the next. For example, Zechariah's
vision VI (5:1-4) will straddle our first and second stages.
Throughout, a major theme will be the continuity in pattern and
content from the earliest and simplest examples of our form to
the latest and most complex. This being said, the three basic
stages break down as follows.

Stage I includes Am 7:7-9, 8:1-3, Jer 1:11-12, 1:13-19,
and 24. The core pattern of seeing-questioning-answering is
particularized as follows: 1) indication of a vision; 2)
description of the vision; 3) the deity's question to the seer,
"What do you see?"; 4) the seer's reply which repeats the initial description; 5) interpretation of the vision by God. The
two visions from Jeremiah 1 omit step 2, so that the description of the vision occurs for the first time in the seer's
response (step 4). Key language for each step of the pattern
is shared by the five visions as is a simple but rhythmic style
characterized by the repetition of key terms. We refer to this
style as "economical-rhetorical." It is grounded in the frame
of the dialogue and in the way the symbol is related to its
meaning. The symbol, which is an everyday object such as a pot
or a basket, is connected to its meaning via word-play or metaphor. The symbol term is thus nuanced or re-used in the process of interpretation. Building on previous scholarship, we
will show that this associative linguistic device is not merely

---

versus pictorial visions, Jeremias places Zech 2:1-4 (horns)
and 5:1-4 (scroll) in the latter, static category. This view
of the horns and scroll visions leads Jeremias to declare them
"less developed" in imagery than Ezekiel's visions and as
throw-backs to the visions of Amos and Jeremiah; they show
"keine klare und ungebrochene Entwicklungslinie" towards Daniel
(*Die Nachtgesichte*, p. 45). In fact, each of these visions
displays important trends in the direction of Daniel 7 and 8.

a convenient method of unifying the structure of the work, but
also a reminiscence of a divinatory technique in widespread use
throughout the Near East, a means of interpreting dreams. The
concept of divination will be important as our work progresses.
Stage II is characterized by five visions of Zechariah:
1:7-17; 2:1-4; 4:1-6a, 10b-14; 5:1-4; and 6:1-8.[22] As mentioned above, the sixth vision of Zechariah (5:1-4) exhibits
only subtle changes from stage I. With the vision of the
menorah (4:1-6a, 10b-14), the question motif is significantly
nuanced; for this vision contains not only the question of the
Lord to the seer (4:2), but also the seer's own request for an
explanation of his vision (4:4). In all remaining examples of
the symbolic vision form, the seer will ask for an interpretation. At this point in the tradition, the action of the vision,
"the plot" if you will, becomes more like a scene of divination.
In stage I the seer is merely a passive tool through which Yahweh reveals his message; he asks no questions. With the
visions of Zechariah he becomes more of a protagonist, the
dreamer who requests enlightenment. He wants to know the significance of what he sees. The content pattern of the form
thus becomes more recognizably divinatory. At the same time
that the description of the vision experience grows to look
more like a divinatory proceeding, the associative technique,
so reminiscent of dream interpretation methodology in stage I,
virtually disappears. The symbol is not related to its meaning
via word-play or metaphor. The seer simply asks, "What is

---

22. We regard Zechariah visions III (2:5-9) and VII (5:5-
11) as experiments which are not in the direct line of development towards Daniel. These two visions are certainly related
to our form, sharing a number of content elements, rubrics,
and structures found in the other visions of Zechariah. Yet
Zechariah visions III and VII are, in a sense, more complex,
innovating upon the basic shared elements so much that they
have strayed off the mainstream of development. Each combines
elements in a rather individual way, including nuances which
do not flow with the continuing course of development. We will
discuss these visions briefly at the end of ch. 2.

this?" and is answered. No particular methodology seems to be involved. (See below.) The first and last visions of Zechariah (1:7-17 and 6:1-8) extend the question/answer pattern with a complex motif, "the observation of divine events." The dramatic happenings found in this motif will be of special importance in the visions of stage III which Zechariah 1:7-17 and 6:1-8 anticipate.

The style of Zechariah's visions is more prose-like and strung out than that of the visions in Amos and Jeremiah, as the author appears to take more time in describing the vision experience. While these visions contain no trace of divinatory technique, repetition is not abandoned altogether as a structuring device. At the same time, the symbols themselves become more mythologized; their meaning is not always explained in the vision's motif of interpretation. Instead, one must use a comparative approach and seek the background of the symbols in the fund of ancient Near Eastern mythology. An interesting phenomenon which makes its appearance in the visions of Zechariah is that of the real-mythic symbol discussed above. A simpler equation between symbol and meaning is re-established in the visions of Daniel and the four post-Biblical works with which we will deal. The visions of Zechariah, in fact, make one reflect upon the interrelationship between the individual author and the tradition in any one example of a form. An author draws from and fits into a tradition; yet he himself can contribute to its ongoing path of development. Alternatively, he can break with the tradition. These issues will arise in the discussion of stage II.

Stage III of the symbolic vision form is represented by Daniel 7 and 8 and by 2 Baruch 35-43; 53-76; 4 Ezra 11:1-12:39; and 13:1-53. Daniel 7 and 8 further extend the narrative quality of the vision. The divinatory pattern which asserted itself in the visions of Zechariah is now filled out with a description of the seer's emotional state and with a better indiction of setting. The dreaming aspect of the vision is all the more emphasized as the symbols themselves become intricate and dramatic scenes observed by the seer. The style of Daniel 7 has a rythmic story-telling quality. The length of some of the motifs is of note. Thematically, the symbolic

vision form becomes the medium of the apocalypticist whose
mythologically charged symbol scenes are like a strange language, intelligible to his circle of the saved. This narrative
thread of the symbolic vision tradition continues with the four
visions of 2 Baruch and 4 Ezra with which we will deal schemati-
cally.
In this way, we trace the development of the symbolic
vision form from its simplest and earliest examples in Amos and
Jeremiah to its more prosaized, yet more mythologized, relatives in Zechariah to an even more baroque and narrative stage
in Daniel and some apocryphal works. This approach discourages
the creation of synchronic categories which do not account for
changes which occur in the form through time. Such an approach
also takes into account developments in Israelite history and
trends in the larger fund of Biblical literature.

The broader Biblical perspective and divination
        Visions and dreams of many varieties are found in the
early layers of OT. The Elohist, in particular, portrays characters who receive information from God via dreams: Abimelech
(Gen 20:3, 6), Jacob (Gen 28:12, 46:2), and Laban (Gen 31:24)
all receive divine communications through dreams. The folktale
cycle in Genesis 37-41 which describes Joseph's rise also contains a number of dream scenes. Joseph himself, the baker, the
wine steward, and Pharaoh all have symbolic dreams. The Deuteronomist also has preserved a number of dream-vision accounts:
1 Kgs 3:5 (Solomon's dream); Jud 7:13 (a symbolic reference to
Gideon in someone else's dream); and 1 Kgs 22:19-23 (the vision
of Micaiah, a ninth century B.C. prophet who prophesies disas-
ter for the war of Jehoshaphat of Judah and Ahab of Israel).
None of the above passages are examples of our form, though the
symbolic dreams in Genesis 41 and the vision of the divine
council in 1 Kgs 22 will be relevant to the discussions below.
By tracing key dream-vision terms such as *ḥlm*, *r'h*, and *laylâ*,
one is led to numerous dream and vision references in early
non-prophetic materials in OT. In contrast, an examination of
Amos, Hosea, Isaiah, Micah, Jeremiah, Deutero-Isaiah, and Ezekiel yields relatively few references to vision experiences when
compared with the large number of direct communications via

oracle. The symbolic visions of Amos and Jeremiah with which we will deal are some of the few instances in which prophets receive divine revelation through visions. Ezekiel includes a few more vision experiences than some of his predecessors. With Zechariah 1-6, however, vision experiences have a new literary life. Following in the symbolic tradition found sparingly in Amos and Jeremiah, Proto-Zechariah employs symbolic visions almost exclusively. By the time of Daniel, visions have become the respectable means of receiving divine revelation, and in post-Biblical works visions and dreams of many varieties abound. What are the causes of the waxing and waning of dreams and visions in Biblical literature? The problem is a complex one and we offer no solutions, only hypotheses.

It can be no coincidence that the waxing and waning of visions and dreams in OT roughly corresponds to the waxing and waning of certain ancient mythic traditions. Frank Moore Cross has shown that "the language of theophany and the imagery of revelation derived from the mythology of the storm God largely fell out of use, beginning in the ninth century, and including two centuries to follow, in prophetic Yahwism."[23]

The religion of Israel in its first lusty and creative impulse absorbed mythic elements readily into its language of faith and into its cult, its dynamic transforming these elements into the service of Yahwism. By the ninth century B.C., however, Israel had become vulnerable to a less wholesome syncretism, and in fact the religion of Yahweh began to give way to the popular cult of Ba'l. Mythical elements in the old language of the Yahwistic tradition were no longer harmless, but were used as conduits through which to introduce the full, sophisticated mythology of the Canaanite Ba'l.[24]

These mythological traditions find a home in royal cult and temple ritual, glimpses of which remain visible in the Psalms (see Ps 29, 93, and 89:6-19). The prophets, however, become self-conscious about using mythic traditions which had

---

23. *Canaanite Myth and Hebrew Epic* (Cambridge: Harvard University Press, 1973), p. 191.

24. *Canaanite Myth*, pp. 190-191.

become so identified with non-Yahwist religious practice and
which, in some senses, had become the property of the ruling
monarchic establishment. The same "foreign-usage/royal-
identification" problem may have applied to the use of dreams
and visions to express the word of the Lord. From 1 Kgs 22 and
from a variety of foreign sources it would appear that court
prophets or shrine priests employed dreams to advise the king on
matters of war and other issues of state. The king's own
dreams, which could if necessary be interpreted by court diviners, served a similar purpose.[25] It might be that the classical prophets simply wanted no part of this aspect of court
life; perhaps they considered it another example of foreign
influence in the ways that Israel and her kings were relating
to Yahweh. Jeremiah, in fact, implies that the use of dreams
provides false propaganda for kings who would involve the people in wars and in forbidden entangling alliances with foreign
powers. His condemnation of foreign policy thus intermingles
with the condemnation of dreamers and their visions (Jer 23:16;
27:9; 29:8; also see Ezek 13:3-4, 7, 9; 22:28). While the
dreams of seers who predicted victory over Babylonia should
probably be regarded as examples of Freudian wish-fulfillment,
Jeremiah and his party suspected them of and accused them of
more evil political motives. Political parties and fears of
foreign contagion aside, the simpler factor of changing tastes
and styles also enters the discussion of forms of divine
revelation. It may be simply that in the period from the 8th
to the late 6th century B.C. poetic oracles were regarded as

---

25. See, for example: the dream of a priest of Ishtar
concerning the successes of Assurbanipal (A. Leo Oppenheim, *The
Interpretation of Dreams in the Ancient Near East* [TAPA 46/3
(1956), p. 249, par. 10); the dream of the Egyptian king Merenp-
tah concerning his own victory (Oppenheim, *The Interpretation*,
p. 251, par. 16); the symbolic dream of the Egyptian monarch
Tanutamun (Oppenheim, *The Interpretation*, p. 251, par. 17);
Sethos' dream of his success against the Assyrians (Herodotus
2:141); and Xerxes' dream which court wisemen interpret to mean
his world conquest (Herodotus 7:19).

the highest form of divine revelation in Israel. Passages such
as Mic 3:5-8, Jer 23:25-32, and Num 12:6-8[26] imply such a value
judgment. Poetic styles change, even deteriorate. With the
loss of the old poetic styles comes the new popularity of the
dream vision. As we will note below, the renewed popularity of
dream visions coincides with an increasing belief that the
divine realm is somehow more difficult to reach than "in the
old days." Intermediaries are deemed necessary in the communication process. Prophecy of the old variety has died.
    Another factor which complicates the vision-revelation
phenomenon is that of divination. As discussed by Burke O.
Long, divination seems to have been practiced in the early
period of Israel's development and in the early monarchy.[27]
Under the heading of divinatory practice, Long places not only
the use of instruments such as the 'ûrîm and tummîm, but also
stylized requests for help or information from God. We might
consider divination more narrowly as a variety of magical
practice whereby one attempts to gain information pertaining to
the future. Such divinatory practices include the reading of
animals' internal organs (extispicy), the reading of oil on
water (lecanomancy), and divining by observing the patterns of
smoke (libanomancy).[28] As noted by Oppenheim with reference to
the Babylonians,[29] and by A. Finet and G. Dossin with special
reference to divination in Mari,[30] such activities were considered scholarly, even scientific. Dossin, in particular,

---

26. See Robert R. Wilson, "Early Israelite Prophecy,"
Interpretation 32 (1978), 12.
    27. "The Effect of Divination upon Israelite Literature,"
JBL 92 (1973), 490-491.
    28. See Oppenheim, *The Interpretation*, p. 242.
    29. "Perspectives on Mesopotamian Divination," *La Divina-
tion en Mésopotamie Ancienne et dans les Régions Voisines*
(Paris: Presses Universitaires de France, 1966), 40.
    30. Finet, "La place du devin dans la société de Mari,"
La Divination en Mésopotamie, 93; Dossin, "Sur le prophétisme à
Mari," *La Divination en Mésopotamie*, 86. On divination at Mari
and in the OT see M. Weinfeld, "Ancient Near Eastern Patterns
in Prophetic Literature," *VT* 27 (1977), 178-195.

emphasizes the pragmatic, utilitarian aspect of mantic wisdom. It must be such methods of divination that are condemned or spoken of as sinful in Deut 18:10, 14, 1 Sam 15:23, 28:8-9 and 2 Kgs 17:17. The people are to listen to the prophets whom God appoints and not to diviners as do the other nations (Deut 18:10, 14). Such "scientific" methods of finding out about the future must have seemed the very embodiment of hubris to one stratum of OT theologians. Could dream interpretation have been included among these suspiciously scientific means of divination? The picture is cloudy.

In Egypt, dream interpretation appears to have been a highly developed skill.[31] One might therefore suggest that the prophets were self-conscious about employing a form of divine revelation which smacked too much of foreign "scientific" practice. On the other hand, dream interpretation was not considered one of the scientific divinatory skills at Mari.[32] Generally in Mesopotamia, the interpretation of dream omina was not considered the most reliable of the divinatory methods available, and it does not appear to have been the most popular means of divination.[33]

C. J. Gadd notes that divinatory practice falls into two categories, "natural" and "artificial."[34] Artificial means include extispicy, lecanomancy, and libanomancy. These methods might be compared to scientific, scholarly experiments which one can set up at will. Natural means include sudden ecstatic experiences of the divine, and very possibly divination through dreams; for dreams are not humanly controllable. One cannot force oneself to have a dream, whereas one can slaughter an

---

31. See A. Volten, *Demotische Traumdeutung=Papyrus Carlsberg No. XIII & XIV* (Analecta Aegyptiaca 3; Copenhagen: Munksgaard, 1942), pp. 41ff.; E. L. Ehrlich, *Der Traum im Alten Testament* (Berlin: Töpelmann, 1953), p. 68.

32. See A. Finet, "La place du devin," 93.

33. See Oppenheim, *The Interpretation*, pp. 238, 242.

34. "Some Babylonian Divinatory Methods and their Interrelations," *La Divination en Mésopotamie*, 22. See also the excellent discussion in R. Flaceliere, *Greek Oracles*, trans. D. Garman (London: Elek, 1965), pp. 4-5.

animal on purpose and rationally examine its entrails.[35]
Moreover, in literary texts such as the Gilgamesh Epic and
the Dream of Tammuz, deities or divinely inspired humans seem
to provide interpretations of dreams without the aid of
rational scientific methods.[36] Even the Gudea text, which may
record a real-life experience of the Sumerian ruler, contains
no reference to a human expert dream interpreter or to some
other rational means of decoding the symbolic dream. The
interpretation is provided by the goddess Nanshe in another
vision.[37] Thus dreams fall into a grey area as regards their
scientific value. Presumably, the less scientific and rational
the better in terms of the OT prophet's view of them; for a
means of telling about the future which seemed like rational,
inductive divination would be anathema along with other overtly
magical, non-Yahwistic activities.

As hints of storm-god mythology never completely disappear
in classical prophecy, so too dreams and visions. Even hints
of "artificial" divinatory technique emerge in the texts from
Amos and Jeremiah with which we will deal. Interestingly, it
is Yahweh who makes the word-play, who is put in the role of
diviner. The seer never asks for an interpretation of his
vision as noted above. Once the seer does request an interpretation of his vision in Zechariah 4:1-6a, 10b-14 and in the
remaining visions with which we will deal, the actual divinatory technique disappears. As in the Gudea Stele, the god-
given quality of the interpretation, its mystery, is underlined.
In fact, throughout OT, dream interpretation is safely described
as a God-sent, God-inspired event. In the Elohist's account of
Joseph's rise to power, the hero actually practices dream

---

35. Plato considered the more inspirational, natural
means the higher form of divination. See Flaceliere, *Greek
Oracles*, pp. 5, 20-21.

36. See Oppenheim, *The Interpretation*, pp. 246-248, pars.
4-7 and p. 246, par. 2. On the Dream of Tammuz, cf. A. Falkenstein, "«Wahrsagung» in der sumerischen Überlieferung," *La
Divination en Mésopotamie*, 64.

37. See Oppenheim, *The Interpretation*, pp. 245-246, par.
1.

interpretation; but E takes special pains to have Joseph insist
that his powers come from the Lord (Gen 41:16). With these
qualifications, the activity of dream interpretation seems to
be made permissible. Even in the 8th-6th centuries B.C. it is
clear that the symbolic vision, a literary form whose background must lie in the activity of dream interpretation practiced as a more scholarly activity at court and as a less self-
conscious aspect of folklore by ordinary people, was not completely ignored by the prophets as a means of expressing the
experience of divine revelation. This form, found in the simple pattern and style of the visions of Amos and Jeremiah,
awaited a renaissance of interest in the late 6th century B.C.

The time of Zechariah is a period of tremendous changes in
Israel. The Solomonic temple is destroyed to be replaced with
a less magnificent structure; kingship will never be the same
as the role of the priest changes and gains new political clout.
Various groups vie for power in the land. The struggle between
returned Babylonian exiles and those who had remained in the
land is just one of the many sociological and political divisions which must have existed in the late 6th century B.C. The
old-style prophet disappears and with him the old-style poetic
oracle forms. These vast sociological changes allow for the
development of new prophetic forms,[38] and for the blossoming of
an old form, that of the symbolic vision as found in Amos and
Jeremiah. This form suits the now more transcendent view of
God so evident in the concerns of P. One receives the word of
God filtered through symbols which must be interpreted to be
understood. Whatever kept the symbolic vision in the background previously, it now has a new popularity as an expression
of man's communication with the divine.

The question/answer divinatory pattern in the Near East

Before beginning detailed analysis, one should emphasize
that the pattern, which consists of seeing a dream or vision, a
question about that vision, and an explanation, is very common
throughout the Near East and is found in a variety of contexts.
In the Gilgamesh Epic, for example, the pattern fits the dream

---

38. See F. M. Cross, *Canaanite Myth*, pp. 343-344.

occurrences through which the author creates effective foreshadowing of major events in the narrative.[39] In Genesis 37-41
the dream interpretation pattern plays an important literary
role in the folktale cycle about Joseph's rise at court.
Joseph's ability to answer dreamers' requests for interpretation furthers his career and on a more basic level advances the
plot of the narrative as a whole. The dreams of Gudea, the
Sumerian monarch, and of Tanutamun, the Egyptian Pharaoh, may
be more historical records of kings' dream experiences.[40] In
the former, the interpretation of Gudea's symbolic dream moti-
vates him to build a temple for Ningirsu; in the latter, the
ruler is given assurances of his successful conquest of Egypt.
Herodotus employs the question/answer dream interpretation pattern in numerous contexts as well.[41]
    Thus the question/answer pattern found also in our form is
not at all unique to it. By the same token, no Biblical writer
need have borrowed the pattern from some non-Biblical dream
source or indeed from the Elohist's tales of Joseph. The pattern, which is grounded in real-life situations, is common
property to a full gamut of Near Eastern prophets, priests,
princes, peasants, and scholars. In the symbolic vision form,
the basic pattern appears with particular nuances of content
and language and for specific prophetic revelatory purposes.
The vision form is infused with a peculiarly prophetic coloration. All examples of our form have much more in common with
each other than with other Biblical and non-Biblical works
which employ the basic question/answer pattern for their own
purposes. The special formal relationship between the visions
of this study will emerge as our work unfolds.

---

    39. Thus Gilgamesh dreams of his soon to be found friend
Enkidu (A. Heidel, *The Gilgamesh Epic and Old Testament Parallels* [Chicago: University of Chicago Press, 1963], Tab. I, col.
5, ll. 25ff.); he dreams of their victories against Huwawa (*Gilgamesh Epic*, Tab. V. col. 3, ll 32-col. 4, ll. 1-22); and
Enkidu dreams of his own death (*Gilgamesh Epic*, Tab. VII, col.
4, ll. 14ff.).

    40. See Oppenheim, *The Interpretation*, pp. 245-246, par.
1 and p. 251, par. 17.

    41. See Herodotus 1:107 for a good example.

Chapter One
STAGE I OF THE SYMBOLIC VISION FORM

Am 7:7-9

			Test for balance
(7)	Thus the Lord showed me	כה הראני ^aאדני (7a	7
	And behold, a man stationed	והנה ^bאיש נצב על (7b	9
	at the wall	חומה^c	
	In his hand, a plumb-line.	ובידו^d אנך (7c	6
(8)	And the Lord said to me,	ויאמר YHWH אלי (8a	7
	"What do you see, Amos?"	מה אתה ראה עמוס (8b	7
	And I said, "A plumb-line."	ואמר אנך (8c	5
	Then the Lord said,	ויאמר אדני (8d	6
	Behold I am placing a plumb-line	הנני שם אנך (8e	6
	In the midst of my people Israel	בקרב עמי ישראל (8f	7
	I will no longer continue to	לא אוסיף עוד (8g	7
	forgive him.	עבור לו	
(9)	Desolate are the high places	נשמו במות ^eישחק^f (9a^g	7
	of Yishaq		
	The sanctuaries of Israel	מקדשי^f ישראל נחרבו (9b	9
	are waste,		
	For I am arising against the	וקמתי על בית ירבעם (9c	10
	house of Jeraboam with a	בחרב	
	sword.		

^aInsert *'ădōnāy* with G. So Harper, McKeating, Cripps, Robinson, and Wolff. In MT *'ădōnāy* has been misplaced after *wĕhinnēh*. See below.

^bWith G(A-V) και ιδου ανηρ εστηκως. So McKeating. Cripps, Robinson, and Wolff prefer G(B-Q^{txt}) = G^{Zi}, και ιδου εστηκως, "And behold one standing." Yet elsewhere in OT the participle *niṣṣāb* is never found in a true nominal role, standing alone as a subj. or obj. Instead, *niṣṣāb* appears in a verbal role, with a pronoun or noun as its subj. as in "I am standing" or "God

21

was standing." See Gen 24:13, 43; 28:13; Ex 17:9; Num 22:23,
31.
    ^cOmit the first *ʾănāk* as a dittography and restore *ḥômâ* to
a non-bound state. So Weiser, McKeating, Hammershaimb, Cripps,
and Robinson. Sellin, Wellhausen, and Wolff suggest that *ḥômat*
ʾeben may be original, but no strong reasons support this view.
Even less likely is Weiser's suggestion that the line once read,
wĕhinnēh ʾănāk niṣṣāb ʿal ḥômâ.
    ^dScholars have suggested various translations and emenda-
tions for *ʾănāk*. A. Condamin ("Le prétendu fils à plomb de la
vision d'Amos," *RB* 9 [1900], 586-594) suggests the translation
"weapon," while G. Brunnet ("La vision de l'étain," *VT* 16
[1966], 387-395) suggest "tin." For him, tin becomes a symbol
of war and destruction because of this metal's role in the
forging of arms. With Wolff, we agree that such a meaning for
the term *ʾănāk* is doubtful; for unalloyed tin is, in fact, a
weak, bendable metal. Ultimately, plummet or plumb-line would
seem the best translation. The measuring device is appropriate
to the meaning of the passage. Its usage as a metaphor for
judgment is comparable to the usage of measuring symbols in Is
28:17 and 2 Kgs 21:13. In Zech 2:5f., a measuring device held
in the hand is nuanced with new positive meaning. F. Horst's
suggestion to emend *ʾănāk* to *ʾănāḥâ* is untenable and unnecessary, as discussed below ("Die Visionsschilderungen der alttestamentlichen Propheten," 201-202).
    ^e*Yiśḥāq* is an unusual designation for Northern Israel used
only here and at Jer 33:26, Am 7:16, and Ps 105:9. It is an
equivalent to *Yiṣḥāq* and a parallel term for Israel in this
passage.
    ^fOmit the prosaizing *waw*.
    ^gA number of scholars regard vs. 9 as a redactional addi-
tion. Weiser believes that its style differs from that of vss.
7 and 8. J. D. Watts (*Vision and Prophecy in Amos* [Grand
Rapids: Eerdmans, 1958], p. 41) feels that its content and form
are out of place in this context. Wolff writes that vss. 9-14
interrupt the five visions of Amos which once formed a whole.
We see no need to exclude vs. 9 from the pericope on thematic,
structural, or contentual grounds. This tricolon provides a
poetic recapitulation of the interpretation of the symbols, a

summation which creates additional emphasis. The tricolon's lack of poetic perfection is fully in tune with the stylistic goals of the author.

Pattern of Content Elements		Rubrics
7:7	Indication of a vision	כה הראני אדני
7:7	Initial description	...והנה
7:8	Question of God to seer	ויאמר YHWH אלי מה אתה ראה
7:8	Reply of seer and repetition of description	ויאמר
7:8-9	God's explanation of seen object(s)	ויאמר אדני

The above pattern of elements and the terms in which the elements are presented describe the version of the symbolic vision form shared by Am 7:7-9, 8:1-3, Jer 1:11-12, 1:13-19, and 24.[1] While a full discussion of this stage of the form will be more appropriate after detailed analysis of each of its examples, we make a few points at the start concerning structure and the unity of structure in Am 7:7-9.

External criteria of form

Amos 7:7-9 and the other visions of this simplest stage of the form exemplify the prophet's response to the demands of his tradition. The traditional composer is subject to a long history of literature and to the requirements of accepted modes of expression. Sociological realities may well provide the models

---

1. Zech 5:1 employs a variant of this rubric *wě'er'eh wěhinnēh*, "And I saw and behold...," while Jer 1:11, 1:13 employ an alternate rubric, *wayyěhî děbar yahweh 'ēlay*, "And the word of the Lord happened to me...." Such choices are to be expected in traditional literature, and indeed evidence a rather economical use of language. That is, there are only a few ways to introduce a vision. We would not go so far as to suggest that the visions of our form have been oral formulaically composed. Nevertheless, written traditional literature may have much in common with oral traditional material. The use of rubrics in this form is not unlike the use of formulas in orally composed works.

for literary traditions, but once specific literary forms
coalesce and take shape, they have their own definable reality. A stylized way to present a certain scene or event has
an integrity of its own whether or not it neatly corresponds
to some real-life model. A law-suit scene, as it might occur
in court, is thus transformed into a prophetic oracle with
its stylized patterning of call to witnesses, accusation, and
sentencing. This oracle has its own integrity of form apart
from the real-life court situations which are its model. A
traditional enthronement psalm conforms to certain prosodic
norms, certain modes of expression, and to a certain set of
motifs which may or may not have all that much correspondence
to a real-life ritual. The literary creations derived from or
inspired by these real-life activities become formalized traditions in their own right. Such traditions themselves make
rather definite demands on the composers of literature. Certainly, there is much flexibility in traditional literature,
but flexibility comes within certain predetermined borders. A
combination of content elements which is found again and again
in a large body of literature and which consistently reveals
similar nuances of language has developed its own stylized
unity of structure. In this case, the phrase which indicates
that a vision has been experienced will necessarily be followed
by *wĕhinnēh* and a description. We have observed similar phe-
nomenona in folk tale patterns and their language when one particular tale type is shared by a number of stories in the same
culture.[2] The same kind of flexible conformity characterizes
all traditional forms of literature.

The above point of view has important implications for our
work. A number of scholars have sought psychological explanations for the ways in which the vision scene is described.[3] We
too will examine aspects of world-view and real-life activities
to gain a sense of the background behind the process of symbol
interpretation which is so evident in this stage of the symbolic

---

2. See S. Niditch and R. Doran, "The Success Story of the
Wise Courtier: A Formal Approach," *JBL* 96 (1977), 179-183.

3. S. A. Loewenstamm, "כלוב קיץ לטפולוגיה של חזון נבואה"
Tarbiz 34 (1964/65), 319-322.

vision form. Important as such considerations are, however,
one must never forget that Amos sets down visions and presents
their interpretation in a certain way because of the demands of
the literary tradition. Amos is not only grounded in a certain
life setting and subject to a certain group-psychology; he is
also very much within a literary tradition. A variety of
accepted ways exist to describe a vision, and Am 7:7-9 conforms
to the boundaries of one of these accepted typologies. In this
way, an inner tension exists between the elements of Am 7:7-9,
unifying it and giving it a wholeness of structure. This wholeness is based not only on prosodic relationships in the passage
or on the use of repetition, or on any other solely internal
criteria of structure contained within this version of the symbolic vision form. Its unity of structure also depends on the
patterning, language, and style which it shares with a number
of other visions.

Internal criteria of form

Having established the notion of external or typological
criteria, we examine specific internal criteria of structure
for Am 7:7-9.

One possible structurer for a vision of the 8th century
B.C. might be the adherence to the prosodic norms of classical
poetry. These rules include: 1) basic balance in line length,
determined by syllable count; 2) a preponderance of non-
enjambed lines; and 3) the use of *parallelismus membrorum*. In
order to test the vision for an adherence to these prosodic
rules we have divided it into cola and have created four units
of roughly the same number of lines each. These units are composed of thematically appropriate clusters of content elements
as follows: 1) indication of vision and description (7:7a-c);
2) God's question and prophet's reply/description (7:8a-c); 3)
God's explanation of the vision (7:8d-g); and 4) the recapitulation of the message of the vision (7:9a-c).

The length of each colon is determined by content. Generally, when the thought is completed the colon is completed.
Thus we are looking for periodic lines such that the thought
and the sentence end with the line or for non-periodic enjambement of lines such that the thought is completed at the end of

the line, though the grammatical sentence may continue on to
the next line. Both of the above are typical of traditional
poetry.[4] Am 7:7-9 yields an unmistakable if imperfect balance
in syllable count between lines, and the untraditional "necessary enjambement" is found only once between 8e and 8f.

A more important factor in the prosodic analysis of this
vision, however, is the complete lack of parallelism in vss.
7a-8d. Parallel constructions are found in the recapitulation
of the vision's message (vs. 9) and to some extent in 8e-8g,
which contain the interpretation of the symbols, the initial
revelation of the vision's meaning for the future. Vs. 9 has
genuinely poetic style with the following parallelistic arrangement: a b c / b c a / (a) b c (a). Note the chiasm in the
first two cola and the shift from third person to first person
in the final line for emphasis. We consider the whole action
image to be *wĕqamtî bĕḥāreb* and therefore refer to *bĕḥāreb* with
the verbal designation "a."

In order to perceive parallelism in 8e-g one must join
together 8e and 8f to parallel 8g.

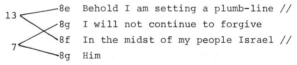

13
     8e Behold I am setting a plumb-line //
     8g I will not continue to forgive
7
     8f In the midst of my people Israel //
     8g Him

The resulting 13/7 metrical arrangement is obviously impossible.
Enjambement must be allowed between 8e and 8f. Nevertheless,
parallelism is present if obscured.

Admittedly, the arrangement of Am 7:7-9 as if it were
classical poetry is somewhat artificial. The division of the
vision into cola is useful, however, as means of determining
the true structural make-up of the vision. We will apply a
similar "test for prosody" in future studies. In Am 7:7-9 the
test for prosody has revealed the clipped, reasonably balanced,
if non-poetic, style of the dialogue pattern in 7a-8d. This
dialogue is then climaxed by the passable poetry of 8e-9. The
poetic section is not ideally classical in style; for 8e-8g
evidences the presence of enjambement and imprecise parallelism,

---

4. A. B. Lord, *The Singer of Tales* (New York: Atheneum,
1968), p. 54.

while vs. 9 displays metric imbalance.

Ultimately, one must conclude that the writer has conformed to certain prosodic norms, but that his major stylistic
goal is not to compose classical poetry. It is significant
that God's word, revealed in vs. 8 and re-emphasized in vs. 9,
is expressed more poetically. This tendency to set the word of
God in poetry will be found in a number of the visions of the
form and may reflect the pro-oracle value judgment mentioned in
our introduction. We suggest that the classical prophets, in
particular, may have assessed revelation through poetic oracle
to be of greater value than revelation through visions. Thus
Amos presents the word of the Lord more poetically than the
dialogue portion of the vision. Nevertheless, the rules of
classical poetry do not seem to be the chief unifiers and
structurers of the passage as a whole. What then is?

The repetition of forms of '*mr*, a factor of the dialogue
pattern itself, is one unifier. The rhyme between *qereb* (8f)
and *ḥereb* (9c) also may be of some small significance. The
most important structurer in the passage, however, is the play
on '*ănāk*. The plumb-line appears in the description of the
vision (7c), in the prophet's reply to God's question (8c), and
finally in the interpretation of the vision (8e). In Genesis
41 Pharaoh's dream is repeated at three comparable junctures.
The difference in genre between Gen 41 and Am 7:7-9 precludes
closer structural comparisons, but it is interesting that
Pharaoh's dream, like Amos' vision, is initially described,
then repeated to the one who will interpret it, and then again
re-used in the explanation or interpretation. In both works,
the repetition serves to unify the whole and to emphasize the
theme contained within the symbols.[5]

The use of the same lexical items to create the same image
several times within one work is evidence of a traditional-
style economy of language.[6] The pithy style which results from

---

5. For a discussion of the role of repetition in traditional literature, see A. Olrik, "The Epic Laws of Folk Narrative," *The Study of Folklore*, ed. A. Dundes (Englewood Cliffs:
Prentice-Hall, 1965), pp. 129-141.

6. See Lord, *The Singer*, p. 53.

the repetition of key terms is a constant throughout the simplest stage of the symbolic vision form. This style which we
call "economical-rhetorical" is not classically poetic, but in
its own way exhibits an equally traditional use of language.

The symbol term and dream interpretation

H. W. Wolff notes that all details of the vision are not
emphasized in Am 7:7-9.[7] The symbol of the plumb-line is the
quintessential element of the vision. It is re-used, nuanced,
and played upon in the nearly transparent metaphor (8e-8f) by
which God reveals its deeper meaning. The metaphor which
describes a process of "measuring up" or judging is immediately
followed by a definitive and sober indication of sentencing:
lōʾ ʾ ôsîp ʿ ôd ʿ ăbôr lô, "I will not continue to forgive him."
Indeed, Israel has been weighed and measured, and found lacking.[8] The theme of judgment in turn is re-emphasized by the
poetic and possibly formulaic description in vs. 9.[9]

Some scholars have emphasized the literary aspects of this
passage, built as it is upon the nuanced repetition of *ʾ ănāk*.[10]
Lindblom, Wolff, and Volz regard the passage as a stylized,
catechetical form and emphasize the question/answer dialogue,
which they consider didactic in style and intent.[11]

---

7. *Dodekapropheten, Amos*, p. 347.
8. The thematic thrust is not unlike that of Daniel's
interpretation of the handwriting for Belshazzar (5:27).
9. One would have to make a thorough study to ascertain
that these poetic phrases are formulaic, but the neatness of
the parallelism, the commonness of the *šmm/ḥrb* pair in OT literature (see Zeph 3:6, Ezek 6:6 for use in parallelism, Is
49:19, Ezek 36:35 for use in synonym chain), and the simplicity
of the syntax of each phrase are hints that one might be able
to identify a formulaic pattern, "verb of destruction + construct, indicating what is to be destroyed." This formula-
pattern would be appropriate within a theme of punishment/
destruction.
10. F. Horst, "Die Visionsschilderungen," 201-202.
11. J. Lindblom, "Wisdom in the Old Testament Prophets,"
Wisdom in Israel and in the Ancient Near East, ed. M. Noth and

Two scholars have noted that the play-on-words is a technique used within a number of cultures to divine dream symbols.
S. Loewenstamm, who deals primarily with Am 8:1-3, is most concerned with the psychological implications of dream symbols and
the Freudian-style skill involved in decoding them.[12] A.
Guillaume is more intrigued by the relationship of prophetic
visions to forms of magic. Guillaume's arguments are weakened
by an insensitivity to the boundaries of literary form.

He places under the heading of sympathetic magic and divination numerous prophetic sign acts, plays-on-words, allegories,
as well as Biblical patterns of lex talionis.[13] Such an

D. Winton Thomas (Leiden: Brill, 1955), p. 202. H. W. Wolff,
Dodekapropheten, p. 347; Volz, *Der Prophet Jeremiah* (KAT 10;
Leipzig: Scholl, 1928), p. 9.

12. כלוב קיץ.

13. *Prophecy and Divination among the Hebrew and Other
Semites* (London: Hodder and Stoughton, 1938), esp. pp. 149-151.
A *"mashal,"* as Guillaume calls the association of like with
like, is involved in any play-on-words, in any allegory, or in
any sign act; yet each of these is a rather distinct literary
type. G. Fohrer has shown that the sign act, for example, is a
form distinguished by certain content elements, certain language, and so on. (*Die symbolischen Handlungen der Propheten*
[Zurich: Zwingli, 1968]) Surely the sign act is to be differ-
entiated from our form, which also happens to employ *"mashal."*
To further complicate matters, each of the above literary types
(play-on-words, allegory, etc.) can be incorporated into larger
forms. For example, the play-on-words in Ezek 25:16 *(wĕhikratî
ʾet kĕrētîm)* is part of an oracle against the nations, a rather
stylized form, used by Ezekiel several times in ch. 25. Similarly, Nathan's allegory about the lone sheep in 2 Sam 12 is
contained within the larger prophetic rebuke/judgment scene.
The allegory equating Bathsheba with the sheep provides the
element of accusation. We might add that Guillaume considers
vss. 11, 12 of this scene, the sentencing element, an example
of sympathetic magic, since the nature of the crime is associated with or brings about the nature of the punishment.

approach leads to generalization and misinterpretation. Indeed Guillaume does not properly distinguish between forms of magic. For example, he discusses Moses' use of a magically sympathetic uplifing of arms to assure victory in Ex 17:11, under the heading of divination. Moses' action is not divinatory at all. That is, it is not a means or process by which the future is revealed, though it may magically help to bring about a certain turn of events. Nevertheless, Guillaume's emphasis on dream interpretation technique and the divinatory process which are found in Am 7:7-8 is not to be ignored. While Am 7:7-9 is ,a vision and not a dream or night vision, certain definite links exist between it and the symbolic dream.

In Am 7:7-9 a person is made to see an object; then the person receives an interpretation which relates the object to future realities. Thus we find 1) symbol, 2) interpretation, and 3) future orientation. The same elements are found in Daniel 2 and Genesis 41, two of the few Near Eastern examples, however fictionalized, of the divinatory process in action.[14] An even more interesting parallel between Am 7:7-9 and dream divination is found in the way the symbol is made to relate to its meaning. We disagree with Long's characterization of the relationship between the symbol and its interpretation as "casual," "unpredictable," and "fortuitous."[15] The word-play on 'ănāk is reminiscent of the inductive methods of dream interpretation. Such methods were well known throughout the Near East as the work of a number of scholars has shown. A. Leo

---

14. Daniel 2 and Genesis 41 incorporate these elements within a folktale of Thompson type 922. The elements are thus contributing motifs within a larger narrative pattern, which itself conforms to a universal tale type. For further discussion, see S. Niditch and R. Doran, "The Wise Courtier." While these narratives do fit the form of traditional, stylized folk fiction, we need not exclude the possibility that they reflect elements or combinations of elements (actions, character roles) which might have had some correspondence to real-life situations. M. Sister noted this correspondence some forty years ago ("Die Typen der prophetischen Visionen").

15. "Reports of Visions," 357, 359.

Oppenheim deals with Assyrian material, A. Volten with Egyptian evidence.[16] B Ber 55a-57a also contains interesting examples of dream interpretation methodology, which nicely parallel the methods abstracted from dream omina by Volten and Oppenheim.

One such method of relating symbol to reality is word association. In order to interpret the symbol, one looks for the symbolic object's sound-alike or for a term which rhymes with it. One might also seek an interpretation based on an alternate meaning of the term for the symbolic object. The Hebrew term *'ap* may mean "nose" or "anger"; *šm'* may mean "to hear" or "to understand." If one dreams of one of these objects or actions, one might interpret the true meaning to be the other object or action. This method of interpretation exhibits the process of "creative philology"[17] found in the Rabbinic interpretation of Scripture. Such a method will be relevant for our discussion of the play on *qāyiṣ* and *qeṣ* in Am 8:1-3. The process in Am 7:7-8, however, is more akin to another equally exegetical divinatory technique.

Oppenheim and Volten employ the general heading "idea association" to refer to this other method of dream interpretation. The meaning of the object(s) or action(s) seen is drawn from some intrinsic aspect of them. One associates certain ideas with the seen elements or is led to certain elaborations. A ripe bunch of grapes makes one think of fullness and fertility. Thus if a man sees ripened grapes in his dream, his wife will soon have a child. Often idea association leads to creation of a more specific metaphor. B Ber 56a (middle) relates that when Raba dreams of a lettuce on the mouth of a jar, Bar Hedya, the dream interpreter, explains, "Your business will be bitter like a lettuce." Thus the lettuce is re-used in a metaphor.

In another variety of idea association, the object in the

---

16. *The Interpretation*, esp. p. 241; *Demotische Traumdeutung*, esp. pp. 60ff.; for Greek evidence see Artemidori Daldiani, *Onirocriticon Libri V*, ed. R. A. Pack (Leipzig: Teubner, 1963), 4.80.

17. I. Heinemann, *Darke ha-Aggadah* (Jerusalem: Hebrew University, 1954), pp. 96-107.

dream is employed in a brief narrative or elaboration which
nuances it and gives it specific meaning and relevance. When
Raba dreams a cask fell into a pit, Bar Hedya tells him that
his goods will be spoilt and thrown into a pit (b Ber 56a middle). This interpretation involves some metaphorizing as
"cask=goods." The action of throwing nuances the action of
falling by making the verb transitive, but the pit is simply
incorporated into a possible tale about future events.

We have discussed "idea association" at some length because it is into this category that the re-use of 'ănāk falls.
The plumb-line is used in an elaboration which nuances and
colors it. Indeed this re-use makes the plumb-line a simile
for judgment. F. Horst is mistaken in his attempt to turn this
passage into an *Assonanzvision*, by emending 'ănāk to 'ănāḥâ
(see note "d" above).[18] He would thereby place this passage in
the same formal category as Am 8:1-3. Not only is Horst's
emendation completely unsupported by manuscript evidence; a
more basic problem is his assumption that Am 7:7-9 requires
emendation in order to be formally like the other symbol vision
in Am 8:1-3. There is no need to formally differentiate between
Am 7:7-9, where the symbol is linked to its meaning via idea
association, from Am 8:1-3 or Jer 1:11-12, where the symbol is
linked to its meaning via word association. Amos has simply
varied the associative technique, employing idea extension in
this passage and a sound play in ch. 8. Horst's *Assonanzvision*
and *Wortsymbolvision* are distinctions which do not apply to the
passages which here interest us.[19] As our study proceeds, it
will become clear that Am 7:7-9, Am 8:1-3, Jer 1:11-12, etc.,
share a form, being identical in terms of patterning and
rubrics. Am 7:7-9, like these other passages, unfolds the
interpretation of the symbols by means which evoke divinatory
magic.

A question comes to mind: Do we have a Near Eastern parallel to the dialogue in Am 7:7-9 in which a man who has had a

---

18. "Die Visionsschilderungen," 201-202.

19. While Hans Walter Wolff would not accept this emendation, he too accepts the formal distinction between the "symbol
vision" and the "word-play vision."

dream is in the presence of an interpreter? The interpreter
asks him, "What do you see," and when told, the interpreter
uses divinatory technique to explain the symbolic content of
the dream. The answer is, we have no such parallel.[20] In Am
7:7-9 and the other passages which share its form, God is not
simply a nominal motif which replaces a shrine priest or oracle
in a well-attested Near Eastern divination form. The prophetic
form has its own integrity and undergoes further development
within the Biblical tradition, as examination of the visions in
Zechariah 1-6 will show. Nevertheless, we agree with Guillaume
that the play on 'ănāk does have a divinatory thrust. It is
more than a literary device. The appearance of a divinatory
technique in a vision which tells the future is no coincidence.

The divinatory aspect of the passage adds to its power;
for the interpretation of the symbols has the power of a curse.
As certain texts analyzed by Oppenheim show, a bad interpretation of a dream, like a curse or charm, was countered by a
counter-charm or counter-ritual. Some of these texts include
instructions for warding off the evil consequences of the given
interpretations.[21] When a simple plumb-line is associated with

---

20. Burke O. Long ("The Effect of Divination upon Israelite Literature," *JBL* 92 [1973], 489-497) attempts to establish
a formal connection between the narrative in 2 Kgs 8:7-15,
where a question about recovery from illness is addressed to
the prophet, and the Assyrian "tamītu" texts which are oracular
queries addressed to Šamaš and Adad. The "tamītu" texts (discussed by W. G. Lambert, "The ≪tamītu≫ Texts," *La Divination*,
119-123) have a set structure which to some degree parallels
Long's example from 2 Kings less well than the second half of
the motif pattern of the symbolic visions in Daniel 7, 8 and
2 Baruch, 4 Ezra. In each of these passages, the seer's
address to God and his request for an interpretation of the
vision are reminiscent of the address to Šamaš and request for
answers, found in the Assyrian texts. Professor Long does not
take into account the dream interpretation techniques which we
have discussed either in "The Effect" or in his recent article,
"Reports."

21. *The Interpretation*, pp. 295-307.

a judgment of doom, a sympathetic magical relationship is set
up. The same concept is behind the prophetic use of sign acts,
as Fohrer has shown.[22] The plumb-line means doom; in a divinatory framework, its appearance to the prophet predicts doom.
In terms of magic, the very verbalization of the prediction
helps to bring it about. God's pronouncement, set within the
language and mechanism of divination, gains extra strength and
penetration.

Thus far, we have examined the play on 'ănāk on a literary
level, noting that structurally, via repetition, the term uni-
fies the passage while nuancing ahd emphasizing meaning. We
have also noted the deeper significance of the way in which
'ănāk is interpreted. A magical divinatory technique can be
seen behind the metaphoric re-use of 'ănāk, which fortells doom
for Israel. One further point must be made. God inspires Amos
to see the symbol, God asks the prophet what he sees, and himself interprets the vision, unsolicited by the prophet. The
entire proceeding is inspirational. Even though one can associate the first description of the plumb-line with its interpretation via inductive, rational, human reasoning, one need
not. No interpreter is called in; the answer is given. The
associative interpretation, like the vision, comes from God.
In other words, God sends the symbol and performs his own divination. This inspirational quality of the vision scene makes
divination suitable for prophetic use.

Am 8:1-3

			Test for balance
(1)	Thus the Lord showed me	YHWH ⟨ ⟩ᵃ כה הראני (1a	6
	And behold a harvest basket.	והנה כלוב קיץ (1b	6
(2)	And he said, "What do you see, Amos?"	ויאמר מה אתה ראה (2a\nעמוס	10
	And I said, "A harvest basket."	ואמר כלוב קיץ (2b	6
	Then the Lord said to me,	ויאמר YHWH אלי (2c	7
	The cut-off point has come for my people Israel.	בא הקץ אל עמי ישראל (2d	9

---

22. *Die symbolischen Handlungen der Propheten*, esp. ch.4.

I will not continue to for- give him.	לא אוסיך עוד עבור לו (2e 7
(3) The court singers will wail on that day.	הילילו[e] שרות היכל (3a 11 ביום ההוא [f]< >
The corpses are a multitude. Throw (them) anywhere.	רב הפגר בכל מקום (3b 9 השליך[g]
Silence!	הס[h]

[a]Omit the expansionary 'ădōnāy in MT and read with G, ουτως εδειξε μοι κυριος. So Wolff and others.

[b]On the etymology of kĕlûb, see W. Baumgartner, "Die Etymologie von hebräischem kelûb Korb," *Th. Z.* 7 (1951) 77-78.

[c]We have chosen "harvest" as a translation for qāyiṣ instead of "summer fruit," the choice of most scholars. Qāyiṣ is used in synonymous parallelism with qāṣîr, "harvest" or "harvesting" in Jer. 8:20, Prov 6:8, 10:5, and 26:1. The use of qṣ in the Gezer Calendar is also helpful. In this inscription various periods of the year are defined by the agricultural activities which take place in them. There are "two months of ingathering ('sp), two months of sowing (zr'), two months of late sowing (lqš)," and so on. The final period, yrḥ qṣ, refers to the summer fruit harvest. Like its parallels, 'sp, zr', and lqš, the term qṣ may refer to the agricultural activity, not simply to the agricultural product. Compare B. Rahtjen, "A Critical Note on Am 8:1-2," *JBL* 83 (1964) 416-417, and Robert Coote, "Ripe Words for Preaching: Connotative Diction in Amos," *Pacific Theological Review* 8 (1976) 13-19.

We do not suggest that the harvest basket has ritual connotations as does the Greek liknon, a basket carried at the Dionysiac festivals. It is rather a receptacle into which the fruit might be placed. The translation "harvest basket" is preferred because the emphasis on the harvest nicely complements the notion of qēṣ, "set time" or "end." While qēṣ is not etymologically related to qāyiṣ, its root qṣṣ which means "to cut" nicely plays on the activity of the harvest when one cuts down fruit. In a sense, qēṣ is a temporal cutting off, while the harvest, qayiṣ, involves the physical action of cutting. Amos sees a harvest basket, but ironically it is Israel who is to be harvested; her time has come.

^dDelete the prosaizing *waw*.

^eMost scholars, including Weiser, McKeating, Hammershaimb, Edghill, and Wolff, accept the emendation *šārôt*, "female singers." The image thus becomes one of ritual mourning at harvest time. G reads φατνωματα, "coffered work in a ceiling." One possibility is that MT *šîrôt*, "songs" is a corruption for the *qôrôt*, "rafters." G does not translate *qôrôt* by φατνωματα elsewhere in OT, but the Greek term is used to translate *rāhît* which parallels *qōrôt* in Cant 1:17. McKeating mentions the *qôrôt* emendation but rejects it as impossible. The image of the rafters weeping is rather effective and would accommodate the more difficult reading contained in G. Such an interpretation, however, misses the ambiance of the seasonal festival evoked by the image of professional female mourners.

^fWolff omits *nĕ'um 'ădōnāy yahweh* as a secondary expansion. Robinson suggests placing the phrase at the end of 3c for a supposedly better metric arrangement. We agree with Wolff's decision which is based on the fact that the phrase is found three times in Amos 8, at vss. 3, 9, and 11, but only two times in the whole rest of the book (3:13, 4:5). Some, if not all, of the usages in Amos 8 must be additions.

^gHarper, McKeating, and Hammershaimb suggest emending *hŏšlyk* to *hošlak*, the hoph. perf. The subj then becomes *rōb happeger*, "the multitude of the corpses is flung." Driver, Sellin, Wolff, Cripps, and Edghill accept *hŏšlyk* and vocalize *hišlîk*, the hiph. perf.: "he has cast, thrown." The problem then becomes the identification of the subj. None of the solutions is compelling, though the impersonal "one has cast" is a possibility. We prefer to read *hašlîk*, the hiph. impv., an alternative reading mentioned by Edghill. This command which ends the passage has the ritualistic thrust of magic. The bodies are to go unburied. "Throw (them) anywhere." See the discussion below.

^hDriver and Cripps take *has* as an adv., "in silence." Such a translation, however, is not possible. In other OT usages, *has* is an interjection meaning "Hush" or "Keep silent." The use of this term in Am 6:10 is of importance (see below). G, επιρριψω σιωπην, is either an attempt to make sense of an unclear Hebrew tradition preserved in MT or a reflection of a

differing textual tradition. We consider the MT reading the
better.

Pattern of Content Elements	*Rubrics*
8:1 Indication of a vision	כה הראני
8:1 Initial description	והנה...
8:2 Question of God to seer	ויאמר מה אתה ראה עמוס
8:2 Reply of seer and repetition of description	ואמר...
8:2, 3 God's explanation of seen objects	ויאמר YHWH אלי

The pattern of elements in this vision is identical to
that of Am 7:7-9. The framing or rubric language is also
shared. We note small, expected variations: the use of *yahweh*
instead of *'ădonāy* in the introduction of the vision; the
shortening of the introduction to God's question to simply
wayyō'mer; and the address to the prophet by his name, "What do
you see, Amos?" Am 8:1-3 shares a simple version of the symbolic vision form with Am 7:7-9. Participation in such a formal tradition provides Am 8:1-3 with the external or typological criteria of structure discussed earlier.

As in Am 7:7-9, adherence of the rules of classical poetry
is not a primary unifier or structurer of the piece. The motifs
of indication of vision and initial description (vs. 1) do
create a metrically balanced bicolon, but no parallelism is
found. Lines a-b of vs. 2, which contains the motifs of question and answer/explanation, cannot be made into units of equal
length if one wishes to avoid enjambement. The demands of the
dialogue pattern and its rubrics supercede prosodic norms. As
our work continues, it becomes clear that even in a period in
which classical-style poetry is a popular and possibly preferred mode of expressing prophecy, this particular form is
essentially non-classical. Unlike various oracle forms, this
vision form does not demand adherence to classical prosodic
norms in the time of Amos.

Even the explanation of the vision, the word of Yahweh, is
not expressed in finely balanced classical poetry, though the
tricolon in 2c-2e exhibits passable metric balance (7/9/7)
and parallelism between the two lines which follow the rubric
line:

בא הקץ verbal action // verbal action עוד עבור לא אוסיף עוד

אל עמי ישראל object // object לו

The final graphic summation and elaboration of God's explanation of the symbol (vs. 3) is a bicolon with an 11/9 metric
arrangement, one rather too long for this piece and unusually
long for 8th century Hebrew poetry in general. One might
attempt to shorten 3a by omitting *bayyôm hahû'* as a later expansion. One is then left with a 9/9 count if one excludes the
interjection *has* from the bicolon. Yet more basic problems
exist. These two lines, while roughly parallel in intent, are
not really parallel in terms of syntax or individual building
blocks. In short, this bicolon is not a good example of classical poetry, though it and 2d-2e do reveal the tendency to re-
vert to a more poetic medium in declaring the word of the Lord.

As in Am 7:7-9, a basic internal structurer of the passage
is the repetition of forms of *'mr*, which set forth the pattern
of speakers. The play on *qāyiṣ/qēṣ*, however, is the structural
and thematic core of Am 8:1-3. As in Am 7:7-9, the play-on-
words can be analyzed on three levels: the literary level; the
level of magical praxis and divinatory technique; and the level
of divine inspiration.

On a most basic literary level, the play on the terms for
"harvest" and "end" has the same unifying effect as repetition.
Significantly, in Northern Israel, *qāyiṣ* and *qēṣ* would have
been pronounced in identically the same way.[23] Each time one
said the one term, one said the other. This singly-heard,
doubly-meant term is found in the motifs of initial description,
prophet's reply, and explanation; it links motif to motif,
structuring and unifying the work. Thus the economy of language which characterized Am 7:7-9 is found once again in this
example of the symbolic vision form. Each time the symbol term
is repeated, it is re-emphasized. The third mention of *qāyiṣ=
qēṣ* reveals the theme of the work by which "harvest" becomes a
"cut-off time" for Israel.

Without repeating the discussion of the methods of dream

---

23. L. Rost takes note of the pronunciation and orthog-
raphy of *qāyiṣ/qēṣ* in "Bermerkungen zu Sacharja 4," *ZAW* 63
(1951) 216, n. 4.

divination, we note that this passage evidences the specific
technique of word association. Like Am 7:7-9, 8:1-3 contains a
prediction about the future based upon the interpretation of
symbols. The identification of the harvest, $q\bar{a}yi\varsigma$, with its
sound equivalent $q\bar{e}\varsigma$ ("cut-off in time") not only reveals the
future, but also effects a magical process which helps to bring
about the revelation. As in Am 7:7-9, no human employs this
divinatory, magically potent technique. Both the symbolic
image and its interpretation are initiated by God. The seer is
merely the tool of God. The visionary process is totally inspired by the divine.

Thematically, Am 8:1-3 is an even more neatly structured
example of the symbolic vision form than Am 7:7-9. Am 8:1, 2,
and 3 interrelate such that the theme of harvest = the end of
Israel crescendoes in the final imagery of mourning and death.[24]
The ritual mourning which accompanied Near Eastern harvest
festivals - a custom originating in myths of the dying fertility God whose manifestations in nature were cut down in the
harvest season[25] - intermingles with the image of mourning over
actual human death, "a multitude of corpses." Harvest leads to
end leads to ignoble death.

Robert Coote notes that the term $^{\flat}\partial s\hat{\imath}p$ in 2e, "I will not
continue $(^{\flat}\partial s\hat{\imath}p)$ to pass him by," also has a double meaning
based on its unmentioned sound-alike $^{\flat}\bar{a}s\hat{\imath}p$, another term for
harvest.[26] We recall that this seasonal term, like $q\varsigma$, is
found in the Gezer Calendar. Like B. Rahtjen, Coote suggests
that the seasonal list of the calendar would have been familiar
folklore to Amos' audience, and thus the terms $q\bar{a}yi\varsigma/q\bar{e}\varsigma$ and
$^{\flat}\partial s\hat{\imath}p$ gain additional nuance and affect. Israel will be gath-
ered in, harvested.[27]

The use of the term $\check{s}lk$ in the hiph. is of special

---

24. As in the case of Am 7:9, a number of scholars consider Am 8:3 to be secondary. So Wolff and Weiser. We disagree and consider this verse an intrinsic part of the pericope
in terms of style, content, and theme.

25. Cf. J. D. Watts, *Vision and Prophecy*, pp. 41-42.

26. "Ripe Words," 16.

27. "Ripe Words," 15; "A Critical Note."

importance. As in Jos 8:29, 10:27, 2 Kgs 9:25, 26, and Jer
22:19, the casting out of the dead, leaving them without proper
burial, is an ultimate form of punishment and curse. It is
"the burial of an ass" (Jer 22:19). The cursing quality of the
final line of the vision helps to explain the meaning of the
enigmatic *has*.

Has is a brief counter charm, an attempt to "silence" the
curse or turn it away. It has the same effect as saying "God
forbid" after hearing of some horrible event. One should view
the use of *has* in Am 6:10 in a similar light. As in 8:1-3, the
setting is one of death. We suggest the following translation
and emendations.

And one's kinsman and the one who takes account of him
(mĕsapprô ?) will be left *(niš'ărû ?)* to bring the bones
out of the house. And one says to the one who is in the
recesses of the house, "Are there any more with you?" And
he replies, "None, silence!" - in order not to remind God
with a name.

The G reading, υπολειφθησονται, *niš'ărû* has been accepted
as correct. MT *nĕšā'ô* results from a confusion with *niš'ărû*,
the *resh* having dropped out. A form of *nš'* may also be a
doublet for *lĕhôṣî'*, since the notions of "carrying" and "bringing out" are comparable. The MT reading *msrpw* reflects a let-
ter reversal of *r* with *p*. We read a piel participle of *spr*.
If one considers the third *wĕ'āmar* in the MT version to be
dittographic, the speakers do not change. The one who is
counting up bodies in the house does not wish to mention the
name of anyone with him who might be alive, lest he remind God
that he missed a person. He is practicing a form of preventative magic.

While the command "silence" is less specifically directed
in Am 8:1-3, it has the same preventative thrust. In Am 6:10,
has is an attempt not to involve anyone else in the curse which
has already been fulfilled; in Am 8:3, it expresses, however
hopelessly, a wish to ward off the curse. A. Leo Oppenheim
lists a number of Assyrian counter-charms to be chanted in the
event of a bad dream. The interjection *has* is a much simpler
example of the same human response to a bad vision experience.[28]

28. *The Interpretation*, pp. 295-307.

Sellin suggests that the term *has* may be an attempt to
keep away the "plague demon." He believes that the "Pestdämon"
or "Würgengel" is the subject of *hᵉlyk*.[29] While there is no
need to bring in the pest demon, our own conclusions about the
nature of *has* are not unlike those of Sellin. The use of this
term is more than expression of horror, as suggested by Wolff,[30]
and is not simply a command to avoid mention of God's name in a
place of death, as suggested by Hammershaimb and others.[31] It
is an appropriate response to a curse or a prediction or doom,
which stems from a very basic if not completely conscious participation in a tradition of magic.

Jer 1:11-12

			Test for balance
11)	The word of the Lord came	ויהי דבר YHWH (11a	7
	to me saying,	אלי לאמר (11b	5
	"What do you see?"	מה אתה ראה ⟨ ⟩ᵃ (11c	5
12)	And I said, "An almond rod."	ואמר מקל שקד ⟨ ⟩ᵇ (11d	7
	Then the Lord said to me,	ויאמר YHWH אלי (12a	7
	"You have seen well,	היטבת לראות (12b	5
	For I am watching over	כי שקד אני (12c	5
	my word to do it."	על דברי לעשתו (12d	7

This passage is the briefest example of our form, and can
be discussed in an abbreviated manner. The only text critical
notes are as follows:

ᵃWith the shorter reading in G, omit *yirmᵉyāhû*.
ᵇWith the shorter reading in G, omit *'ănî rō'eh*.

The order of content elements in Jer 1:11-12 parallels
that of Am 7:7-9 and 8:1-3, but the element of initial description is missing. In this slightly condensed version we find:

1:11 Indication of vision/communication ויהי דבר YHWH אלי לאמר
1:11 Question of God to seer   מה אתה ראה
1:11 Reply/description   ואמר...
1:12 God's explanation of the object   ויאמר YHWH אלי

---

29. *Das Zwölfprophetenbuch*, pp. 295-307.

30. *Dodekapropheten*, *Amos*, p. 369.

31. *The Book of Amos*, p. 121.

Note that an alternate rubric introduces the vision.

Reminiscences of classical poetry are absent. Lines are
in the short 5-7 syllable range, but bicola are not neatly balanced, nor is there parallelism between lines. There is a succession of equally brief phrases with enjambement in the introductory rubric and between the last two phrases of the vision.
There is, moreover, no attempt to poeticize the explanation
motif, the word of the Lord. 1:12 thus contrasts with the
somethat more poetic Am 7:8e-g and 8:2d-e. Absent is the
nuanced recapitulation of the message which was poetic in style
in Am 7:9 and 8:3. On the other hand, the role of repetition
and economy of word choice is an even stronger and more obvious
structural unifier in this brief piece. A certain homogeneity
of language emerges in *rō'eh* (11), *lir'ôt* (12); *dĕbar* (11),
dĕbārî (12); *yahweh 'ēlay* (11, 12); and *lē'mōr, wā'ōmar* (11),
wayyō'mer (12). The play on *šqd* is, of course, the major unifier of theme and structure.

The literary, divinatory, and "inspirational" levels, discussed for the word-plays found in Amos, are still operative.
The unifying literary quality of the sound-alikes, *šāqēd/šōqēd*,
is only one aspect of this play. The vision of the almond rod
(šāqēd) provides symbolic assurance that God will indeed act
(šōqēd la'ăśôt), that he is watching. There is no need to
posit that the rod itself contains magical mantic power, as
suggested by Volz in a comparison with Hos 4:12 and Gen 30:37.
The mantic aspect emerges when an ordinary object, a stick from
an almond tree, is interpreted to have definite significance
for the future. Through word association a message about God's
actions is revealed; herein lie hints of mantic divinatory
practice.

The thematic progression achieved by the word-play on *šqd*
is not so sophisticated or stylish as that of *qāyiṣ/qēṣ*. Nevertheless, the message in Jer 1:11-12 is presented succinctly and
unmistakably. The quick progression of alternating speakers, a
rhetorical feature of the dialogue, and economy of word choice
assert a style which is powerful by its very terseness and
immediacy.

Jer 1:13-19

				Test for balance

13) And the word of the Lord came   ויהי דבר YHWH (13a   7

    To me a second time saying,   אלי שנית לאמר (13b   6

    "What do you see?"   מה אתה ראה (13c   5

    And I said, "A boiling pot,   ואמר סיר נפוח ⟨ ⟩a (13d   6

    And it faces from the north.   ופניו מפני צפונה (13e   9

14) Then the Lord said to me   ויאמר YHWH אלי (14a   7

    From the north will blow forth   מצפון bתפיח הרעה (14b   8
        the evil

    Upon all the inhabitants of   על כל ישבי הארץ (14c   7
        the land.

15) For behold I am calling
    To all the kingdoms of the north
    And they will come and each will set his seat
    At the entrance of the gates of Jerusalem,
    Around all her walls,
    And against all the cities of Judah.

                 כי הנני קרא (15a   6

              ⟨ ⟩d cלכל ממלכות צפון (15b   7

               ובאו ונתנו איש כסאו (15c   11

               פתח שערי ירושלם (15d   8

               ועל כל חומתיה סביב (15e   9

               ועל כל ערי יהודה (15f   8

16) And I will speak with them in judgment
    About all their evil, that they left me
    And they sacrificed to other gods,
    And bowed down to the makings of their hands.

               eודברתי להם במשפטe (16a   9

             על כל רעתם אשר עזבוני (16b   11

               ויקטרו לאלהים אחרים (16c   11

               וישתחוו למעשי ידיהם (16d   11

17) But you, gird up your loins,
    Arise and speak to them
    All which I shall command you.
    Do not be dismayed by them
    Lest I cause you to be shattered before them.

8   ‏ואתה תאזר מתניך‏ (17a
9   ‏קמת ודברת אליהם‏ [f] (17b
8   ‏את כל אשר‏ [g⟨ ⟩] ‏אצויך‏ (17c
7   ‏אל תחת מפניהם‏ (17d
8   ‏פן אחתך לפניהם‏ (17e

18)   Behold I am making you this day into a fortified city,
       Into a pillar of iron and walls of bronze
       To all the kings of Judah,
       To its princes and to the landed gentry.

12   [h⟨ ⟩] ‏הנה נתתך היום לעיר מבצר‏ (18a
12   [f] ‏לעמוד ברזל ולחמות נחשת‏[i⟨ ⟩j] (18b
7   [k] ‏לכל מלכי יהודה‏ (18c
9   ‏לשריה‏ [k⟨ ⟩] ‏ולעם הארץ‏ (18d

19)   They will fight against you, but not overcome you,
       For I am with you to save you.

12   [f] ‏נלחמו אליך ולא יוכלו לך‏ (19a
11   ‏כי אתך אני‏[l⟨ ⟩] ‏להצילך‏ (19b

[a]With shorter reading in G, omit *'ănî rō'eh*.

[b]With G, εκκαυθησεται. This term is often used to translate hiph. of *pwḥ*. See G Prov 14:5, 25, 19:9, 29:8. With Or.,
Volz reads *nāpaḥtî*. Rudolph also suggests reading a form of
npḥ. As seen in Am 8:1-3, the play on words need not involve
terms which are the same etymologically. The play is achieved
via sound. *Nāpûḥ* and *tāpîḥ* provide suitable sound-alikes,
while allowing for the use of a common MT equivalent for εκκαιω
εκκαιω is never used to translate a form of *npḥ*. We disagree
with Bright, Weiser, and Driver who accept MT *tippātaḥ*. MT may
be the result of an eye-slip to vs. 15 on the part of a scribe.

[c]MT *lĕkol mišpĕḥôt mamlĕkôt ṣāpônâ* and G πασας τας βασιλ-
ειας απο βορρα της γης reflect two variant readings: *lĕkol
mamlĕkôt ṣāpônâ* and *lĕkol mišpĕḥôt hā'āreṣ*. So Janzen, *Studies*,
p. 10. Most scholars omit *mišpĕḥôt*, though some with Rudolph
simply regard MT as an expansion of Jer 25:9, *kol mišpĕḥôt
ṣāpôn*. The *h* ending on *ṣāpôn* has been copied from *ṣāpônâ* of
vs. 13.

[d]Omit *nĕ'um yahweh* with Syp. So Volz.

[e]Weiser and Volz emend MT *'ôtām* to *'ittām*. G, και λαλησω
προς αυτους μετα κρισεως, *wĕdibbartî lāhem bĕmišpāṭ* seems the

shortest and best reading. Rudolph accepts the unmarked form
of *mišpāṭ*, but prefers the basic syntax of MT with the emendation *'ittām*: *wĕdibbartî mišpāṭ 'ittām*.

 ᶠOmit prosaizing *waw*.

 ᵍOmit *'ănōkî* with G.

 ʰOmit *wa'ănî* with G.

 ⁱWe accept MT which contains the three parallel expressions for strength. So Bright, Weiser, Rudolph, and Janzen.
Volz deletes *lĕ'ămmûd barzel* with G. With Janzen we agree that
G is haplographic (*Studies*, p. 119). G ως τειχος χαλκουν
οχυρον is an addition from 15:20 or a scribal error caused by
the proximity of the expression *'îr mibṣār*.

 ʲOmit *'al kol hā'āreṣ* with G. This phrase is unnecessary
in its present context in terms of sense and metric balance.
The addition may have been occasioned by the nearby use of
hā'āreṣ in *lĕ'am hā'āreṣ* combined with a displacement of *kol*
which modifies *malkê yĕhûdâ* in the tradition preserved by G,
πασι τοις βασιλευσιν Ιουδα.

 ᵏOmit *lĕkōhănêhā* and follow the shorter reading in G, πασι
τοις βασιλευσι Ιουδα και τοις αρχουσιν και τω λαω της γης. We
agree with Janzen, Cornill, and Streane against Bright, Volz,
Weiser, and Rudolph. Janzen wisely notes that 1:18 contains a
"stereotyped list of officials." By studying the natural
groupings or pairs into which fall these traditional parallel
elements, Janzen concludes that *lĕkōhănêhâ* is not paired off
with a traditionally proper element (*Studies*, pp. 35-36). It
is intrusive in MT 1:18.

 ˡOmit *nĕ'um yahweh* as a redactor's addition. Bright and
Weiser follow G, where the phrase is less intrusive than in MT.
We agree that G contains the earlier reading, but it too is expansionary. The phrase is a common redactor's marker and adds
nothing to the meaning of the vision while upsetting metric
balance. G has preserved a redactor's closing rubric.

 Jer 1:13-19 poses problems not only of form but also of
redaction. While elements of content found in this pericope
basically parallel those which describe other examples of our
form, close analysis reveals that the literary style of vss.
15-19 differs significantly from that of vss. 13-14, which we
regard as the original unit of the passage. The two-layered

quality of Jer 1:13-19 and the significance of nuances in the
final redacted form of this vision will emerge in our study.[32]

Pattern of Content		Rubrics
1:13	Indication of vision	ויהי דבר YHWH אלי שנית לאמר
1:13	Question of God to seer	מה אתה ראה
1:13	Reply and description	ואמר...
1:14	Explanation of seen objects	ויאמר YHWH אלי...
(1:17	Charge	no rubric)

The pattern of motifs is as expected as is the language used to
present them. As in Jer 1:11-12, the motif of initial description of the vision is absent. The first rubric is especially
long.

---

32. Bright and others have suggested that vss. 15-19 may
be a continuation of vss. 4-10, but this suggestion is belied
by 1) thematic and 2) stylistic considerations: 1) We believe
that the reference to the north in vss. 15-19 picks up the
theme of vss. 13-14. Vs. 15f. would not follow vs. 10 with
nearly so much effectiveness or meaning. 2) While vss. 4-10
contain some textual and poetic difficulties, they do display
some characteristics of true classical style, good parallelism,
disenjambement, and flexibility in the use of traditional language. That is, the expected parallel pairs and syntactic
arrangements are combined with freshness and variety. See vss.
5 and 7c, d in particular. Dialogue between God and the prophet may lead to departures from classical style, such that the
alternation between speakers provides the frame and structure
for the poetry rather than more usual classical criteria. This
phenomenon may in part explain the structure in our examples of
the symbolic vision form and in Jer 1:4-10. Still, the latter
does contain some nice classical touches. In contrast, vss.
15-19 are neo-classical in style, displaying the traits of late
poetry analyzed by Paul D. Hanson (*The Dawn of Apocalyptic*
[Philadelphia: Fortress, 1975], esp. pp. 105, 118, and 143.

One might characterize vss. 4-10 as semi-classical, 11-14
as non-classical, and 15-19 as neo-classical. While the first
and second varieties can exist contemporaneously, 15-16 is a
later addition.

The motif, "explanation of seen objects," covers vss. 14-
16 and joins the original unit with the redactional material.
The redactor has simply filled out the theme of judgment evoked
by the play on *sîr nāpûḥ/miṣṣāpôn tāpîḥ*.[33] The evil from the
north named by the punchline at vs. 14b, c is specified further
by sub-motifs: 1) the call to the judges who are the *mamlākôt*,
"the kingdoms" (vs. 15); and 2) the review of accusations against
the people (vs. 16). Such elaborations are natural extensions
of the basic judgment theme. In fact, vs. 15 skillfully evokes
a double image of war-preparation and invasion on the one hand
and of court and judgment on the other. The gates of the city
are traditionally a place for judgment, where the king sits to
hear cases (2 Sam 19:9), where suits are settled (Ruth 4:11),
where punishment is meted out and justice done (2 Kgs 7:20; see
also Am 5:10, 12, and 15). Yet here the judges at the gate are
the invading nations. The coming and sitting at the entrance
of the gate intermingles with images of setting about the walls
and against the cities of Judah. The flexible meaning of the
preposition *ʿal*, "at/against," serves the double image well, as
judgment and invasion are evoked simultaneously.

This lengthy and descriptive enrichment of the explanation
of the symbols should be kept in mind as our study continues;
for the baroque explanation of the symbol will become a regular
feature of later symbolic visions.

Jer 1:13-19 also contains an additional motif which concludes the pattern, "the charge to the prophet" (vss. 17-19).
Such concluding commands and/or encouragements, found in a number of prophetic oracles (Jer 18:2, Ez 11:4, 12:28, etc.), is
fully at home at the end of this piece and does not disturb
the typological form. Yet there is no doubt that the charge
motif does extend the pattern beyond the boundaries of the
other examples of our form. A charge motif concludes the symbolic visions at Zech 1:14, Dan 8:26, 2 Bar 43:1-3, 76:3-4, and
4 Ezra 12:37-39, and like the baroque explanation of the vision,
found in the redactionally later portion of the passage, may
indicate a direction in which the symbolic vision form is developing. The redactor may feel that the vision should end

---

33. See text critical note "b."

with a charge, whereas Jeremiah did not. He thus fills out
Jeremiah's original vision in accordance with modes becoming
popular and accepted in his day.

In any event, the basic motif pattern and the introductory
rubrics of the piece are formally fully predictable. Even the
extension of the explanation motif contains no shift in theme.
Indeed vss. 15-19 cannot stand alone as an individual composition. The passage simply has no context without the earlier
reference in vs. 14 to the evil from the north. Given then
that the piece does adhere to our external or typological criteria of form, why do we insist on redactional layers? It is a
discussion of form and literary style which leads to the reali-
zation that, while Jer 1:13-19 does have a formal and thematic
integrity, it has undergone a process of development in tradition.

The original vision

Jer 1:13-14 is an uncomplicated example of the form which
includes the indication of a vision experience, question and
reply/ description motifs, and the explanation motif. In
visions as brief as Jer 1:13-14 or Jer 1:11-12, we do not
attempt to divide the piece into units of lines. The composers
of the pieces and those to whom they were addressed probably
required no such breaks in the material, nor do we in our
attempt to understand issues of structure and form.

Once again there is little evidence of classical poetics.
In order to allow for balance in the line length between 13a
and 13b and between 14b and 14c one creates non-traditional
enjambement. Vs. 13 contains no balance in the seer's reply-
description (6/9). More important, no real parallelism between
cola is found. Thus on the lowest level of structure, rules of
classical prosody do not unify this piece which we consider to
be the earliest redactional portion of Jer 1:13-19.

As in the other examples of the form, there is a repetition of forms of *'mr (lē'mōr, wā'ōmar* (13), *wayyō'mer* (14))*,
the rhetorical pattern which helps to unify the piece. The
sound-play on *pānāyw mippĕnê* creates a catchy rhythm in 14c
which completes the tricolon in a euphonic if not classically
poetic way. The most important structural unifier of the piece

is the play on ṣāpônâ/miṣṣāpôn and nāpûḥ/tāpîḥ. We are less
surprised when a boiling pot from the north leads to an interpretation of evil blowing from the north than when a harvest
basket leads to an interpretation of the end (Am 8:1,2). The
association here is less subtle. The notion of something hot
and fiery from the north may be common enough in Biblical tradition to convey an already transparent meaning in vs. 13. The
north is the historical locus of Near Eastern super-powers and
also the mythic locus for Yahweh's abode, the place where he
begins his march as divine warrior. In any event, formally the
process found in Jer 1:13-14 is identical to that found in the
other passages.

Once again the association of like with like smacks of
divinatory technique. If the tāpîḥ emendation is correct (see
note "b"), the interpretation of the vision involves word and
sound association as well as idea association. One sort of
blowing, usually associated with heat and flames, leads to the
idea of another sort of blowing, usually associated with breath-
ing or blowing out. The blown, fired pot leads to evil which
snorts or puffs forth like an evil wind.[34] Once the symbol is
clearly divined, its eventuality becomes all the more likely.
The curse has been cast.

In this vision, as in the others, God both presents the
symbol and interprets it, while the prophet is a tool made to
experience the vision so that he can report it. This inspirational use of divinatory technique - such that God is the true
diviner - differs from the use of scientific divination as explained in Egyptian and Assyrian dream books.[35]

---

34. In a later period the fiery sense of nph is possibly
attributed to its sound-alike and mean-alike puḥ. Hence the
sense of "inflaming the city" in Pr 29:8. Yet the phrase, parallel with yāšîbû 'ap, might as well be translated in our own
idiom, "cause the city to blow up," i.e. "to be angry."

35. We recall that such "scientific" methods of dream
interpretation are simply not found in the literary texts
adduced by Oppenheim (The Interpretation). In symbolic dreams
of the Gilgamesh Epic (Oppenheim, 247-249) the interpretation
seems to be based on a very free method of idea association.

It is clear that Jer 1:13-14 is fully in accord with the
other passages in our study both in terms of its use of the
divinatory associative technique - with all its levels and
implications - and in terms of style. Its structural unity is
based on economy of language and the repetition of sounds as
opposed to more classical criteria. What then of vss. 15-19,
which continue the motif of explanation and add the element of
charge?

The redactional additions

One might suggest that vss. 15-16 are akin to the summation and recapitulation of the vision's interpretation, found
at Am 7:9 and 8:3. Unlike Am 7:9 and 8:3, however, Jer. 1:15-
16 and vss. 17-19, which contain the element of charge, are
different in style from the rest of the vision. While it is
likely that the Amos visions took form all at once, Jer 1:13-19
has undergone a process of development in tradition, a process
which extended but did not disrupt the original form of the
vison. Close analysis sets the date of the redactor's con-
tribution to the passage at the late sixth century B.C.

The same is true in the symbolic Dream of Tammuz (Oppenheim,
246) in which the deity's sister Gestinanna acts as dream interpreter and in the Dream of Gudea (Oppenheim, 245-246) in which
the goddess Nanshe serves as interpreter. One cannot make
assumptions about real-life practice, of course, from these
literary works, but it is interesting that divine intervention
is portrayed as a means of receiving the interpretation of
dreams in the case of the Tammuz dream and the Gudea dream.
The latter, in fact, may actually record a real experience of
the king, his reason for undertaking building projects. One is
again led to the speculation that dreams are on the grey area
between "natural" and "artificial" phenomena. They are not
necessarily dealt with scientifically (contra A. Falkenstein,
"《Wahrsagung》 in der sumerische Überlieferung," *La Divination*,
p. 64). The symbolic visions in Amos and Jeremiah *combine* the
natural aspect of a dream sent by the deity and interpreted by
him with the artificial method of dream interpretation such
that he becomes the diviner.

First note the frequent presence of enjambement between
lines: between 15a and 15b; 15c and 15d; *15c and 15e; *15c
and 15f; 16a and 16b; 17b and 17c; *18a and 18c; *18a and 18d.
Certainly enjambement is common in the form and has been noted
as an example of non-classical style; yet in several of the
above instances we find an unusual and complex variety. One
grammatical or syntactic unit is not carried simply to the next
line but to two beyond it. See the starred examples above.
Paul Hanson has indicated that the "intricate interweaving of
grammatical elements"[36] is one of the distinctive traits of
late poetry. Neater, more classical canons have broken down.
This baroque style of poetry which we call neo- or mock-
classical evidences the movement towards a more prosaic and
literary medium. This style seems almost a parody of truly
classical or good archaizing modes. Vss. 15-19 also exhibit
other traits which Professor Hanson has observed in Trito-
Isaianic material.

While some acceptable parallelism is found in 16c/16d,
17a/17b, 17d/17e, and 19a/19b, for the most part parallelism is
of an easy-to-compose variety. Hanson has discussed the use of
"recurring grammatical elements" in Trito-Isaiah.[37] Here the
monotonous repetition of syntactic arrangements provides a
rather unimaginative method of parallel construction. Vss. 15e
and f and 18c and d are examples of such parallelism. The
parallel elements do not create an impressionistic picture, but
instead have a list-like quality. The list quality, another of
the characteristics of late poetry, is also found in vs. 15c,
which contains a rather unnecessary piling up of verbs, and in
18a, b. This "prose-like succession of elements"[38] leads to
long prosodic units, comparable to those in Isaiah 58 and 59.
In general, while individual bicola and tricola are balanced in
length, the overall metric pattern is erratic, interspersed
with some extremely long units. See especially vss. 18a, b and
19a, b.

The above style clearly differs from classical style,

36. *The Dawn of Apocalyptic*, p. 105.
37. *The Dawn of Apocalyptic*, p. 105.
38. *The Dawn of Apocalyptic*, p. 105.

conforming in all respects to Paul Hanson's description of late
sixth century B.C./early fifth century B.C. poetry. Yet the
repetition of grammatic constructions, the excessive length of
prosodic units, and the list-like quality of vss. 15-19 differs
just as greatly from the style which has emerged in our studies
of the symbolic vision form. Like much of the material from
Trito-Isaiah, Jer 1:15-19 has a baroque, strung-out quality,
whereas the earliest examples of our form display a rather nice
tightness of structure, a neat unity of form, based primarily
on an economy of language and on the centrality of one basic
image. For the most part, bicola and tricola in our vision
form exhibit far less metric balance than the material in Jer
1:15-19. Parallelism of any kind is minimal. The visions do
not display classical style or a classical style which has
become baroque. The symbolic vision form displays an alternate
style of prophetic expression which existed in the classical
period, but which did not conform to norms of classical poetry.
The significant variation in style between Jer 1:13-14 and vss.
15-19 points to the likelihood of the latter's being a late
sixth century B.C. addition to the original vision.

     We should emphasize, however, that the piece as it now
stands may point toward the development of the symbolic vision
form in tradition. The charge, included in the redactional
portion of the above piece, will become a frequent element in
the pattern of later versions of this form. Similarly frequent
will become the baroque embellishment of the explanation motif.
This lengthening and elaboration of the explanation may simply
result from the fact that the symbols themselves become more
complex. On the other hand, it is possible that the redactor
of the late sixth century B.C. finds the Jeremiah passage a bit
bare as it stands. Without changing the original form or the
thrust of the symbol, he is still able to fill out the piece,
concluding with a charge to the prophet as do the authors of
Zech 1:14 and Dan 8:26.

Jeremiah 24

		Test for balance
הראני YHWH	(1a	5
והנה שני דודאי תאנים	(1b	11
⟨ ⟩ מועדים^a לפני היכל YHWH b⟨	(1c	9

⟨אחרי הגלות נבוכדראצר מלך
בבל את יכוניהו בן יהויקים
מלך יהודה ואת ^cהשרים ואת
החרש ואת ^dהמסגר מירושלם
ויביאם בבל⟩

הדוד אחד תאנים טבות מאד	(2a	11
כתאני הבכרות	(2b	8
והדוד אחד תאנים רעות מאד	(2c	12
אשר לא תאכלנה מרע	(2d	9
ויאמר YHWH אלי	(3a	7
מה אתה ראה ירמיהו	(3b	9
ואמר תאנים	(3c	6
^eהטבות טבות מאד	(3d	7
והרעות רעות מאד	(3e	8
אשר לא תאכלנה מרע	(3f	9
ויהי דבר YHWH אלי לאמר	(4	11
⟨ ⟩^f כתאנים הטבות האלה	(5a	10
כן אכיר את גלות יהודה ⟨ ⟩ לטובה	(5b	12

⟨אשר שלחתי מן המקום
הזה לארץ כשדים⟩

ושמתי עיני עליהם לטובה	(6a	11
והשבתים על הארץ הזאת	(6b	10
ובניתים ולא אהרס	(6c	8
ונטעתים ולא אתוש	(6d	8
ונתתי להם לב לדעת אתי	(7a	12
כי אני YHWH	(7b	5
והיו לי לעם	(7c	6
ואנכי אהיה להם לאלהים ⟨ ⟩	(7d	11

⟨כי ישבו אלי בכל לבם⟩

וכתאנים הרעות	(8a	8
אשר לא תאכלנה מרע^g⟨ ⟩	(8b	9

12   (8c   כן אתן את צדקיהו מלך יהודה

13   (8d   ואת שריו ואת שארית ירושלים⟩ ⟩

⟨הנשארים בארץ הזאת
והיושבים בארץ מצרים⟩

(9   ⟨   ⟩

⟨ (9a   ונתחים ⟩ לזרועה

(9b   לכל ממלכות הארץ

(9c   לחרפה ולמשל

(9d   לשנינה ולקללה

(9e   בכל המקמות

⟨ (9f   אשר אדיחם שם ⟩

8   (10a   ושלחתי בם את ־ החרב

8   (10b   ואת הרעב ואת הדבר

9   (10c   עד תמם מעל האדמה

7   (10d   אשר נתתי להם ⟨ ⟩ ⟩

1) The Lord showed me
   And behold two baskets of figs
   Set before the temple of the Lord ⟨   ⟩.
⟨after Nebuchadrezzar, king of Babylon,
exiled Jeconiah son of Jehoiakim, king
of Judah, and the princes, and the
craftsmen, and the goldsmiths from
Jerusalem, and brought them to Babylon.⟩

2) One basket was of very good figs
   Like the figs of first-ripening,
   But the other basket was of very bad figs
   Which could not be eaten, so bad were they.

3) And the Lord said to me,
   "What do you see, Jeremiah?"
   And I said, "Figs.
   The good ones are very good,
   But the bad ones are very bad
   So that they could not be eaten, so bad are
       they."

4) And the word of the Lord came to me saying,
5) Like these good figs
   I will recognize the exile of Judah ⟨ ⟩ for
       good.

⟨whom I sent from this place to
the land of the Chaldeans⟩

> 6) And I will set my eyes upon them for good.
>   And I will return them to this land
>   I will build them up and not tear down,
>   I will plant them and not uproot.
>
> 7) And I will give them a heart to know me,
>   That I am the Lord.
>   They shall be for me a people,
>   And I for them a god. ⟨ ⟩

⟨For they will return to me
with all their heart.⟩

> 8) But like the bad figs
>   Which could not be eaten, so bad are they,
>   Thus will I make Zedekiah, king of Judah,
>   And his princes and the remnant of Jeru-
>   salem ⟨ ⟩.

⟨who remain in this land
and who dwell in the land of Egypt.⟩

9) And I will make them like seed scattered   ⟨   ⟩
   Toward all the nations of earth
   To be a reproach and a byword
   A taunt and a curse
   In all the nations
   Where I drive them.

> 10) And I will send against them the sword,
>   And hunger and plague,
>   Until they are completely destroyed from
>   the land
>   Which I gave to them.

[a]With Bright and against Volz and D. Winton Thomas ("A
Note on מועדים in Jeremiah 24, 1," *JTS* 3 [1952], 55) we see no
need to emend $mû'ădîm$. As at Ezek 21:21, the hoph. part. of
$y'd$ means "set" or "placed." G. R. Driver suggests reading
$mô'ădîm$ from the Arabic usage, "fresh, tender," hence "freshly
ripened figs." His suggestion, however, ignores the fem.

gender of *těʾēnîm*, "figs." ("Hebrew Notes on the Wisdom of
Jesus Ben Sirach," *JBL* 53 [1934], 233.)

[b]This date-setting rubric which contains a list of those
exiled to Babylon seems out of place in MT and G contexts, from
the point of view of syntax and form. Like the comparable date-
list in Jer 29:2, it is, no doubt, an editorial addition, possibly based on the more complete list of exiles in 2 Kgs 24:14-
16. In this passage and in Jeremiah 29, the date-line is inserted after the initial indication of the vision (in Jeremiah
24) or message (in Jeremiah 29), possibly in order to have it
seem a more intrinsic part of the form in each case. Of interest for our study is that a date-line will become a regular
expected element of later versions of the symbolic vision form.
See Zech 1:7, Dan 7:1, 8:1, 4 Ezra 11:1, 13:1, 2. As in Jer
1:13-19, a later redactor has filled out the original work,
leaving us hints of the form's direction in development. It is
interesting that the redactor did not feel that the rubric of
date should be placed at the beginning of the vision. Perhaps
the date-line was not yet a completely regular part of the form,
and so was inserted after the initial motif.

[c]With shorter reading in G, και τους αρχοντας.

[d]As noted by Rudolph, Weiser, Bright, and others, the meaning of *msgr* is not at all certain. Since *hammasgēr* is linked
to *heḥārāš* in the lists at Jer 24:1, 29:2, and 2 Kgs 24:14, 16,
the tendency has been to assign some sort of craftsman's meaning to the term - either "locksmith" from the *sgr* root meaning
"to close" or "goldsmith" from the sometimes use of *sāgûr* in
connection with gold-work (1 Kgs 6:20, 21; 7:49, 50; 10:21).
The translation "goldsmith" is preferred because the profession
of locksmith does not seem appropriate to the list of exiles of
court status. (Noted also by G. R. Driver, "Linguistic and
Textual Problems: Jeremiah," *JQR* 28 [1937], 116.)

The issue is complicated by the G translation for *msgr*,
δεσμωτης, "captive, one in bonds" in the Jeremiah verses and
συνκλειοντα, "the one who shuts up, closes up" (ms. acc. part.
of συγκλειω), in 2 Kgs 24:16. The latter seems to be a slavish
translation of the Hebrew, based on its etymology and nominal   form; the translator does not comprehend the true meaning or usage of *msgr*. On the other hand, the translations in

Jeremiah are clear enough. Of additional interest and possible
relevance are other members of the list of exiles found in the
G, but not reflected in the MT tradition.

Jer 29:2 (36:2) ... και παντος ελευθερου και δεσμωτου και
      τεχνιτου

Jer 24:1 ... και τους τεχνιτας και τους δεσμωτας και τους
      πλουσιους.

Who are the πλουσιους and who is the ελευθερου? The
"wealthy," the *ʿăšîrîm*, and "the freeman," the *ḥopšî* or *ḥōr*,
seem to refer to societal statuses or roles rather than to
positions in the royal household as do the other terms in each
of the vss. from Jeremiah. On the other hand, the longer passage from 2 Kgs 24 does seem to include larger definable groups
in society such as *ʾēlê hāʾāreṣ*. Could the G reflect a pair
"freeman/bondsman" *(mešuggar?)* in Jer 29:2? Is Jer 24:2 contrasting the wealthy with their bonded servants, all of whom
were exiled together as households? Indeed, is *ḥārāš* a later
corruption for *ḥōr*, so that 2 Kgs 24:16 (now corrupt in G and
MT) once read

שבעת אלפים (πλουσιους ?) ואת כל אנשי חיל

אלף (δεσμωτην) ואת המסגר (ελευθερον) וההר

The two verses in Jeremiah G would thus preserve some earlier
readings, lost in the G of 2 Kgs 24:16 and in the MT tradition
of Jer 24:1 and 29:2.

    The above susggestions while interesting cannot be proven.
We have therefore opted for the MT reading in Jer 24:2, accept-
ing with reservations the translation "goldsmith" for *msgr*. G.
R. Driver's suggestion that *masgēr* is a later corruption for a
form of *sigrite* (Akkadian "palace women," i.e. those closed in,
as in a harem) is highly speculative.

    [e]With G omit *hattě'ěnîm*.

    [f]Omit *kōh 'āmar yahweh 'ĕlōhê yiśrā'ēl* as expansionary.
So Weiser, Rudolph, and Volz.

    [g]Omit *kî kōh 'āmar yahweh* as an expansionary addition. So
Weiser, Rudolph, and Volz.

    [h]Omit *rā'â* with most scholars. Janzen suggests that the
presence of *rā'â* is best explained as a conflation from mss.
in which *zw'h (zawǎ'â)* was transcribed as *r'h (rā'â) (Studies,*
pp. 12-13). This explanation, however, does not account for

the G reading, διασκορπισμον, "a scattering, dispersal." Could
G reflect some form of *zrh*, "to scatter, winnow" or of *zrᶜ*, "to
sow, scatter seed"? *Zrh* is often translated by a form of διασ-
κορπιζω, while that Greek term is not used to translate *zrᶜ*.
Nevertheless it is possible that in this case διασκορπισμον is
translating a noun-form such as *zērûᶜa*, "sowing" found in Is
61:11. Better yet, there may have been a noun-form *zērûᶜâ*
after the pattern of *sᵉmûᶜâ*, "report." This term *zĕrûᶜâ* could
have easily split off into two misreadings, *lĕzawĕᶜâ* and *lĕrāᶜâ*.
There are other advantages in taking the G reading seri-
ously. The sense of "scattering" fits in well with the final
words of vs. 9, לכל המקמות אשר אדיחם שם. As a whole, vs. 9
deals in a negative way with those who have left the land.
Such an attitude is at variance with the central theme of Jeremiah 24: contrast between the good exiles and the evil ones
who stay behind in the land. The latter will perish in the
land (see vs. 10). It is unlikely that a redactor added only
the final words of vs. 9 (*lĕkol hamĕqōmōt....šām*) which are so
obviously out of place within the theme of punishment to those
left in the land, but pardon for those who have been exiled.
It is more likely that a redactor added a whole section which
properly introduces this new notion of punishing some who leave
the land in exile. A form of *ntn* in vs. 9a echoes the sentencing use of the same verb in vs. 8c. As suggested by Rudolph,
vs. 9 may well be a reworking of Deut 28:37. This vs. from
Deuteronomy contains not only the motif of being sent to foreign lands, but also the elements of becoming a mockery and byword in these lands. It would seem that more than lines e and
f of vs. 9 are secondary additions. Nevertheless, Rudolph himself and Weiser consider only the last bicolon to be secondary.
Volz goes further, believing 9c-g to be secondary; yet all
three believe 9a-b to be part of the original piece, reading
zawĕᶜâ as "horror, Ensetzen." These solutions do not deal with
the basic problem of the thematic inappropriateness of the
final bicolon of vs. 9. The redactor was not so completely
insensitive to the theme of the larger piece. Punishment in
exile and the notion of bad exiles is introduced, as a new additional aspect of sentencing. They will be sown among the
nations and become a source of derision. The ones who initially

avoided exile and stayed in the land will get their just de-
serts too.

In a fuller discussion of redactional layers of Jeremiah
24, we will show that the whole of vs. 9 comes from a later
period than the original piece, a period in which bitterness is
expressed not only for those who stayed in the land under Zede-
kaiah, but also for those who eventually escaped to Egypt and
elsewhere in the following years.[39]

[i]Accept shorter reading in G and om. *wĕla'ăbōtêhem*.

Redactional additions in Jeremiah 24

Jeremiah 24 contains a number of redactional problems
which divide into the following groups.

1) The brief rubrics which indicate the announcement of a
word of God (notes "f" and "g") are the least complex secondary
additions in the piece. These phrases, omitted from vss. 5 and
8, are not of content-importance and do not add to the theme of
the work in any way. Rather, as rubrics, they indicate that a
certain element of content is coming.

The rubric in vs. 5, *kōh 'āmar yahweh 'ĕlōhê yiśrā'ēl*, may
be a doublet for the equivalent introductory rubric in vs. 5.
Inclusion of both readings is cumbersome and unnecessary.

In vs. 8, the phrase *kî kōh 'āmar yahweh* has been inserted
to emphasize and heighten the interpretation motif *(kēn 'ettēn
...)* which follows the repetition of the symbol in 8a, b. In
fact, this phrase interrupts the syntactic flow of the verse
and is counter to the tight, neat style seen in other examples
of the symbolic vision form.

Thus both of the above rubrics, variants of *kōh 'āmar*

---

39. Jeremiah 29, which also develops the theme of good
exiles vs. evil ones at home, re-uses Jer 24:8, 9, copying vs.
9 almost verbatim (see Jer 29:17-18 in particular). These vss.
not found in G are a late addition to the MT from Jeremiah 24,
where vs. 9 itself is an addition to the original text. It is
clear that any hints to the original reading of this expansionary vs. are to be found in Jeremiah 24 and the G to that chapter. Jeremiah 29 contains only a later smoothed out version of
the expansion and is of no help.

yahweh, are secondary additions; yet the date of these additions or their authorship is indeterminable. Such stock rubrics provide no sure handles; we have simply omitted them with notes. The other suspicious material which does contain content and is not purely a marker or heading has been included to the left of the text.

2) The addition in vs. 5b, *'ăšer šillaḥtî...kaśdîm*, and in vs. 7 (following our 7d), *kî yāšûbû...libbām*, do contain content, but of an essentially elaborative variety. In 5b, the phrase interrupts the syntactic flow, as does the rubric in vs. 8 discussed above. Moreover, it destroys otherwise passible, if not classical, long metrical balance. This interpolation originally may have been a marginal note, explaining the *gālût* in more detail. While *kî yāšûbû...libbām* does not create syntactic problems it has the appearance of a redactor's expansion, explaining the pardon of Israel, the transitional *kî* being a common marker of explanatory redactional activity.

The phrase in vs. 8, *hanniš'ārîm bā'āreṣ hazzō't*, is in the same category as *'ăšer šillaḥtî...kaśdîm* in vs. 5. That is, it is an explanatory *peshat* interpretation or specification of the *šĕ'ērît yĕrûšālaim*.

The content of the above additions is not datable or identifiably polemical. In midrash terminology, they are *peshat*, simple literal explanatory notes, a very basic way to expand the text.

3) The lengthy date-setting element, inserted uncomfortably in vs. 1 has been discussed in text critical note "b." It does provide a context for the vision, but in its position in G and MT is clearly intrusive, injecting a long prose passage into a more rhetorical medium and disrupting the even, direct movement from the description of the symbol to the explanation.

As noted earlier, such date-lines introduce a number of later relatives of this vision form, and indeed had the date segment begun Jeremiah 24, we might have considered it an original part of the vision, an alternate introduction to the vision form in the time of Jeremiah. Since it is unlikely that the whole date section was dislodged from the opening of the vision, we must assume that a redactor placed the indication of

date within the initial description of the vision in order to
make it seem more a part of the whole. Such a suggestion
becomes more plausible if one assumes that originally the date
element was considerably shorter, and not such an eyesore.
This hypothesis is supported by some briefer textual variants
which omit some of the members of the list of those exiled.
(See the miniscules in the "C" group.) It is of special importance, however, that the introductory date motif will become a
completely common and unintrusive part of later revelatory symbolic visions. In Jer 24:1, the date/list provides no internal
information which allows one to decide when it was added to the
original vision. At some point, an orderly redactor sought to
place this vision in its proper chronological place. His date-
line would place it after the exile of 597 B.C. We, like
Bright, see nothing wrong in this dating of the vision material
and can be no more explicit than the redactor.

  4) Vs. 8 contains more intriguing and specific content.
The phrase, *hayyōšĕbîm bĕ'ereṣ miṣrāyim*, is a rather interesting addition which does somewhat alter the theme at hand. The
mention of those in Egypt provides the passage with a new
dimension. While the bad figs symbolize those who were not
exiled in contrast to the good figs, the *gālût yĕhûdâ* of vs. 5b,
this phrase tacks on to the metaphor, those who dwell in Egypt.
They too are like bad figs. This addition may be a product of
the period after the fall of Jerusalem and the assassination of
Gedaliah when those who had remained in power fled to safety in
Egypt (2 Kgs 25:26, Jer 41:17). They too have not submitted
themselves to the required punishment and must be included in
the earlier condemnation. On the other hand, this addition may
well reflect an even later animosity between Babylonian and
Egyptian Jews during the period of the restoration. In any
event, it is likely that this addition formed one bicolon with
the previous line; the redactor thus eases in his nuance in
theme via a bicolon which pairs those remaining in the land
with those who are dwelling in Egypt.

  5) The most interesting addition of the piece is vs. 9.
We have already discussed thematic reasons for considering the
verse an addition and, in turn, our reasons for emending to
zĕrû'â. Stylistic considerations are also important. Minus

redactional additions, Jeremiah 24 does conform to the
economical-rhetorical style of other examples of our form; yet
the style of Jer 24:9 is much like the neo-classical style of
1:15-19. Granted, Jeremiah 24 provides less material with
which to work, but note the repeated use of the preposition *lě*
in vs. 9 to create a list-like succession of prepositional
phrases. Vss. 9c and 9d are particularly monotonous. The
whole is reminiscent of Jer 1:18. Thus the style of Jer 24:9
would seem to support a rather late date.

If the above suggestion is correct, vs. 9 presents a late
6th century date and a theme which emphasizes not the healing
aspects of exile (in that the punishment leads to eventual salvation and pardon, vss. 5-7), but the punishment itself. In
vs. 9, exile means derision and curse, a scattering, not a
means of redemption. Could this vs. belong to the same redactional tradition as the addition concerning "those dwelling in
Egypt" found in vs. 8? Does vs. 9 reflect a strain of anti-
Egyptian-Jew sentiment on the part of the orthodox Babylonian
returnees? In any event, whoever the author and whatever the
specific polemic, this vs. attempts to direct the passage in a
new way, tempering the simple dichotomy between good exiles and
bad non-exiles, found in the original vision. The attempt is
not entirely successful; the fissure between the original
vision and the addition is still visible from both a stylistic
and a thematic point of view.

This passage and its redactional problems have been far
more difficult than those of Jer 1:13-19. The latter contains
homogeneous redactional material in one block, which in no way
interrupts the syntax of individual cola or the form as a whole.
If the content of vss. 15-19 is not distinctive, polemical, or
datable, their style is distinctive and identifiable. In contrast, the material which we consider redactional in Jeremiah
24 has been intertwined into the piece in snippets. How many
hands are responsible for the various additions or how many
different periods is indeterminable.

The *kōh ʾāmar* rubrics are common redactional stock and
have been omitted when redundant in vs. 5 or intrusive in vs.
8. Such additions fall into the same category as *něʾum yahweh*,
omitted in Jer 1:15, 19. The additions in our groups 2 and 3

above are more significant. These are not stock phrases; nor
is their content in any way inappropriate to the piece as a
whole; yet our examples from vss. 1 and 5 are clearly intrusive
on various structural levels, and are to be considered interpo-
lations. The suggestion that *kî yāšūbû...libbām* in vs. 7 is an
addition is more difficult to justify, though frankly we question the originality of the whole of the verse.

The metric balance of vs. 7 is even worse than that of all
the other bicola and tricola in the piece. More importantly,
without the vs. the form of the piece would be much neater.
Vss. 4 and 5 parallel the intent of vs. 8, providing the explanation of the symbol through simile *(kēn 'akkîr//kēn 'ettēn)*.
Then vs. 6 parallels the intent of vs. 10; both provide a small
poetic elaboration of the explanation, comparable to Am 7:9 and
8:3. A third section explaining the symbol of the good figs is
thus composed of two essential parts as is a final section explaining the bad figs. What is the purpose of vs. 7? It seems
only to interrupt the compact structure of the piece, adding
little. However, without ms. support or evidence that its
style and content are inappropriate to the piece, we hesitate
to list the vs. as secondary.

The additions in our groups 4 and 5 are the most interesting. Both nuance the image of the exiles, presenting them in a
negative light. While the date of the smaller addition in vs.
8 is not certain, vs. 9 is clearly late in style.

Once the additions are explained, a good neat example of
the symbolic vision form remains, similar to other examples in
terms of content, order of content elements, and style. Segments considered secondary are listed at the side of the text
to visually present a conception of original and later contributions to the piece. As noted, one cannot be precise about
the chronological order of development. The secondary segments
are now a significant part of the whole and in some cases are
as interesting and valuable as the original form itself.

The secondary date-line in vs. 1 indicates a direction in
which the content of the form is developing; for the date will
become a popular introductory element in later versions of the
symbol form. Vss. 8 and 9 contain hints of later polemic, even
if the exact circumstances may not be clearly ascertainable.

Thus the simple vision form has grown and been rebuilt in Jeremiah 24. The basic structure of the work, however, is still
fully identifiable as that of the symbolic vision form.

Pattern of Content Elements		*Rubrics*
24:1	Indication of vision	הראני YHWH
24:1-2	Initial description	והנה...
24:3	Question of God to seer	ויאמר YHWH אלי מה אתה ראה ירמיהו
24:3	Reply/description	ואמר...
24:4-10	Explanation of seen objects	ויהי דבר YHWH אלי לאמר...

The ordering of motifs and the rubrics used to present
them parallel those of other examples of the form. Once again
the piece adheres to "external criteria of form."

In analyzing this slightly elongated version of the form,
it is useful to divide the piece into four major sections.
These larger units have been determined on the basis of content.
We have attempted to establish logical breaks or pauses at thematically and visually appropriate intervals. The sections
thereby created allow us to see the larger structural building
blocks of the vision. Grouped together are the motifs of indication of vision and initial description (24:1-2). Section II
is formed by the motifs of question and answer (24:3). The
motif of explanation forms the lengthiest portion of the piece.
In Jeremiah 24, the metaphor is not built on one basic symbol
image as are those of other visions, but on two contrasting
symbol images: a basket or jar of good figs and a container of
bad figs. In the explanation of the symbols, increased emphasis is placed on this contrast by discussing the significance
of each symbol separately. Thus section III (vss. 4-7) develops the simile, good figs = exiles, and section IV (vss. 8, 10)
creates the simile, bad figs = those who remain in the land.
This splitting of the symbols' explanation leads to greater
length of the form. The lengthening process, however, does not
lead to a loosening of structure.

Use of language and unity of structure

Vs. 2a which initially describes the good figs has a close
parallel in vs. 3c-d, the prophet's description of what he sees,

and in vs. 5 where God explains the symbol. Similarly, vs. 2c-
d, the initial description of the bad figs, is repeated almost
verbatim in vs. 3e-f, the prophet's reply/description, and in
vs. 8a-b, where God explains the significance of the bad figs
via simile. The repetition or partial repetition of one or
both of the symbols' descriptions in each section leads to a
tight unity of structure and evidences an economy of language
expected in the most traditional literature. Thus not only
the symbol-images and their slowly revealed significance unify
the piece, but also the fact that similar and often identical
language is used to describe the symbols.

While the good/bad fig imagery and the repeated language
are the chief unifiers of the piece, we should also take note
of other elements of structure in the passage and apply our
test for adherence to classical style.

We quickly confirm that metrical balance is not a major
means of structural organization. As in other examples of our
form, a number of bicola and tricola display rough metrical
balance with a fairly even syllable count per line. See vs.
3d-f: 7/8/9; vss. 4-5b: 11/10/12; vs. 6a-b: 11/10; vs. 6c-d:
8/8; vs. 8a-b: 8/9; vs. 8c-d: 12/13; vs. 10a-b: 8/8; and vs.
10c-d: 9/7. Nevertheless, there is no overall patterning system; shorter bicola (e.g., 2b, 2d, 6c, 6d, 7b, 7c, 8a, 8b) are interspersed with very long bicola with no apparent arrangement in
mind. The lengthiness of some of the lines anticipates trends
which will become more prominent in the visions of Zechariah.

Several bicola and tricola are not balanced (1a-c; 2a-b;
2c-d; 3a-c; 7a-b; and 7c-d) while necessary enjambement is
found between 5a and 5b and 8a and 8c.[40] It is of special

40. The primary criterion for identifying necessary enjambement is the continuation of the thought to the next line.
A. B. Lord notes that unperiodic enjambement (the sense is complete at the end of the line, but not the sentence) is allowed
within traditional literature. Thus in identifying a case of
necessary enjambement, the challenge is to decide where the
thought ends. We consider 1b and 1c, 2a and 2b, 2c and 2d, 3e
and 3f, 8a and 8b, and 10c and 10d to be examples of unperiodic
enjambement. The second line in each case adds a nuance to the

interest that the demand to repeat descriptions in exactly the
same terms seems to override other rules of traditional style.
Thus the thought begun in vs. 8a carries to 8c. Does this
extended carry-over evidence the complicated neo-classical
style seen in Jer 1:18? We think not. The need to describe
the bad figs according to their usual terms of description is
simply the more important yet equally traditional organizing
factor.

The creation of parallel cola is also more involved in the
repetition of the symbol images and their language than in
classical methods of building parallel pairs. Thus 2a + 2b
parallel 2c + 2d and 3d parallels 3e. The traditional pairing
of *tôbâ* and *rā'â* certainly helps to create the parallelism in
each of the above cases. However, vss. 2a-d and 3d-e remind
one less of classical poetry than of the account of the little
English girl: "When she was good, she was very, very good, but
when she was bad, she was very, very bad." This repetitious
parallelism has a rhythmic ring and creates an effective doubly
emphasized contrast in images. Note the rhyme between *tôbôt*
and *rā'ôt*; for the use of rhyme, like the lengthiness of line
mentioned above, point in the stylistic direction of Zechariah.[41]
The variety of parallelism found in Jer 24:2, 3 differs significantly from the parallelism of 24:6 which displays genuinely
classical style. As in the two symbolic visions of Amos, a
classical-style poetry is used to re-emphasize the message of
the symbols, to underline the word of the Lord.

Vss. 8c and 8d and 10a and 10b contain a ballast form of
parallelism, where the verb is understood in the second colon.

---

first line or explains it further; yet the first line does not
hang, conceptually incomplete without the second line. In contrast the import of 5a and 8a does not emerge until 5b and 8c.
These are examples of necessary enjambement. For a full discussion of enjambement, see A. B. Lord, *The Singer*, p. 54.

41. As noted by A. Ehlen, rhyme and lengthiness of lines
are also traits of late poetry ("The Poetic Structure of a
Hodayah from Qumran: an analysis of grammatical, semantic, and
auditory correspondence in 1QH 3, 19-36" [unpublished doctoral
dissertation, Harvard University, 1970], pp. 259-307).

Parallelism is achieved via a chain of equivalent direct
objects. Is this chain a hint of list-like neo-classical style
or does it have the punch of a true traditional refrain? We
opt for the latter, especially in vs. 10. Vs. 10 does not display the monotonous re-use of a lengthy grammatical unit as
does Jer 1:15e, f. In Jer 24:10, the chain of plague-like
curses adds to the power of the prophecy. These various direct
objects of *wĕšillaḥtî* have the same chanting, curse-power as the
words of haughty Pharaoh in Ex 15:9, where first person verbs
form the chain: *'erdōp 'aśśîg 'ăhallēq šālāl*. The chain of
direct objects in vs. 8c, d has a less literary and more historical explanation. The author seeks to include specific
groups and individuals in his metaphor and does so within certain poetic bounds such that they form a parallelistic bicolon.

Thus certain classical or semi-classical elements of style
do contribute to the structural wholeness of Jeremiah 24: parallelism of a kind; rough metric balance in the majority of
bicola and tricola; and a use of chanting refrain. Yet these
elements of style are subordinate to the more central unifier,
the contrast between good and bad figs, repeated in key language at key points in the passage.

Symbolic usage

The nature of these symbols and the manner of their interpretation compares with those of other examples of the form and
with Genesis 41 in some interesting and significant ways. The
symbols themselves are agrarian, like the harvest basket in Am
8:1-3. The setting of the basket of figs *lipnê hêkal yahweh*
does not imply a ritual or sacred context. These are ordinary
figs.[42] The split between good and bad agricultural products
is reminiscent of the dream symbols in Genesis 41. Contrasting
agricultural symbols convey effective messages and are not unusual, as the two dreams in Genesis 41 show. However, while
the good and bad grains and cows signify years of plenty followed by years of famine, the good and bad figs refer to saved
and doomed members of the Israelite community. The theological
import of the latter must be emphasized; for in all the earlier

---

42. Cf. Volz, *Der Prophet Jeremia*, p. 249.

examples of the form, the symbol is explained to mean judgment
for all the people; in Jeremiah 24, a select group is bound for
salvation. The use of a contrastive symbol-image thus supports
a specific theological purpose and evidences a significant new
direction in the view of the nation. Well before Ezra and the
restoration, this example of the vision form exhibits the
Palestinian/Babylonian division of the people, with a pro-
Babylonian bias. A view of the saved and the unsaved, with increasing emphasis on predetermination and decreasing emphasis
on historical rationales, will be a major theme of later versions of the symbolic vision form, works which fall within the
category of apocalyptic.

Also significant is the relationship in Jeremiah 24 between
the symbols and the predicted realities. In contrast to other
examples of this form, no play-on-words creates the link between
symbol and explanation; nor is a specific term which expresses
the symbol re-used to create a linguistic and conceptual association with its meaning. Re-use of ʾănāk serves such a purpose in Am 7:7-9. Jeremiah 24 contains a freer non-philological
association between the symbol and the explanation, a simile
introduced by kĕ, "as, like." Such a free-associative extension of the symbol is as common a method of dream interpretation as the more philologically bound varieties. We recall Bar
Hedya's interpretation of the lettuce seen by his client in a
dream, "Your business will be bitter like a lettuce" (b Ber 56a,
middle). This passage from Berachot includes a number of
interpretive similes introduced by kĕ, as are the explanations
of the symbols in the Jeremiah passage above.

We should emphasize, however, that the results of this
method of interpretation are less predictable than the results
of methods which employ rhyme, sound-alikes, or the incorpora-
tion of the term for the symbol in a new usage. That is, the
latter methods of interpretation have certain philological
limits which help one to predict what the explanation might be.
Granted there are numerous rhymes and sound-alikes for any one
word, a number of ways in which any specific term can be
nuanced in re-use and/or by inclusion in a metaphor; yet these
options are still bounded by philological considerations. To
compare a symbol image such as a jar of figs with anything else

in the world in order to interpret its meaning is a very free
and wide-ranging technique. The options would be much fewer if
one had to find a rhyme for *tĕᵃēnîm* or *dûd* or if one had to
include one of these terms in a more direct metaphor which does
not employ "like" or "as." The reduction in options would thus
make the interpretation more scientifically or rationally de-
ducible. As this vision stands, however, the results of interpretation are not so predictable. The solution of the symbols'
meaning places more emphasis on the level of divine inspiration.
God provides an answer which even the cleverest literary play-
maker might not be able to predict. The logical and poetic
significance of the relationship between symbol and explanation
is thus diminished while the non-rational inspirational level
is heightened.

The particularly unpredictable quality of the symbols in
Jeremiah 24 is illustrated by a contrast with the interpretation of dream symbols in Genesis 41, another example of non-
philological association between symbols and explanation. We
have noted that both Jeremiah and Genesis 41 deal with good and
bad agricultural elements. That such symbols all refer to good
and bad occurrences to take place in the future is a logical
enough guess since dreams and visions are potentially divinatory, future-telling media, and the positive and negative implications of the symbols are obvious. Yet what are these occur-
ences to be? Genesis 41 contains the sympathetic association
between agricultural products (the symbols) and the success or
failure of agricultural production (the explanation). With
God's help (according to E), Joseph links like with like in a
neat, logical association of ideas. Conceptually, the connection is more difficult between good and bad figs and a promise
of salvation for one group, but a set of curses for another
group. Bad figs in themselves are not an immediate symbol for
judgment as are the plumb-line (Am 7:7-9) and the boiling pot
from the north (Jer 1:11-12). That is, bad fruit are not regularly employed in such metaphors as are measuring instruments
or images of fiery substances.[43] Thus the use of symbols in

---

43. Jer 29:18, where bad figs are found as a symbol of
punishment, is a late addition based on Jer 24:8,9 (note "h").

Jeremiah 24 simply differs from that of other examples of our
form and from the use of contentually similar agricultural symbols in Genesis 41.

The increased necessity to rely on God's interpretation in
order to understand the meaning of the symbols indicates a new
direction in the development of the symbolic vision form; for
the meaning of the God-sent symbols in Zechariah will be even
less predictable, even more obscure than those of Jeremiah 24.
All neat literary play and definable divinatory technique will
disappear as one must await the word from God's intermediary in
order to understand. Mystery is heightened in Zechariah's versions of the form as the literary structure becomes less tight
and neat.

The element of curse is as powerful in Jeremiah 24 as in
other examples of the form; for once the metaphor is made, the
curse against those in the land is assured. In this passage,
sympathetic magic also leads to promise and blessing for those
who do submit to exile. Stylistically and structurally, Jeremiah 24 is another example of the symbolic vision form. However, it displays 1) a significant new theological direction,
as the good and bad symbols highlight a split in the community,
and 2) additional implicit emphasis on the role of God's inspiration in divining the symbols with an accompanying de-
emphasis on logic and word-play.

A Summary of Findings from Five Studies

1. All five passages conform to what we have termed "external criteria of form." They share a pattern of content elements and employ the same basic rubrics to present these elements. The two passages in Jeremiah 1 employ a variant introductory rubric and eliminate the motif of initial description
of the vision, but these are allowable, minor variations.

2. Criteria of structural unity are not metrical balance,
disenjambement, parallelism, and formulaic composition, the
prosodic rules of classical Hebrew poetry. Unity is based
primarily on a nice economy of language such that repetitions
of key terms occur at key points in the passage. The dialogue
frame itself adds to the unified effect in a style which we
call "economical-rhetorical."

3. Another interesting aspect of the use of language in
these visions has been the authors' tendency to present the
word of the Lord in a more poetic medium. This tendency is
found in Am 8:2d-3b, 7:8e-9c, and in Jer 24:6.

4. In dealing with symbolic usage, we have rejected the
catechetical emphasis which Lindblom, Wolff, and Volz place on
the question/answer pattern.[44] The process through which the
symbols are given meaning is better understood within the context of dream interpretation technique.

While emphasizing the divinatory import of the symbols, we
reject the view that these symbolic objects have ritual or
magical significance in and of themselves. The boiling pot is
not a temple vessel, nor the almond rod a magic wand, nor the
setting of Jeremiah 24, *lipnê hêkal*, a ritually significant
context. The transcendent or sacred quality of these passages
is achieved by the simple fact that a man is in communication
with the divine. This communication removes him from ordinary
profane time and places him on the border between this world
and the other world. The prophet thus has the liminal status
of an intermediary. A sacred quality is also achieved by the
divinatory process which interprets the everyday object to be
something other than it appears. This sympathetic association
is not only a literary device but also a form of magic. As the
Rabbis say in b Ber 55b (end) כל החלומות הולכים אחר פה, "All
dreams follow the mouth," that is, follow the interpretation
placed upon the dreams. Once the association between symbol
and explanation is made, the given prediction has the power to
fulfill its own prophecy. Acting like a curse or a blessing,
the stated prediction helps the predicted event to come about.

5. The analysis of this simple stage of the symbolic
vision form has uncovered directions in content, structure, and
theme in which the form will grow. The 6th century B.C. redactional portion of Jer 1:13-19, vss. 15-19, includes the element
of charge and a lengthening of the explanation motif, features
of later versions of the symbolic vision form. A redactional
segment of Jeremiah 24 includes the date-line, another element
which will become a regular feature. Moreover, Jeremiah 24

---

44. See ch. 1, note 11.

evidences a lengthiness of individual lines and the use of
rhyme, traits of late poetry which will also be found in the
increasingly prosaized visions of Zechariah. In Jeremiah 24,
the community is viewed as bi-partite, composed of those who
were exiled and those who were not, those to be forgiven and
those to be condemned. This view of the community has important implications for future versions of the symbolic vision
form. The reliance on God's inspiration as a means of con-
necting the symbol with its meaning is emphasized more in Jeremiah 24 than in the other examples of the earliest stage of the
symbolic vision form. In Jeremiah 24, the association between
symbol and explanation is freer and less predictable by "scientific" and "rational" means. The heightened mystery of the
symbols will also be a feature of later versions of the symbolic form.

Chapter Two

STAGE II, A LITERARY-NARRATIVE DIRECTION
IN THE VISIONS OF ZECHARIAH

The symbolic vision form remains relatively stable in the
works of Amos and Jeremiah, that is, from the 8th to the 6th
centuries B.C. In the late 6th century B.C., the time of the
restoration, the form undergoes growth and change. This growth
is reflected in the redactional layers of Jeremiah 1 and 24
discussed in ch. One, and in the visions of Zechariah which we
are about to discuss. In Zechariah, the motif pattern is expanded as the question motif is significantly nuanced.

On a hypothetical line of formal development a course may
be traced from Zechariah vision VI (5:1-4) to vision V (4:1-6a,
10b-14) to vision II (2:1-4) to visions I (1:7-17) and VIII
(6:1-8). These hypothetical stages in Zechariah's works are
not to be understood as evidence for a datable growth process.
Vision V (the menorah), for example, was not necessarily composed before vision I (the horses). Zechariah's visions reflect differing points on a formal line which we can trace in
retrospect. Such stages all may have existed contemporaneously
from the point of view of chronology. The author or authors no
doubt constantly tried out new variations, new departures from
simpler versions of the form in order to present their own
messages. Beneath all innovations, of course, precursors in
the literary tradition remain fully visible. We simply posit a
logical order of formal development for the symbolic visions of
Zechariah, given that the visions of Amos and Jeremiah provide
formal antecedents and those of Daniel 7 and 8 formal descend-
ents within the same literary tradition.

Certain experiments en route to the form as found in
Daniel may have worked better than others. Zechariah visions
III (2:5-9) and VII (5:5-11) are experiments which do not point
as clearly towards Daniel as do the other symbolic visions of
Zechariah. These two visions are certainly related to our
formal tradition, sharing a number of content elements, rubrics,

73

and structures found in the other visions of Zechariah. Visions
III (the man with the measuring line) and VII (the 'êpâ) are
interesting in that they evidence greater influence exerted by
the individual author than by the tradition. These are complex
visions which employ elements of the symbolic vision in a
rather singular way. We will discuss these visions briefly at
the end of ch. Two.

Taken as a group, Zechariah visions VI (scroll), V
(menorah), II (horns), I (horse-rider teams), and VIII (horse-
chariot teams) reflect other significant trends in the development of the symbolic vision form. One is the movement from the
economical-rhetorical style, found in Amos and Jeremiah, to a
more clearly prose medium. The lessening of concern with
traditional-style repetition and with economy of language, key
factors in the earliest stage of the form, is evident in all
the Zechariah visions to varying degrees.

Secondly, Zechariah's visions evidence increasing mythologization both in the symbol objects and in the way the symbols are related to their meanings. One might compare the sta-
tionary, mundane, non-ritualistic symbol objects of Amos and
Jeremiah with the flying scroll of vision VI or the temple
paraphernalia of V. Moreover, in the visions of Zechariah one
cannot relate the symbol to its explanation via rational pseudo-
science, as in the visions of Amos and Jeremiah. Finally, as
noted earlier, the symbols of Zechariah visions II (horns), I
(horse-rider), and VIII (horse-chariot) are explained within
their own mythic terms; they are not declared a representation
of something else. This symbol-interpretation coalescence
disappears in the symbolic visions of Daniel, 2 Baruch, and 4
Ezra where the neater and simpler equation is preferred such
that the symbol represents something other than itself. In any
event, the "symbol=itself" equation in the visions of Zechariah
is evidence of genuine mythic mentality.

Thus the visions in Zechariah reveal exciting and creative
change. The role of these visions in the development of the
symbolic vision tradition will emerge more fully in individual
case studies. We begin with the vision closest in patterning
and language to the symbolic visions of Amos and Jeremiah, Zech
5:1-4.

Zech 5:1-4

			Test for balance
(1)	Again I raised my eyes and saw	ואשרב ואשא עיני ואראה (1a	11
	And behold a flying scroll	והנה מגלה^a עפה (1b	8
(2)	And he said to me,	ויאמר אלי (2a	5
	"What do you see?"	מה אתה ראה (2b	5
	And I said, "I see a flying scroll,	ואמר אני ראה מגלה עפה (2c	12
	Its length twenty cubits	ארכה עשרים באמה (2d	7
	And its width ten cubits."	ורחבה עשר באמה (2e	7
(3)	Then he said to me,	ויאמר אלי (3a	5
	"This is the curse which goes forth	זאת האלה ^bהיוצאת (3b	7
	Over the face of the whole land.	על פני כל הארץ (3c	6
	Everyone who steals	כי כל הגנב (3d	5
	For this reason is as inno-cent as death,	^cמזה כמות נקה^c (3e	6
	And everyone who commits perjury	וכל הנשבע ^dלשקר (3f	7
	For this reason is as inno-cent as death."	מזה כמות נקה (3g	6
(4)	I will bring it forth, says the Lord of hosts,	^eהוצאתיה נאם YHWH צבאות (4a	11
	And it will go to the house of the thief	ובאה אל בית הגנב (4b	8
	And to the house of the one who swears in my name falsely	ואל בית הנשבע בשמי לשקר (4c	11
	And it will lodge in the midst of his house	ולנה בתוך ביתו (4d	7
	And destroy it, its sticks and stones.	וכלתו ואת עציו ואת אבניו (4e	12

^aG reads δρεπανον, a term used to translate *maggāl*, "sickle," in G Joel 3(4):10 and Jer 27(50):16. G either re-flects scribal error or preserves an alternate reading. MT

mĕgillâ creates a good rhythmic rhyme with ʿāpâ, its participial modifier, and with ʾālâ, its interpretation. In our opinion, this rhyme is intended.

[b]Note the use of the article as a relative pronoun. This
is a late usage found also in 1 Chron 26:28; 29:8, 17; 2 Chron
29:36; and Ezra 8:25; 10:14, 17.

[c]This phrase, twice used as an apodosis, is the most difficult problem in the vision. MT reads מזה כמות נקה while G
has a quite different reading, εκ τουτου εως θανατου εκδικηθησεται. Rignell suggests that G reflects the Hebrew במות מזה
נכה. It is more likely that the Greek εκδικηθησεται from
εκδικεω, "to avenge, punish," reflects the Hebrew *niqqam*, the
niph. of *nqm*, "to avenge." A form of εκδικεω is used to translate a form of *nqm* in G more than once, whereas the Greek term
is never used to translate a form of *nkh*. Moreover, epigraphi-
cally it is more likely for *h* to be mistaken as final *m* than
for *q* to be mistaken as *k*. It is also unlikely that εως θανατου translates *bĕmāwet*. εως usually translates ʿad. In Greek,
the notion of "with/by death" would be conveyed either by the
use of the dative or possibly by δια + genitive, but certainly
not via εως. Thus while Rignell's Hebrew composition reads
nicely, it is unlikely as a text behind this Greek translation.
On the other hand, the literal retranslation of the Greek back
into Hebrew reads מזה עד מות נקם, "from here unto death he will
suffer vengeance" - an uncomfortable and non-idiomatic phrase.
Nevertheless, G may preserve hints of an original reading.

The problem of this phrase as found in MT consists of
three component parts: how to deal with *mizzeh*, with *kmwh*, and
with *nqh*.

1) There are two basic suggestions for *mizzeh*. Köhler,
Rothstein, Nowack, and Sellin take it to mean "from this place,
from here" as is often the usage in OT. See for example Gen
37:17, 42:15, Ex 13:3. This literal meaning is the most common in OT.

Rignell, Chary, and Horst translate the double *mizzeh* "on
the one side/on the other side," in accordance with OT usage in
Ex 17:12; 26:13; 32:15; Ezek 45:7; 48:21; etc.

Neither of the above suggestions is ideal.

We view *mizzeh* = G εκ τουτου as the transition-maker or
causal link between the protasis and the apodosis, and translate "on account of this" or "for this reason." Such a meaning
for Greek εκ τουτου is allowed by Liddell and Scott, C, VIII,
5 under ουτος. *Min* has this causal sense in Ex 2:23; 6:9;
15:23; Deut 7:7; Prov 20:4; Ru 1:13; and Cant 3:8. While OT
contains no example of *min* used in this way with the demonstrative pronoun *zeh*, there is no reason why it might not be.

2) Two basic suggestions have also been made for MT *kmwh*.
Marti and Mitchell, after Wellhausen, emend *kāmôhā* to *kammeh*
and take the expression *mizzeh kammeh* to mean "how long can..."
Literally, they are reading "It is how much that...." With
Zech 7:3 *(zeh kammeh šānîm)* in mind, Mitchell suggests further
emendation, shortening *mizzeh* to simply *zeh* so that the phrase
reads *zeh kammeh niqqâ*, "How long can he be let free?"

Other scholars, including Rignell, Horst, Chary, and
Sellin, read *kāmôhā*, "according to it." The "it" would refer
to the scroll/curse. Yet *kĕmō* "like, as" is never really used
elsewhere in OT to mean "according to."

In contrast to both views above, we accept G θανατου,
"death," as the original reading. Due to scribal error, *h* has
been mistaken for *t*. We will discuss the ironic twist rendered
by this reading in a moment after dealing with the third piece
of the puzzle.

3) Most scholars accept the usual meaning of *niqqâ* in OT,
"free, guiltless," though a few like Sellin take *niqqâ* the
niphal of *nqh* to mean "purged out," that is, "cleaned out" in a
definitive punishing sense. The only comparable usage is found
at Is 3:26 where the sense is less "purged out" than "emptied
out" via plundering. With most scholars, we are compelled to
accept the translation for *niqqâ*, "free of guilt." Given the
textual choices discussed above, we read,

Everyone who steals,	כל הגנב
for this reason, is as innocent as death.	מזה כמות נקה
Everyone who commits perjury,	וכל הנשבע לשקר
for this reason, is as innocent as death.	מזה כמות נקה

One might also render the conditional protasis, "If anyone
steals...." As Glendon E. Bryce has noted in his work on pro-
verbs and omen texts ("Omen-Wisdom in Ancient Israel," *JBL* 94

[1975], 19-37), "A survey of usage of the participle (in OT)...
indicates that it may function as a conditional statement in
wisdom literature. This is also true of legal texts...." (27).

The reading above reveals the transformation of a casuis-
tic formula into the prophet's own ironic statement about the
guilt of the wrong-doers. Death is personified in Hab 2.5,
Cant 8:6 and Lam 1:20. In each of these passages death is considered a devouring, insatiable killer. Here death is described
as a criminal. Rather than include the sentencing, the apodosis contains the verdict, repeated after each accusation like a
refrain. The punishment or sentencing follows in vs. 4. Thus
an ancient form has been re-used, stretched to fit the prophet's
message.

   ᵈMT is haplographic. G has επιορκος, "perjurer." Most
scholars, including Wellhausen, Mitchell, Nowack, Sellin, Rothstein, and Horst, fill out the Hebrew according to vs. 4 הנשבע
בשמי לשקר. With Chary we accept the shorter G επιορκος, נשבע
לשקר.

   ᵉG has και. With most scholars we accept MT.

   The pattern of content elements in Zech 5:1-4 and the language used to present the elements basically parallel those in
Am 7:7-9, 8:1-3, Jer 1:11-12, 1:13-19, and 24.

	Pattern of Content Elements	*Rubrics*
5:1	Indication of vision	ראשוב ואשא עיני ואראה
5:1	Initial description	והנה...
5:2	Question of divine being to seer	ויאמר אלי מה אתה ראה
5:2	Reply of seer and description	ואמר אני ראה...
5:3,4	Explanation of seen objects	ויאמר אלי זאת...

The initial rubric refers back to earlier visions of the
Zechariah cycle (ואשוב...) while retaining a form of *r'h*. The
substitution of an angel for God himself, in the character role
which carries over from the preceding visions, is a new and
significant feature which will be found in the other visions of
Zechariah and in Daniel 7 and 8.[1] Also new is the use of the

---

   1. Noted also by C. Jeremias, *Die Nachtgesichte*, pp. 228-
229.

demonstrative in introducing the explanation motif. This usage
has subtle significance for the development of the form. Essentially, however, the sixth vision of Zechariah adheres to the
same external criteria of form as the prophetic symbolic visions
analyzed in ch. One.

The attempt to divide Zechariah 5:1-4 into clusters of
content elements is revealing. In the longer visions we have
looked for building blocks of content, each made of roughly the
same number of lines. As we view the structure of Zech 5:1-4,
it contains six of these building blocks or units. The first
three brief units are as follows: 1. the indication of the
vision and initial description (5:1); 2. the question of the
divine being (5:2a-b); and 3. the prophet's response (5:2c-e).
Three more definable units are all part of the explanation
motif. A fourth unit includes mention of the roving curse,
which hunts for criminals like a detective (5:3a-c); a fifth
declares the verdict on those criminals (5:3d-g); and a sixth
includes their final sentence (5:4). The explanation motif is
thus lengthy and can itself be divided into units which are
reminiscent of the lawsuit form. The length of this final
three-part motif causes it to dominate the vision to some extent. The explanation motif was similarly long in Jeremiah 24;
yet it was skillfully related to the earlier portion of the
vision via the method of repetition of key motif language.
Structure and balance between content elements did not break
down; the tension between these elements remained constant. An
examination of the internal criteria of form of Zech 5:1-4 will
indicate if its elements of content are equally well integrated.

Use of language and emerging changes in style

As in Amos and Jeremiah, the syllable counts of lines
vary. Thus vss. 1a, 2c, 4a, 4c, and 4e are rather lengthy intrusions in the more usual 5-7 syllable range of the piece.
One is tempted to shorten the count of 2c by deleting *'ănî
rō'eh* as expansionary in accord with our decision in Jer 1:13c.
In Zech 5:2, however, there is no text critical support for
such a decision. Similarly, one might consider deleting *nĕ'um
yahweh ṣĕbā'ôt* as a prosaizing rubric in vs. 4. The *nĕ'um*
phrase, however, does serve a purpose in vs. 4 as an indicator

of the word of God which will announce the punishment. The
12/11/7/12 meter resulting from such a deletion would be no
great improvement in any event. Line length in this piece as
in the visions of Amos and Jeremiah is variable. We pause,
however, to note the extreme length of some of these lines.
One does not find the 11-12 syllable line as frequently in the
Amos and Jeremiah material, with the one exception of Jeremiah
24, the latest of the three symbolic visions in Jeremiah. The
line length factor is important for further work.

     Like its predecessors in Amos and Jeremiah, Zech 5:1-4
has some cases of enjambement between lines, between 3b and 3c,
3d and 3e, and 3f and 3g. This vision has three cases of
necessary enjambement, more cases than any of the visions discussed thus far. Jeremiah 24, the longest vision with which we
have dealt, has only two cases (5a + 5b, 8a + 8c).

     Again as in Amos and Jeremiah, *parallelismus membrorum* is
not found throughout the vision. Parallelism is found in 2d a
and 2e, where '*ārkâ/rāḥbâ* and *ʿeśrîm/ʿeśer* create directionally
contrastive pairs, and more important in the explanation motif.
In 5:3 the two varieties of evil-doers, the *gōnēb*, "thief," and
the *niśbāʿ laśśeqer*, "perjurer," are held in tandem by the repeated refrain about their guilt. In 5:4b-3 verbs and prepositional phrases (an obj. in 4e) create a synonymous, impressionistic[2] picture of punishment. These examples of parallelism
which come within the explanation motif further exemplify the
tendency to reveal the word of the Lord in poetry.

     In the vision as a whole, however, we should expect to
find the unifying factors of repetition and economy of language,
the economical-rhetorical style which characterizes the symbolic visions of Amos and Jeremiah. And in fact once again we
do find the pattern of '*mr* forms (2a, 2c, 3a), the dialogue
frame which spans from the question to the explanation motif.

---

     2. Frank Moore Cross uses the term "impressionistic" in
a somewhat more technical sense than intended here to describe
"overlapping" parallel images which create one impression and
do not imply a sequence of activities. See "Prose and Poetry
in the Mythic Epic Texts from Ugarit," *HTR* 67 (1974), 1-15.

The terms for the symbolic image, the key organizers in previous examples of the form, appear in the motifs of initial description and in the prophetic reply/re-description. In each *mĕgillâ ʿāpâ* is found, but these terms are not found in the explanation motif. The explanation does not re-invoke the symbol image via repetition, but merely begins, *zōʾt...*, "this is," and later refers to it by the pronoun in vs. 4. Herein lies a subtle but significant shift away from the earlier visions toward a new stage in the symbolic vision form.

The establishment of a connection between the symbol and its explanation has been the key structural joint of the vision. Here we find that *mĕgillâ ʿāpâ*, "flying scroll," leads to *zōʾt hāʾālâ*, "this is the curse." What creates the link? As we will later discuss, the notion of a scroll having to do with a curse has a good thematic pedigree in the history of OT tradition, but here we are looking for a possible connection on a lower structural level. Such a connection, however tenuous, does exist: One cannot miss the rhyme on long *a*'s between the terms for the symbol and the term for the explanation, and as one examines the vision as a whole one notices more and more of these *a* sounds: *ʾārkâ/rāḥbâ; bāʾammâ/bāʾammâ; hōṣēʾtîhā; ûbāʾâ.* Clearly, the long *a* is common enough in any Hebrew composition where feminine nouns and their modifiers or pronouns are found. Yet as A. Ehlen notes in his study of a late poem, repeated sounds are often used to create a poetically rhythmic effect.[3] The same effect is achieved in Jer 24:3, which may anticipate a trend to be found in Zech 5:1-4 and in late Hebrew poetry. The presence of rhyme in Zech 5:1-4 is not coincidental but planned. Thus the element of repetition once again links motif to motif; yet it is a repetition of sounds, not the re-invocation of a whole semantic unit. The vision ends on a similar play of sounds between *ʿēṣāyw* and *ʾăbānāyw* "its sticks and stones." In fact rhyme is not so far afield from the divinatory techniques discussed in ch. One. We recall that the association of like with like is the key to relating the symbol to its meaning in the symbolic visions of Amos and Jeremiah. Rhyme is also an associative technique; yet play on one phoneme is

---

3. "The Poetic Structure," 259.

less precise, predictable, and scientific than play on a whole
word or group of words. The metaphor-creating technique used
in Jeremiah 24 is also less scientific or predictable than the
neat word-play; even so, Jeremiah 24 does not break with the
tradition of re-using the symbol terminology that third time in
the explanation motif. Terms for the symbol are repeated. Zech
5:1-4 conforms to the traditional re-call of the symbol image
only marginally via the late poetic device of rhyme.

Zech 5:1-4 points toward a new stage in the symbolic vision
form in which word-play between the symbol and the explanation
is not the key to unity of structure. Eventually, in fact, the
rhetorical question of the deity which leads to the middle repetition of the symbol term (or the initial description in Jer
1:11-12; 13-14) is dropped. We find instead: 1) a description;
2) the prophet's question, "What is it?"; 3) a response, "This
is...." The answer motif, as already here in the sixth vision
of Zechariah, is not a quick clever play which may be high-
lighted by a bicolon or tricolon as in Am 7:9 and 8:3, but instead has a drawn out narrative quality: "This is...which...."
It is in this narrative direction that the form is headed. The
explanation in vision VI is a lengthy one like that of Jeremiah
24, which once again foreshadows later development. In Jeremiah 24 the explanation is nicely integrated into the vision as
a whole via the key technique of repetition. With that technique reduced to rhyme, the aesthetic of the neatly balanced
rhetorical form declines. Indeed while the symbol terms are
not repeated in the explanation motif, the terms for the wrong-
doers are found twice. The final motif thus becomes less a
dramatic climax as in the Amos and Jeremiah visions than a
separate piece containing its own unity of form via repetition
of key terms. The vision as a whole becomes bottom heavy.

This change in the simple form ultimately culminates in
prose narratives such as Daniel 7 and 8 where the length of the
explanation motif does not jar a tight, economic structure, but
is balanced by an equally lengthy and narrative description of
the vision. The visions of Zechariah reflect a transitionary
period. The use of repetition as an organizing technique, in
fact, is not completely abandoned in later versions of the symbolic vision form. Zechariah vision VIII (6:1-8), for example,

displays some niceties of word choice, repetition, and traditional economy. Yet the symbolic vision form is being transformed subtly and Zech 5:1-4 shows the first signs of change.

The choice of symbols and the theme

Having dealt with the relationship between the symbol and
its meaning on the level of language, on the "auditory level,"[4]
we turn to the question of their thematic relationship. That
is, why should a flying scroll be chosen as a symbol for a
curse? A *mĕgillâ* is found in two Biblical passages besides
Zechariah 5, the initiation scene in Ezekiel (2:9 and 3:3) and
the story of Jeremiah's relaying of a doom message to Jehoiakim
by way of Baruch in Jeremiah 36. These two passages underline
the relationship between scrolls and divine messages and in
turn the magical power of such documents. When Ezekiel swal-
lows the written scroll, he is literally filled with the word
of the Lord in a sympathetically magical way. He becomes united
with that message and can thus act as its messenger. Ezekiel 2
and 3 like Zech 5:1-4 no doubt reflect the larger belief that
God the king keeps written records and sends royal decrees like
any Near Eastern monarch. His scrolls, however, preserve a
record of man's wrong-doing and affect his fate. The Jewish
tradition of a Book of Life which contains the information of
who will live and who will die in the coming year is a later
folkloristic reflection of this symbol of the scroll, grounded
in an ancient respect for the written word.

The scroll in Jeremiah is not so otherworldly in nuance as
that of Ezekiel, but provides an interesting foil for the
vision in Zechariah. The scroll which Jeremiah dictates to
Baruch contains the divine record of God's previous admonitions
sent since the time of Josiah. God wishes the message recapitu-
lated in the hopes that the people will repent (36:3). The
scroll speaks of certain destruction by Babylon (36:29). Thus
from the king's point of view it is a piece of sedition, encour-
aging his people to submission. With a penknife Jehoiakim
slices the scroll into pieces and throws it into the fire,

---

4. I borrow this usage of the term "auditory" from A.
Ehlen, "The Poetic Structure."

column of writing after column. This is no mere act of dis-
dain; it is an action of magical significance. By destroying
the scroll, he is attempting to destroy the word, the prediction contained in the scroll. God commands Jeremiah to have
the same words written down again (36:28), and he does. The
inevitability of the curse and hence the power of the scroll
emerge in this scene. Fire cannot destroy the curse spelled
out in vss. 30-31.

The same nuance of the unavoidable, indestructable curse
of the Lord, contained in a scroll, is surely evoked by Zech
5:1-4. This scroll/curse visits the evil-doer at his home like
an evil demon, destroying it utterly. The more realistic or
mundane scroll written by human hands in Jeremiah contrasts
with the flying, otherworldly scroll of Zechariah 5, which
appears like an apparition. The flying scroll is evidence of
the mythopoeic quality of Zechariah's symbols, especially when
these are contrasted with the everyday harvest basket of Amos
or the boiling pot of Jeremiah. Another aspect of the scroll's
super-mundane quality is its huge size, twenty by ten cubits.

A number of scholars have noted that the scroll's measurements are those of the porch of Solomon's temple (1 Kgs 6:3).
The measurement *eśer/*eśrîm* may be one with cosmic, heavenly
implications - a magic measurement of wholeness. Thus the 10/
20 measurement is found both in the size of the temple porch
and in the description of the scroll image. The numbers seven
and three have such special implications in other OT contexts.
The association of 10/20 measurements with the temple, the
center of cultic activity, gives the scroll additional power
and pedigree. We do not, like K. Seybold, however, see a hint
of temple-building polemic in the use of these measurements in
Zechariah 5.[5]

Before concluding the present study, one should note that
some scholars have regarded the *gōnēb* and the *nišbā' laśśeqer*
as metaphors or symbols for historically identifiable groups.
To find such a specific identity behind the reference to the
evil-doers, some scholars look to the attitudes of the returnees toward those who had remained in the land after the

_____

5. *Bilder zum Tempelbau* (Stuttgart: KBW, 1974), p. 109.

exile[6] and consider the reference to perjurers to be directed
at the alleged syncretism of those left in the land. To the
returning Babylonian exiles, the non-exiles' intermarriage is a
breach of vows to God - in a sense, participation in a lie or
perjury. The thievery would refer to the land-dwellers' con-
fiscation of homes and properties during the exiles' absence.
The suggestion about the identity of the perjurers is difficult
to accept since the usual OT terms for syncretism, forms of
znh, *'np*, "to commit fornication, adultery" are not found in
this passage. These are the usual metaphors, not references to
swearing falsely. The larger problem with the above suggestions is that clear reference to such an attitude of resentment
towards those who had remained in the land is simply not found
in any of the other visions of Zechariah, and the reference in
Zech 5:1-4 would have to be considered a rather veiled one
indeed. This vision, like the others in Zechariah, is the product of a pro-temple, pro-Zerubbabel and Joshua, and pro-
restoration mentality, but the idealistic emphasis is more on
the new and good kingdom than on the enemies within. Zech 3:10,
in fact, emphasizes peace and friendship among neighbors. It
is possible that this propaganda document naively or purpose-
fully ignores political realities. Indeed if Frank Moore
Cross's recent work on the Chronicler is correct, then portions
of the present Ezra-Neh-Chron document which reflect the returnees' violent feelings against other forces in the land are
of later date than Zechariah and the first layer of Ezra-Chron,
Chr 1, which Cross dates to shortly after 520 B.C.[7] Passages
in Ezra and Nehemiah which strongly reflect inner tension and
difficulty would thus be from a later period, when hope had
turned to frustration, euphoria to reality.[8] The earliest

_____

6. See Sellin, *Das Zwölfprophetenbuch*, p. 512. Cf. our
discussion of Jeremiah 24.

7. "A Reconstruction of the Judaean Restoration," *JBL* 94
(1975), 4-18.

8. The description of the problems concerning intermarriage in ch. 9 would thus be the contributions of Chr 2 (ca.
450 B.C.). The Nehemiah memoirs with its descriptions of the
rivalries and divisions in society and of intermarriage (Neh

layer, as Cross notes, emphasizes hope. The coming of the
kingdom means that each man can sit under his fig tree and the
Davidic monarch on his throne, his power now tempered by that
of the priest.

     The above world-view reflected in the visions of Zechariah
is a rather conservative one. The category of the "cursed" is
not in our opinion based on the sociological and political
divisions in society, as in a number of apocalyptic works. The
emphasis in Zechariah as in Jer 31:30 and Ezek 18:20 is on the
individual's performance of basic stipulations of the covenant.
In the hopeful view of the kingdom to be established, all in-
justice is to be eradicated. This destruction of evil is the
thrust of the condemnation of thieves and perjurers. The throwing of *rišʿâ* into the ephah and the carrying away of her (vision
VII, 5:8-11) has the same emphasis. See also Zech 3:9, *ûmaštî
ʾet ʿăwôn hāʾāreṣ hahîʾ bĕyôm ʾeḥād*, "I will remove the sin of
this land in one day." The same meaning of putting an end to
evil is behind the curse against the thief and the perjurer.
Shining throughout is the Deuteronomic message that all is
peaceful and well when God's commandments are being followed.
If the curse roots out thieves and perjurers, the society is a
better one, the restored relationship with God confirmed and
healthy, *ûbāḥar ʿôd bîrûšālāim*, "he will again choose Jerusalem
(1:17, 2:16).

Conclusions

     To present a message of punishment for those who have dis-
obeyed God's commandments, Zech 5:1-4 employs the motif pattern

---

2:10ff., 3:33ff.) would not have been joined to the work by Chr
3 until ca. 400 B.C., though the memoirs may have circulated
earlier as an independent source (Cross, "A Reconstruction," 11-
14). Cross writes that the original propaganda document ends
at Ezra 3:13, and that Chr 2 (ca. 450 B.C.) is responsible for
joining Ezra 5:1-6:19 to the work. What of ch. 4 which records
the story of the harassment of the temple builders? It too
would seem inappropriate to the piece of propaganda which ends
at 3:13 and therefore perhaps should also be assigned to a
later layer of tradition.

and rubrics which we recognize from the symbolic visions of
Amos and Jeremiah; yet subtle change has taken place. As an
organizing factor, economy of language and repetition of terms
take a back seat to repetition of sounds. The play-on-words
disappears as the message of the vision instead emerges in a
lengthy segment, written in a less concise, narrative style.

Accompanying the above changes in structural criteria is a
shift toward mythologization of the symbol image. The scroll
symbol is one with a previous history in OT tradition and held
an implicit meaning for Zechariah's audience, one which they
could readily accept and understand.

An interesting discovery of our study is that certain
nuances in the vision form are anticipated by Jeremiah 24. The
use of especially long lines, the use of rhyme to create rhythm,
and the expansion of the explanation motif are all found in
Jeremiah 24. In Jeremiah 24, these usages are so well integrated into the older tradition that they do not seem to indicate a major shift in the form. In Zech 5:1-4 real changes
begin to emerge.

Zech 4:1-6a, 10b-14*

1) וישב המלאך הדבר בי וייערני כאיש אשר יעור משנתו ויאמר אלי
מה אתה ראה

2) ואמר^a

ראיתי והנה מנורת זהב כלה ^{b}וגלה על ראשה
שבעה ^{c}נרות עליה ^{d}ושבעה שבעה^d מוצקות לנרות
אשר אל ראשה   3) ושנים זיתים עליה
אחד ^{e}מימינה ⟨ ⟩ ואחד על שמאלה

4) ואען ואמר אל המלאך הדבר בי ⟨ ⟩^{f}
מה אלה אדני

5) ויען המלאך הדבר בי ויאמר אלי
הלוא ידעת מה המה אלה

ואמר

לא אדני

---

*For vision V we have provided two lay-outs of the text,
one which underlines the prose dialogue quality of the vision
and a second which allows for the test for prosody.

ויען ויאמר אלי לאמר   (6
⟨6αβ-10α⟩^g

שבעה אלה עיני YHWH המה משוטטים בכל הארץ   (10

ואען ואמר אליו   (11

מה שני הזיתים האלה על ימין המנורה ועל שמאולה
⟨vs. 12⟩^h

ויאמר אלי ⟨ ⟩^i   (13

הלא ידעת מה אלה

ואמר

לא אדני

ויאמר

אלה שני בני היצהר העמדים על אדון כל הארץ

Zech 4:1-6a, 10b-14

		Test for balance
רישב הלמאך הדבר בי	(1a	10
ויעירני כאיש אשר יעור משנתו	(1b	15
ויאמר אלי	(2a	5
מה אתה ראה	(2b	5
ואמר^a ראיתי	(2c	6
והנה מנורת זהב כלה	(2d	10
וגלה^b על ראשה	(2e	6
שבעת נרות עליה	(2f	7
ורשבעה שבעה^d מוצקות לנרות	(2g	11
אשר על ראשה	(2h	5
ושנים זיתים עליה	(3a	8
אחד ^e מימינה ⟨ ⟩	(3b	5
ואחד על שמאלה	(3c	7
ואען ואמר אל המלאך הדבר בי ^f ⟨ ⟩	(4a	14
מה אלה אדני	(4a	6
ויען המלאך הדבר בי	(5a	10
ויאמר אלי	(5b	5
הלא ידעת מה המה אלה	(5c	10
ואמר לא אדני	(5d	7
ויען ויאמר אלי לאמר	(6	10
⟨6αβ-10α⟩^g		
שבעה אלה עיני YHWH	(10a	8

המה משוטטים בכל הארץ	(10b	10
ואען ואמר אליו	(11a	8
מה שני הזיתים האלה	(11b	9
על ימין המנורה	(11c	7
ועל שמאולה	(11d	5
⟨vs. 12⟩[h]		
⟨ ⟩[i] ויאמר אלי	(13a	5
הלוא ידעת מה אלה	(13b	8
ואמר לא אדני	(13c	7
ויאמר אלה שני בני היצהר	(14a	11
העמדים על אדון כל הארץ	(14b	10

1) The angel who was speaking with me returned
   and awakened me like a man that is awakened from his sleep.
2) And he said to me,
   "What do you see?"
   And I said,
   "I saw and behold a menorah all of gold, a saucer shaped
   feature was atop it. Seven lamps were upon it and seven
   spouts were to each lamp which was atop it. 3) And two
   olive trees were by it, one to its right and one to its
   left."
4) And I responded and said to the angel who was speaking
   with me,
   "What are these my lord?"
5) Then the angel who was speaking with me answered and said
   to me,
   "Don't you know what these are?"
   And I said,
   "No, my lord."
6) Then he responded and spoke to me, saying,
                   ⟨6aβ-10a⟩

10)   "These seven are the eyes of Yahweh. They range through-
       out the land.
11) I replied and said to him,
       "What are these two olive trees to the right of the
       menorah and to its left?"
                   ⟨vs. 12⟩

13) And he said to me,

"Don't you know what these are?"

And I said,

"No, my lord."

14) Then he said,

"These are the two anointed ones who stand by the Lord
of the whole earth."

[a]With most scholars we accept the first person qĕrê reading supported by G rather than the kĕtîb third person reading
found in MT.

[b]We follow G, το λαμπαδιον, which translates an unsuffixed
form of gullâ, "bowl, basin, curved shaped feature." So Horst,
Sellin, Nowack, Chary, and Wellhausen. Torrey ("The Messiah
Son of Ephraim," *JBL* 66 [1947], 253-277), and Mitchell prefer
the suffixed reading of MT. Noting that MT gullâ implies a
suffixed form of a m.s. n. gol and that such a term is unattested in OT, Mitchell suggests emending to gullātâ. Acceptance of G seems the simpler solution. The suffix is unnecessary and probably resulted from the scribe's looking ahead to
the object suffix on rōʾšâ.

[c]With the unsuffixed shorter reading in G, επτα λυχνοι,
nērōt, "lamps." So Wellhausen, Nowack, and Chary. Sellin,
Mitchell, Horst, and Torrey keep the suffix, reading nērōtĕhā,
"its lamps," with MT. The association of the suffixed form of
nērōt with the mĕnōrâ and with the number seven is common in
OT. See Ex 25:37; 37:23 for a usage with šibʿâ in a mĕnōrâ
context and Ex 35:14; 39:37; 40:4; Num 4:9; 8:3; 1 Chron 28:15;
and 2 Chron 13:11 for a usage of nērōtĕhā with the mĕnōrâ alone.
It is on the strength of these passages that the above scholars
keep the MT suffixed reading. In each of the above cases, the
suffix is necessary to indicate which nērōt are meant. The
suffix makes clear that these are the lamps of the aforementioned mĕnōrâ as are the utensils (kēlĕhā) and other paraphernalia listed with the lamps in a number of the above passages.
In contrast, Num 8:2, which also associates the nērōt with the
mĕnōrâ and with the count of seven, employs the unsuffixed form.
For here, the direction is clear:

בהעלתך את הנרת אל מול פני
המנורה יאירו שבעת הנרות

When you raise up the lamps in front of the
lampstand, the seven lamps will give off light.

The reference is clear and the suffix not necessary. In Num
8:3, however, the syntax is varied a bit, making a suffix helpful.

ויעש כן אהרן אל מול פני המנורה

העלה נרתיה כאשר צוה YHWH את משה

Aaron did so in front of the lampstand. He
raised up its lamps as the Lord had commanded
Moses.

Similarly, no suffix is found in Lev 24:4, which contains no
ambiguity concerning the lamps: "Upon the pure lampstand he
will arrange the lamps." The situation is comparable in Zech
4:2. The use of *'al rō'šā* precludes the necessity for a suffix
on *nērōt*. Therefore we consider the shorter reading the more
original. The frequent occurrences of the phrase *nērōtêhā*
šib'â and the frequent use of the suffix on *nērōt* to refer back
to the menorah explains how the suffix crept into this passage.

   [d]MT reads *šib'â wěšib'â*, "seven and seven." G has the
shorter reading, simply *wěšib'â* "and seven." Mitchell and
Nowack follow G and consider MT dittographic. Wellhausen and
Sellin instead suggest omitting the first "seven" of 4:2 so
that the text reads, "The lamps upon it are seven and seven are
the 'spouts' (our translation, in accord with Robert North
below) for the lamps...." Other scholars point to the distributive meaning of a repeated numeral + *lě*, as demonstrated by Num
13:2 and 31:4. These passages are not precisely parallel to
the case from Zechariah. In the former two, the numeral *and*
the modified object are repeated twice.

   Gen 7:2 and Gen 7:9 seem to provide closer parallels. Yet
the sense we want for Zech 4:2 is "seven spouts *for each* of the
lamps." Gen 7:2, שבעה איש ואשתו שבעה, means "seven, male and
female respectively." Gen 7:9, שנים שנים באו, means "two by
two they came...." Neither the "respective" sense which requires that two items be involved nor the "pair" sense exactly
fits the case from Zechariah. Moreover, the conjunction between the two numerals in Zech 4:2 has no parallel in OT usage.
Thus acceptance of the distributive sense for this phrase

requires some minor revision (either elimination of the *waw* or
transferral to the first numeral) and some flexibility about
usages of a double-numeral distribution pattern. Torrey, Rignell, Chary, and Horst make the minor concessions necessary to
adopt the MT reading, translating "seven *mûṣāqôt* for each...."

Ultimately the problem involves making a decision about
the structure and appearance of the lamps. Does each lamp have
one *mûṣeqet* or seven? Herein lies the larger problem of identifying the *mûṣāqôt*. What are they? Leaving text-critical
considerations aside for the moment, one can turn to the archaeological evidence. Robert North ("Zechariah's Seven-Spout
Lampstand," *Biblica* 51 [1970], 183-206) provides the most recent and complete analysis of relevant archaeological data,
while reviewing and continuing the work of Kurt Möhlenbrink
("Die Leuchter im 5 Nachtgesicht des Propheten Sacharja: eine
archäologische Untersuchung," *ZDPV* 52 [1929], 257-286) and of
K. Galling (*Biblisches Reallexikon* [Tübingen: Mohr, 1937]).

With North we take *mûṣeqet* to be from *yṣq*, "to flow,"
rather than from *ṣwq*, "to be in straits" (so Möhlenbrink).
North writes,

> By "spout" we mean the niche or pinch in the lip of
> the bowl which is suited to hold a wick....We do not find
> it far-fetched to interpret "flow" in the sense of "mount
> through the wick to the flame." (185)

The above definition seems a good one to us. North notes that
in excavated examples from the period after 1700 B.C. the *nēr*
itself was a saucer which had a mild pinch in its lip.

> But gradually the pinch became deeper and more complex,
> turning eventually into a real tube or spout. In the
> saucer-lip there could be more than one pinch for a wick...
> The saucer lamp with precisely *seven* pinches was by far
> the commonest. (188, 190)

North includes a drawing of the little chalice from Taʿanak
which has the seven-pinch form. (See his Fig. 6, 189.) This
piece was used by Galling as the model for his BRL reconstruction. Galling drew a lampstand holding seven lamps, each of
which has seven pinches. Galling, and Möhlenbrink before him,
saw the seven-pinch lamp as the key to the Zechariah image and
especially to the obscure reference to *šibʿâ wĕšibʿâ mûṣāqôt*.

North includes other archaeological evidence for the seven-pinch lamp which was extant at least as early as 900 B.C. These examples, however, are of single lamps with seven spouts or pinches. North notes that examples of lampstands which have seven lamps with seven pinches each are dated from the second century, which "is a bit late for Zechariah. But the possibility of some similar or simpler form (in Zechariah's time) may perhaps be left open" (205).

North himself prefers a simpler model for the image in Zechariah. Each of his seven lamps has one deep pinch per lamp, based on a piece from the Bliss-Macalister excavations of 1902 (189, Fig. 1). One might contrast North's drawing (201, Fig. 42) with that of Galling (North, 189, Fig. 7).

What then of our reading? We have tentatively decided in favor of the more complex, baroque image. Archaeologically, it is a possibility and text-critically, it is the more difficult reading. Neither Ex 25:37 nor 37:23, the pentateuchal accounts which specifically mention seven lamps of the menorah, includes a reference to *mûṣāqôt*. Two explanations are possible: 1) these lamps were not seen to have the spout, which must have been a common feature to the Priestly Codifier responsible for the descriptions; 2) the pinch or spout was such a common feature that specific mention of it was not felt necessary. The latter seems the more likely explanation. We suggest that the menorah pictured in Zechariah 4 is markedly more complex than the one tended by Aaron; for this reason, the number of spouts per lamp is especially mentioned. In this way G may be haplographic. We make no claims of certainty for our choice of reading, however. The problem simply may not be solvable.

[e]G^{Zi} (W) and MT read *mîmîn haggullâ*, εκ δεξιων του λαμπαδιου. G(B-S-V A-Q) read εκ δεξιων του λαμπαδιου αυτης, *mîmîn gullâ*. With most scholars we emend to *mîmînâ*. In any event, the menorah must be the point of reference in this phrase, not the bowl-shaped feature atop it.

[f]Omit *lē'mōr* with G(V A) against MT and G^{Zi}(B-S Q)

[g]We agree with most scholars that vss. 6αβ-10α have been interpolated into the vision. They interrupt the flow of the motif pattern which should move directly from the question of the seer (vs. 4) to the rhetorical question/response pair (vs.

5), a unique feature of this vision found also at vs. 13, to
the response of the interpreter. Formally these vss. simply do
not belong, but where do they belong? Scholars have suggested
a number of alternative locations for the vss. elsewhere in the
Zechariah cycle.

The addition at this point in the vision is perplexing.
These vss. must refer to Zerubbabel, whose rise and fall
appears to have taken place within a very short period of time.
(See frank Moore Cross, "A Reconstruction," 14-16.) Therefore
6αβ-10α must be nearly contemporary with the vision itself.
Perhaps these vss. did once belong elsewhere in the Zechariah
material. Yet surely, any redactor would have realized how out
of place they seem here, dividing the question from the answer
with a lengthy excursus. Paul Hanson suggests that 6αβ-10α
belongs to a second stratum in the Zechariah corpus (IDB Sup.,
pp. 982-983).

In any event, unlike the additions to Jeremiah 1 and 24,
these vss. have not been made to blend with the given form of
the original vision. While the additions in Jeremiah point
toward new directions in the symbolic vision form, these additional vss. interrupt the form. Therefore, given the scope of
our present work, we will not deal with 6αβ-10α. For an extensive exegetical and text-critical analysis of these oracular
additions, see A. Petitjean, *Les Oracles du Proto-Zacharie*
(Paris: Gabalda, 1969), pp. 207-267. Petitjean also includes a
good review of scholarship up to 1969.

[h]Vs. 12 is either a variant for vs. 11, the question of
the seer about the olive trees, or an explanatory gloss. We
suspect that the former is the case. In any event, vs. 12 has
undergone some corruption. MT reads, מה שתי שבלי הזיתים אשר
ביד שני הצנתרות הזהב המריקים מעליהם הזהב. MT מעליהו is a corruption for מעלים = G επαναγοντων, "bring up." A term for oil,
šemen or *yiṣhar*, has probably dropped out so that the vs. once
read,

> What are the two olive branches which are beside the two
> golden pipes which let down and bring up the 'oil'
> (assuming *hazzāhāb* to be a dittography)?

With most scholars we omit vs. 12.

[i]With G omit *lēʼmōr*.

Pattern of Content Elements	*Rubrics*
4:1 Indication of vision	Non-traditional introduction
4:2 Question of divine being to seer	ויאמר אלי מה אתה ראה
4:2,3 Reply of seer and description	ואמר ראיתי והנה...
4:4 Question of seer about symbols	ואען ואמר אל המלאך הדבר בי מה אלה אדני
4:5 Rhetorical question of divine being/	ריען המלאך הדבר בי ויאמר אלי הלוא...
Response of seer	ואמר לא אדני
4:6a, 10b Explanation of part of the image	ריען ריאמר אלי לאמר...
4:11 Question of seer about other part of the symbolic image	ואען ואמר אליו מה...
4:13 Rhetorical question of divine being/	ויאמר אלי הלוא...
Response of seer	ואמר לא אדני
4:14 Explanation of other part of symbolic image	ויאמר אלה...

While Zech 5:1-4 basically conforms to the content pattern
and framing language of stage I of the symbolic vision form
(exemplified by Am 7:7-9, 8:1-3, Jer 1:11-12, 1:13-19, and 24),
an outline of Zechariah 4 displays significant changes. Following an indication of the renewed presence of the angel (4:1),
a rubric especially fitted to the Zechariah cycle, comes an
unusual, individualistic, and thus non-traditional introduction
to the vision.

ויעירני כאיש אשר

יעור משנתו

He aroused me like a man that is
awakened from his sleep.

The above introductory phrase implies a vision which has
occurred during sleep, that is, a dream. At least figuratively,
an image of sleep and liminality is evoked. In contrast, in-
troductions to the visions of Amos and Jeremiah imply spontane-
ous waking experiences: "Thus the Lord showed me..." or "The
word of the Lord came to me...."

Like Jer 1:11-12 and 1:13-19, the fifth vision of Zechariah does not have a motif of initial description of the

vision. The absence of a description of the symbols at the
beginning of this longer work has implications for its unity of
form, as we shall discuss below.

The motif of the question to the seer (4:2) is identical
to the question motif of the earlier examples of the form in
terms of content and language. As in Zech 5:1-4, the intermediary, not God, is the questioner. The prophet answers the
question of the otherworldly being with a form of $r'h$ + $w\check{e}hin-$
$n\bar{e}h$, terms more usually found in the indication of a vision and
initial description (see Am 7:7, 8:1, Jer 24:1, and Zech 5:4).
The use of the perfect of $r'h$ may imply that the vision experience is somewhat less immediate than those of Amos and Jeremiah.

The first three motifs of the vision (4:1-3) do display
some divergence from earlier examples of the form, but through
vs. 3 there is a basic congruence in content order and language
between this vision and those of stage I. In vs. 4, however,
enters an entirely new motif, not found in stage I of the symbolic vision form. The prophet himself asks the angel to
interpret the objects described in vss. 2, 3. This request for
an explanation is an extremely important addition to the pattern; for the seer's question will come to replace the question
of the divine being in later examples of the symbolic vision
form. This request for interpretation together with the dreaming nuance discussed above point to a divinatory context.[9]
Zechariah 4:1-6a, 10b-14 evidences an important phenomenon in
Biblical prophecy: revelation through interpretation. The
interpretation of symbolic objects upon the request of the seer
leads to a divine revelation. This mode of revelation says
something not only about the changing nature of prophecy, but
also about the relationship between God and man as perceived by
the author of the vision. Communication with God is less
direct and more difficult than in other prophetic modes (see
below).

---

9. C. Jeremias considers the prophet's questioning to be
an important nuance in the visions of Zechariah, one which dif-
ferentiates his visions from those of Amos and Jeremiah (*Die
Nachtgesichte*, pp. 92, 228). He does not approach the questioning, however, in relation to the phenomenon of divination.

The movement from the seer's question to the interpreter's response is interrupted by a little pause which takes the form of a rhetorical question by the interpreter, "Don't you know what these are?" and the seer's polite response, "No, my lord." This question/answer pair delays for a moment the explanation motif at vs. 5 and vs. 13. Rignell and Baldwin write that the angel's rhetorical questioning serves to heighten the tension of the piece.[10] There is no doubt that the author takes more time to describe the interaction between the seer and the interpreter. The pattern from description to explanation is lengthened as the tight economical version of the symbolic vision form is stretched in a more narrative direction.

The fifth vision of Zechariah shows the vision form in transition. The external criteria of form which described the visions of Amos and Jeremiah do not apply as well. While the formalized language of stage I remains in the motifs of question of the divine being and reply of the seer (4:2), many of the old rubrics are missing. Vision V includes the motif of question of the divine being to the seer, but also includes a new motif, the question of the seer to the interpreter, a motif which plays a key role structurally and conceptually in the on-going development of the form. In vision V, the form is in flux, the content structure of the piece loosened. The presence of two question motifs, one of the angel and one of the seer, complicates the neater and simpler question/answer pattern which characterizes the visions of stage I.

The same transitory quality emerges in an examination of the vision on its lowest level of structure, that is, in terms of its use of language.

Use of language and loss of economy of expression

We have prepared two lay-outs of the text of Zechariah 4, one which portrays the vision as a prose dialogue pattern of alternating speakers and one which allows for our "test for adherence to prosodic norms." The test for line length and

---

10. Rignell, *Die Nachtgesichte*, p. 152; J. Baldwin, *Haggai, Zechariah, Malachi* (Downers Grove, Ill.: Inter-Varsity, 1972), p. 120.

enjambement is useful in this vision specifically to reveal
contrasts between its style and the style of the visions of
stage I. We recall that the neat rhetorical style of stage I
begins to break down in the scroll vision (Zech 5:1-4). The
test for prosody, moreover, revealed some especially lengthy
lines and more cases of enjambement than were found in any of
the symbolic visions of Amos and Jeremiah. In the fifth vision,
the economical criteria of structure are almost completely
abandoned. The piece contains only reminiscences of repetition
and traditional economy of language. Balance in line length
also diminishes appreciably.

A scan of line lengths in vision V reveals an extremely
erratic pattern, the least balance between lines we have seen
in our studies thus far. We have often noted that balanced
line length is no major criterion of structure in stage I of
the symbolic vision form; yet none of the visions of stage I
included a fifteen syllable line as in vs. 1 or a fourteen
syllable line as in vs. 4. Note that the rubric in vs. 4
employs two verbs instead of one to introduce the question.
Two verbs are also used in vs. 5 and in the shorter rubrics in
4:6 and 4:11. Economy of expression does not seem to be a goal
of the author.

Three cases of enjambement occur between 2g and 2h, 11b
and 11c, and 11b and 11d, but are we justified in establishing
these breaks? In previous cases of enjambement in Amos and
Jeremiah, a necessary break in a long line seemed natural and
appropriate because of the length of the complete thought lines
directly preceding and/or following the line in question. For
example, in Am 7:8d-g we had a choice of a 6/13/7 pattern or a
6/6/7/7 pattern; the latter seemed much more clearly the
author's intention. In Jer 1:14 we had the choice of a 7/15
count or a pattern of 7/8/7, allowing for a break before the
prepositional phrase. The latter seemed appropriate. Even in
the more erratically patterned Jeremiah 24, certain breaks in
lines asserted themselves. When confronted with a possible
11/22 count in 24:4-5, one chose to divide the thought-line
before *kēn* and create an 11/10/12 pattern. The choices are
much less clear in Zechariah 4. At 4:2, is a 7/11/5 (2f-h)
pattern with enjambement preferable to a 7/16 pattern without

enjambement? The preceding line 2e has 6 syllables; 3a which
follows had 8 syllables. Where do the breaks come? With such
diversity of line length that one cannot properly decide where
enjambement comes, one must wonder whether Zechariah 4 evidences any attempt to alter normal syntax. The suspicion grows
that Zechariah 4 is composed in ordinary prose. Before making
a final decision, however, we discuss that which has been the
most essential criterion of structure, the economy of language.

   We have already noted the double-verb rubrics which evidence variety of expression rather than economy. What of the
language used to express the key content elements? Do repetitions of the symbol image occur at predictable points as in
Amos and Jeremiah such that the total piece is unified and
framed by them? Even given the changes in content elements
discussed above, we would expect the symbol objects to be mentioned not only in their first description, but possibly also
when the seer inquires about them, and especially when the
climactic answers are given in response to his request for
enlightenment. Yet in his first question, the seer refers to
the symbol objects by the demonstrative pronoun, *mâ 'ēlleh*,
"What are these?" An opportunity to link motif to motif via
the repetition of terms has been lost. The reply of the angel
does repeat the term "seven" found more than once in vs. 2, but
he re-uses no other symbol terms. In the prophet's second
question comes the only good economical re-use of terms in the
piece. The symbol objects, the *zêtîm*, "olive trees," are
described almost exactly as in vs. 3. In this way, the question is nicely linked to the description of the symbolic image.
The angel, however, employs merely the demonstrative pronoun,
'ēlleh, in his response. That which is repeated almost verbatim is the thematically non-essential pausal question answer
pair (4:5, 13). The author chooses to lengthen his description
of the vision-interpretation scene at the expense of economical
structure. He emphasizes these secondary elements via repetition rather than content elements which would better structure
the work as a whole.

   Some homogeneity of language is found in this vision in
the frequent usages of *'mr*, *'nh*, and *'ēlleh*; but no neat system
characterizes these usages. There is no predictable consistency.

The *'mr* forms, for example, do not stand out as responsible for
the tight rhetorical frame. As noted above, forms of *'mr* sometimes share the rubrics with the verb *'nh*. The *'mr* verb is
even found in the non-essential vss. 5 and 13. The rhetorical-
economic style has given way to prose.

It is not merely the prose quality of this vision which
accounts for its lack of economical language. In vision V, the
divinatory technique of associating like with like via re-use
of the symbol terms seems to fade out. This nuance in the relationship between the symbol and its meaning, of course, is
significant on a conceptual level. More mystery is infused in
the symbol-interpretation equation; perhaps the prophet hesi-
tates to have this dream interpretation scene seem even more
like a mundane divinatory proceeding. The nuance in the relationship between the symbol and its interpretation also has
significance on a basic structural level. With the word-play
or simile of the associative technique gone, the use of repetition of the symbol object, if only for purposes of reference,
also diminishes. Dropping the use of repetition of key terms
weakens the structure of vision V.

With Zechariah vision II (horns, 2:1-4), the content pattern simplifies, as certain basic external criteria of structure again assert themselves. Vision II and most of the remaining visions of our study will be characterized by a prose
style, but repetition as a means of linking the symbol to its
meaning or as a means of creating emphasis for certain key portions of the vision does not entirely disappear. A subtle
transition occurs whereby repetition no longer smacks of divinatory technique but does play a role on a literary level of
aesthetics and structure.

Before dealing with the symbols of Zechariah vision V, we
pause to mention a basic problem, the role of the individual
author in the growth of a literary tradition. Do the visions
of Zechariah merely reflect changes in the symbolic vision form
tradition, a loosening of the tighter demands of stage I?
Alternatively, does the author himself break with these demands
and creatively affect the form of the literary tradition as it
continues? Both of these factors operate in the growth of the
symbolic vision form tradition. Literary forms do evolve and

change with the times. The late 6th century was a period of
tremendous changes. Such times must have allowed for the re-
laxation of stricter demands of form, allowing the creative
author to achieve new syntheses, to attach nuances to the old
form, to find his own place within the tradition. Great continuity exists between the symbolic visions of Amos and Jeremiah and those of Zechariah (or his school); the form found in
these earlier prophets provides the late 6th century prophet
with a vehicle of expression. But the author or authors of
Zechariah 1-6 use this vehicle with flair and a certain degree
of freedom. The visions of Zechariah, in fact, indicate a significant nuance in the concept of prophetic revelation.

In oracles and in the visions of stage I, God provides
information which the seer receives as a passive tool. The
receiving process is rather direct and immediate - even in the
stage I visions. Now, however, the seer must seek to know
God's message via a vehicle of symbol-interpretation. The symbolic images sent by God are a code which must be deciphered in
order that the seer truly see. In a sense, God's own prophet,
the one selected to transmit the word of the Lord, is as ignor-
ant before the interpretation of the vision as are the dreaming
Pharaohs of Genesis 41 and the Tanutamun Stele (see our introduction, pp. 14-19). This concept of delayed revelation through
interpretation emerges not only in the symbolic visions of
Zechariah, Daniel, 2 Baruch, and 4 Ezra, but also in the phenomena of Qumran *pešer* and Rabbinic midrash. In these exegetical forms, the very word of Scripture becomes fraught with
mystery, the code which when deciphered leads to insight about
God's message for man. While a discussion of revelation through
interpretation in *pešer* and midrash is beyond the present study,
we wish to emphasize the importance of this phenomenon which
makes its appearance as a normal means of prophecy in the
formative visions of Zechariah.

The creative quality of Zechariah's visions emerges further
in the symbols used to present the message of the restoration.

Symbols: beneath the contextual level

In dealing with the menorah imagery of Zechariah 4, a
first challenge is to decide what sort of object or objects the

author had in mind. As indicated in text-critical note "d," we
are in basic agreement with Robert North's conception of the
menorah. The lampstand which may have been quite tall[11] rises
into a shallow, saucer-shaped feature which holds seven pinched
lamps, the pinches being mounts for the wicks. We have opted
for the MT reading which describes each lamp as containing
seven of these pinches. In this way, the "real" or surface
level of the image is portrayed by North's Fig. 42, but this
menorah, flanked by two olive trees, has deeper levels of meaning.

On the contextual level, that is, according to the vision
itself, the lamps of the menorah represent the seven eyes of
God and the trees, the anointed ones who stand at attention by
the Lord. In each case, a neat equation seems to exist between
symbol and interpretation. One must pause, however; for each
side of these equations has meaning unstated in the text which
goes beyond the words themselves. Unlike the more obvious
metaphoric relationship in Am 7:7-9 between the measuring tool,
a plumb-line, and judgment, the relationship between cultic
lamps and eyes of God moves to a less obvious, even mystical
plane. When announced in Jeremiah 24 that the bad fruit are
those who did not participate in the exile, the listener com-
prehends the meaning of the symbol and is left with a picture
of reality; yet what are "the eyes of the Lord"? Does not the
reply contain another riddle? Clearly the interpretation of
the symbol remains on a mysterious and mythic level. To some
extent the same applies to the symbolic objects themselves.

Unlike the ordinary items in Amos and Jeremiah, plumb-
lines, figs, and pots, the symbolic lamps in Zechariah 4 have a
sacred, liminal[12] status to begin with, as identifiable cult

---

11. "Zechariah's Seven-Spout Lampstand," 202-203.

12. For a full definition of the term "liminal," see Victor Turner, *The Ritual Process* (Chicago: Aldine, 1969), pp. 94-
97. That which is liminal is that which is betwixt and between
neatly defined categories. A boundary status such that the
thing or person partakes of two seemingly opposite categories
at once is often sacred as well as dangerous. (See M. Douglas,
Purity and Danger [New York: Praeger, 1966], esp. pp. 35, 38-40,

objects employed in rituals which link this world to the other
world. The same "boundary" or liminal status applies to each
side of the other symbolic equation between the trees and the
sons of oil (see below). As anticipated by the flying scroll
of Zechariah vision VI (5:1-4), the symbol objects and their
interpretations are increasingly mythological, subtle, and
multi-layered in meaning. To unearth this meaning one must go
beyond the bounds of the text itself and look to the surround-
ing Biblical and Near Eastern tradition.

A number of scholars have been troubled by the fact that
the text offers no specific interpretation for the menorah as a
whole.[13] D. Buzy goes to the extent of dismissing structural
and linguistic considerations in order to regard vs. 7, which
refers to the cornerstone, as the explanation of the menorah.
Thus the menorah is a symbol for the temple in construction.
In Buzy's view, if one considers the usually deleted vss. 6b-
10a as original to the vision, one restores the explanation of
candelabra, lamps, and olive trees to the order intended by
the author.[14] Such machinations are not necessary. The form
does not require that all aspects of the symbolic image be explained. In Am 7:7-9, neither the hand holding the plumb-line
nor the wall is mentioned in the explanation motif. The key
symbol, the '$\check{a}n\bar{a}k$, "plumb-line," is thereby placed in the spotlight. Even in the late baroque visions of 2 Baruch and 4
Ezra, where a rather neat relationship exists between each symbol object and its explanation, not every aspect of each image
is illucidated. On the other hand, the unexplained aspects of
the image may contain as much symbolic value as the aspects
which are explained within the vision. We thus sympathize with
various scholars' attempts to understand what is meant by the
menorah as a whole.

163-165.) "Liminal" in this sense corresponds to Levi-Strauss's
use of the term "intermediary."

13. See, for example, D. Buzy, "Les Symboles de Zacharie,"
RB 15 (1918), 136-191 (esp. 166-167), and J. Boehmer, "Was
bedeutet die goldene Leuchter Sach 4, 2?" *BZ* 24 (1938), 360-
364.

14. "Les Symboles," 166-167.

While Marti,[15] Rignell,[16] and Chary[17] regard the menorah
as an image of the Lord - "ein Symbol der Gegenwart Jahwes" in
Rignell's terms - Boehmer,[18] Bič,[19] and Baldwin[20] consider the
menorah to represent "the worshipping community,"[21] "die fromme
jüdische Gemeinde."[22] Such rather allegorical explanations are
actually less on the track than Buzy's emphasis on the temple,
though certainly he draws his conclusion for the wrong reasons.
An examination of the individual contributing elements of the
menorah points to its significance as an evoker of temple -
more precisely tabernacle - and cult.[23]

First, the menorah is said to be all of gold. A search
for golden lampstands leads to images from Solomon's temple in
1 Kg 7:49 and to the pure golden menorah of the tabernacle tradition employed by P in Ex 25:31; 37:17, 24; and Num 8:4. Each
of these cultic contexts provides a possible background for
Zechariah's imagery. Note that the tabernacle tradition like
Zechariah 4 speaks of only one menorah thus highlighting it

15. *Das Dodekapropheten erklärt*, p. 414.

16. *Die Nachtgesichte*, p. 175.

17. *Agée-Zacharie Malachie*, p. 85. See also C. Jeremias,
Die Nachtgesichte, p. 181.

18. "Was bedeutet," 364.

19. *Die Nachtgesichte des Sacharja* (Neukirchen: Neukirchener Verlag, 1964), pp. 48, 49.

20. *Haggai, Zechariah, Malachi*, p. 124.

21. Baldwin, p. 124.

22. Boehmer, p. 365.

23. For a detailed analysis of the tabernacle menorah see
Carol L. Myers, *The Tabernacle Menorah: A Synthetic Study of a
Symbol from the Biblical Cult* (ASOR Diss. Ser. 2; Missoula:
Scholars, 1976). Dr. Myers is especially interested in the
menorah's relationship to Near Eastern fertility symbolism and
in its role as a "navel of the earth" phenomenon. See pp.
165ff. and 187ff. Some of our conclusions about the role of
the menorah symbol in Zechariah vision V parallel Myers' larger
findings about the centrality of the tabernacle menorah in Biblical traditions.

alone, whereas Solomon's temple has ten, five to the right and
five to the left before the inner sanctuary (1 Kgs 7:49).

The *gullâ* like the menorah itself is not explained in the
vision to be other than what it appears, a structural feature
of the menorah. The terminology, *gullâ ʿal rōʾšâ*, used nowhere
else in OT in relation to a menorah, is interesting. Similar
terms are found at 1 Kgs 7:41=2 Chron 4:12 in reference to
bowl-shaped features of the capitals of the temple pillars:
וגלת הכתרת אשר על ראש העמודים. Is the writer of vision V
attempting to evoke an image of the Solomonic temple in his
description of the menorah through the mention of this structural feature? Though such a motive may be behind the description, it is more likely that this saucer-shaped feature was a
fairly common element of design in the Near East, used in a
variety of vertical structures. Nevertheless, *gullâ* is a rare
term in OT and the possibility of an intentional link between
temple and menorah through it cannot be ruled out.

A simpler hint to the background of the menorah in Zechariah 4 is found in the reference to seven lamps. The number
of lamps per menorah in the Solomonic temple is not mentioned;
only the tabernacle menorah is said to have seven lamps. See
Ex 25:37; 37:23; and Num 8:2, passages included by the Priestly
Codifier in the sixth century B.C. The link between Zechariah's
menorah and that of P is unmistakable.[24] They share a tradition of the seven lamps. While seven, a prime number, has special significance as an indication of wholeness or sacredness
throughout OT, it is especially pervasive in P descriptions of
ritual activity. See, for example: Lev 4:6, 17; 8:11; 14:7,
16, 27, 51; and 16:14, 19. In line with this notion of seven's
being a most perfect number, the menorah is to have seven lamps.
In the Zechariah 4 description we also find a reference to
seven *mûṣāqōt*, "spouts," which presumably hold the wicks of the
lamps. Depending on whether one accepts the MT or G, there are
seven *mûṣāqōt* to each lamp or seven in all, one per lamp. In
any event, a *mûṣeqet* is found in no other account of the menorah

---

24. Rignell does not discuss the P connection, but does
state "Das Vorbild in der Vision beschriebenen Leuchter ist
zweifellos der Leuchter im Exodos." See p. 175.

(indeed nowhere else in OT) and one wonders if these mounts for
the wicks are mentioned only in order to repeat the number
seven.

The P connection to the specific symbols of Zechariah's
visions nicely correlates a basic finding of Paul Hanson's -
namely that Zechariah is in line with priestly tradition, out-
look, and aspirations.[25]   Klaus Seybold rightly emphasizes the
cultic and ritual symbolism of this vision.[26]   The fact that
Zechariah's menorah image is based on the same tabernacle tradition as that of P focuses attention on the attitude toward
cult shared by P and Zechariah.

The Frank Moore Cross writes:

> The prime benefit of the Sinaitic covenent in the view of
> the Priestly tradent was the "tabernacling" presence of
> Yahweh in Israel's midst....
>
> The entire cultic paraphernalia and cultus was designed to
> express and overcome the problem of the holy, transcendent
> God visiting his pervasively sinful people. Zones of
> holiness in the Tabernacle and court, and in the battle
> camp vividly express the paradox of the immanence of the
> Holy One.[27]

How can the Lord come "to tabernacle," *liškōn*, among his
people who were exiled because of their sin? The cult provides
a means of atonement and of re-establishing the positive tabernacling relationship with God. The concern with the removal of
sin, a cultic concern of P, is a theme of Zechariah found in
the scroll vision (VI), the ephah vision (VII), and at Zech 3:9.
The term *škn*, an archaic term employed by P to describe God's
presence in Israel as their God,[28] is also used by Zechariah to
describe the return of God to the midst of his people. See

---

25. *The Dawn of Apocalyptic*. See pp. 228-269 for Hanson's own approach to the connection between priestly traditions and the participants in the restoration. See esp. 256
for a discussion of Zechariah's emphasis on purification of the
land.

26. *Bilder zum Tempelbau*, pp. 77, 81.

27. *Canaanite Myth*, p. 299.

28. See Cross, *Canaanite Myth*, p. 299.

Zech 2:14, 15 and 8:3.[29] This "tabernacling" presence of God
is also invoked by the Deuteronomist in his pro-Josiah, pro-
Davidite document. Employing the term $škn$ in the context of
the Solomonic temple (1 Kgs 6:13, 8:12)[30] allows the Deuteronomist to portray that temple as a continuation of the more
ancient tabernacle tradition.

To return to Zechariah 4, the menorah and its lamps, which
Aaron was to keep in order continually (Lev 24:4), are certainly an element of and hence an effective symbol of cult, the
activity which links man with God. It is significant that the
seven-lamped menorah is a cultic reminiscence which reaches
back not simply to the Solomonic temple but more precisely to
the tabernacle tradition, employed also by P. Within the context of the larger Zechariah cycle, evocation of the tabernacle
places the restored temple which Zechariah advocates in an
ancient line of sacred tradition.[31] As a focal point of wor-
ship, the menorah points not only ahead to a rebuilt temple but
also back to the tabernacle. This is the pedigree which Zechariah would assume for his temple, as did the Deuteronomist who
refers to the Lord's "tabernacling" in the Jerusalem temple,
the focus of Josiah's program of reform and centralization.[32]

29. See Hanson, *The Dawn*, p. 249, and Cross, "A Reconstruction," 15.

30. The poetic piece at 8:12, 13 may be much earlier than
the work of the Deuteronomist. He has incorporated this more
ancient refrain into his composition.

31. On the actual dating of tabernacle traditions see M.
Haran, *Temples and Temple-Service in Ancient Israel* (Oxford:
Clarendon, 1958), pp. 189ff.

32. 2 Chron 13:11, part of an extremely pro-priestly
passage, portrays the priests and Levites as faithful servants
of the Lord, in the midst of much sinfulness. Their positive
behavior is underlined by their service in the temple, an
important aspect of which is to care for the menorah and its
lamps. This reference would seem to be to a single menorah, as
in P's tabernacle account, in contrast to 1 Chron 28:15 and 2
Chron 4:20, where the author clearly refers to the several
menorahs of the Solomonic temple.

Professor Hanson has taken note of the links between

We will discuss Zechariah's contextual explanation of the seven lamps soon, but first let us look at the other symbolic objects, the olive trees which flank the menorah.

Scholars have long emphasized the possible mythic background of the two olive trees.[33] A. J. Wensinck sees them "as a dim remembrance of the cosmological trees."[34] Others point to the frequency in the Near East of an image of an enthroned deity flanked by trees and more specifically to an image of the Egyptian god Min, who is pictured next to an altar upon which two cypresses stand. An additional symbol appears between the two cypress trees and some scholars have attempted to identify it as a candelabra.[35] This identification, however, remains questionable.

The sacred tree is actually a universal symbol. Equally common in folk and primitive art is the image of a deity, king,

---

traditions of the Zadokite priesthood and the Chronicler, though he would date the Chronicler's activities to 400 B.C., a rather late date (*The Dawn*, p. 270). Professor Cross ("A Reconstruction," 15) and J. D. Newsome ("Toward a New Understanding of the Chronicler and His Purposes," *JBL* 94 [1975], 216) point to the connection between the Chronicler's work and that of Zechariah. We are here interested in the third equation between priestly traditions and Zechariah, as it emerges in the symbols employed by the latter. See also Hanson, *The Dawn*, pp. 262-270.

33. Through an emendation of $z\hat{e}t\hat{i}m$ to $\check{s}\hat{e}d\hat{i}m$ and a number of rather unusual translations and interpretations, Paul Haupt transforms Zechariah 4 into an image reminiscent of Near Eastern fertility myths. "The Visions of Zechariah," *JBL* 32 (1913), 107-122. Professor Haupt's arguments are unconvincing to say the least.

34. "Tree and Bird as Cosmological Symbols in Western Asia," *Verhandelingen der koninklijke Akademie van Westenschappen te Amsterdam* (N.R. 22/1), 12, cited in Rignell, p. 173. We have been unable to locate a copy of the article.

35. For a good list of references to the two-tree image in the ancient Near East and for a critique of the supposed candelabra in the image of Min see K. Möhlenbrink, "Der Leuchter," pp. 260 and 260-261, n.4.

or other figure symmetrically bounded by a tree on each side.
A quick examination of examples from Helmuth Th. Bossert's
Ornamente der Volkskunst warns us against finding a specific
origin for the trees of Zechariah 4 in Eden or in Egypt.[36] On
the other hand, given the trees' context within the Zechariah
passage, one is led to a comparison with 1 Kgs 22:19. The triadic image of Yahweh flanked to the right and the left by his
hosts. This approach to Zechariah's total image is best left
for later in our discussion. What we can say at this point,
however, is that the tree, the fruit tree in particular, is a
universal creation symbol because of its greenness, its implicit
fertility and ability to procreate. As a vertical structure,
it grows from within the earth and yet reaches into the sky.
It thus often plays the perfect role as a Levi-Straussian intermediary between heaven and earth in myths dealing with the
relationship between heavenly and earthly beings. In this way,
if a king is portrayed surrounded by trees, he is surrounded by
life and procreation as well as by veritable ladders to the
divine. In Zechariah vision V, these life/liminality symbols
surround a symbol of cult. The special significance of all the
menorah represents cannot be missed.

That which has not been emphasized enough, however, is the
more obvious connection between olive trees and the priestly
initiation and status. Rignell mentions the link between olive
oil, cult, and anointing once almost in passing, while more
recent commentators do not seem to mention it at all.[37] As
indicated by Jud 9:9, the olive tree was the means "by which
gods and men (kings usually) are honored." The P passages Ex
27:20 and Lev 24:2 state that olive oil is to be used in the
lamp which burns continuously in the tent of meeting. Ex 30:22-
33 contains the most interesting priestly link to the olive
tree. In this passage, Yahweh instructs Moses as to the composition of the oil of anointing, an aromatic combination of
spices and olive oil. The oil is to anoint the tent of meeting, the ark, the menorah, the altar, and its utensils.

---

36. (Tübingen: Wasmuth, 1969). See Pl. 5, Fig. 1, 3; Pl.
8, Fig. 4; and Pl. 23, Fig. 6.

37. *Die Nachtgesichte*, pp. 175-176.

30) ואת אהרן ואת בניו תמשח וקדשת
אתם לכהן לי   (31   ואל בני ישראל תדבר
לאמר שמן משחת קדש יהיה זה לי לדרתיכם
32)   על בשר אדם לא ייסך

(30) And Aaron and his sons you shall anoint. You
shall sanctify them to serve me as priests. (31)
And to the Sons of Israel you will speak, saying,
"This shall be for me sacred anointing oil, throughout your generations. (32) Upon the body of any
ordinary man it shall not be poured...."

Thus the oil prepared from the fruit of the olive tree becomes
a symbol which sets the priest apart from the *bĕśar 'ādām*, the
ordinary, common person. The ceremony of anointing in olive
oil makes him, like a king, a liminal being, that is, a human
on the boundary between this world and the other world, a man
with the touch of the divine upon him. In this light, the
relationship between the olive trees as symbol and the anointed
ones as interpretation becomes intrinsic, emphasizing that
Zechariah does place the sacred priest and the secular ruler
on equal levels. A number of scholars refuse to accept that
the vision presents the priest as anointed, going so far as to
view 4:11-14 as a later addition. [38]   If vss. 11, 13-14 are
from a later hand, so must be vs. 3; for the two passages are
integrally related in terms of the form itself and in terms of
the larger meaning of the symbols as shown above. Were these
scholars correct, one would also have to consider Ex 30:30-32,
a Priestly passage, later than Zechariah 4. Such a chronology
for P is difficult to accept, [39] and there is no reason to
believe that these elitist vss. in Exodus 30 like the material
directly before and after them are from any hand other than
that of P.

Having discussed the deeper implications of the vision's
given symbols, let us explore the motifs of explanation provided by the interpreting angel. The seven lamps are said to
be the seven eyes of the Lord, which range throughout the land

38.   See Chary, p. 87; Beuken, p. 274.
39.   With Cross (*Canaanite Myth*, p. 325) we would date P
just before Zechariah, no later than the sixth century.

(vs. 10b). Most scholars have traced the seven eyes to the
seven planets, which played a role in a number of ancient Near
Eastern cultures.[40] Horst writes:

> Die sieben „Befehlsübermittler" (sumerisch) repräsentieren
> ...die Totalität der Weltherrschaft des höchsten Gottes,
> wurden somit das Rangzeichen gerade Jahwes der „der Gebie-
> ter der ganzen Erde" ist.[41]

Philo and Josephus also viewed the seven eyes as symbols for
the seven planets.[42] In these writers' views, God's eyes like
planets represent divine omniscience. This omniscience in the
world includes a special eye for the protection of Israel.

A. Leo Oppenheim offers a beautifully concrete supplement
to these interpretations. He gives evidence for a kind of
"secret service" or spy squad which seems to have been attached
to a number of Near Eastern courts. This service is called in
the various languages "the eyes of the king."[43] The "eyes" are
essentially an extension of the king's own body, allowing him
to see more widely than any ordinary human could.[44] As noted
by Oppenheim, 2 Chron 16:9 gives further insight into the role
of the "eyes of the Lord." Their role is להתחזק עם לבבם שלם,
"to strengthen (people) if their hearts are pure." The conditional quality of this phrase, in our view, creates a dichotomy
between "pure" and "not pure." Again enters the theme of sin
vs. freedom from sin. Oppenheim goes on to trace the roving

40. See Chary, pp. 85-86; Horst, p. 231; and Rignell, p.
172.

41. *Die zwölf kleinen Propheten*, p. 231.

42. *Life of Moses* 2.102-103; *Antiquities* 3.146.

43. "The Eyes of the Lord," *Essays in Memory of E. A.
Speiser*, ed. W. W. Hallo (*JAOS* 88/1; New Haven: American Oriental Society, 1968), 173-180. For specific examples from Egyptian and Greek sources, see Oppenheim, "Eyes," 173.

44. This physical notion of the "eyes" as an actual part
of the king's body may be even more appropriate to the mythologically charged context in Zechariah. It is fully possible
that Yahweh's divine agents or representatives *are* his very
eyes. Cf. K. Mras, ed., *Eusebius Werke*, VIII, part I, *Die
Praeparatio evangelica* (Berlin: Akademie, 1954), I 10,36.

eyes as well as the horse teams of Zechariah (chs. 1, 6) and
the heavenly travellers of Job 1 to a belief in demonic figures.
While such an orientation is appropriate to the trouble-making
śāṭān of Job 1, it is not appropriate to the passages in Zechariah, where the "eyes" and the charioteers seem more the Lord's
reconnaissance troops than bothersome demons. Nevertheless,
Oppenheim is correct in linking the "eyes" to the horse teams
of visions I and VIII. The spy nuance applies to both varieties of rovers. (See the analysis of visions I and VIII
below.)

     When one correlates 2 Chron 16:9 with Zech 4:10b, one sees
that the roving eyes, like the flying scroll of vision VI, are
directed at individuals within Israel. The eyes strengthen those
who are pure, as the scroll/curse rooted out those who were
impure. The curse, יוצאת על פני כל הארץ, "goes forth on the
face of the whole land," while the eyes משוטטים בכל הארץ,
"range throughout the land." Their purposes are complementary,
and again emphasize the priestly concern with sin, its identification and removal. As the political eyes of the king seek
out traitors - possibly disloyal vassals - these heavenly eyes
from Yahweh's court seek out those who are disloyal to the
covenant relationship with Yahweh.

     As we observed in the analysis of the scroll symbol, the
divine realm is seen in terms of the human realm; aspects of
the heavenly court or council parallel those of the human monarch's court. Such an approach may explain why the "eyes" in
Zechariah 4:10 are employed with a m.p. verb, *měśôṭěṭîm*. The
Chronicles passage opts for the more grammatically correct
agreement between the feminine noun, "eyes," and its verb;
Zechariah 4 is the more literal. At any Near Eastern court,
"the eyes of the king" were no doubt male; so in the divine
court. Thus in Zechariah 4, we are dealing with not merely a
reference to the Lord's omniscience, but more specifically with
real members of the divine council. They are a part of the
mythological set-up of the other world. The planets were no
doubt seen as representations of such divine spies, "the eyes"
of the heavenly king, but the concrete courtly origins for the
expression must be appreciated, as must be their larger role in
mythology.

In the context of vision V, the eyes are an explanation of
the lamps of the menorah. It is important to note how the
meanings of these two images blend. A quintessential sign of
cult is interpreted to be an arm of the divine council which
seeks out sinners and non-sinners. Such a meshing of heavily
loaded symbols serves to infuse the cult with tremendous author-
ity and importance. The divine realm is symbolically represented in the temple seeking out men, as the cult carried out
in the temple seeks out God. The two realms, divine and manmade, overlap on this boundary of symbols which encompass both.

The explanation of the two olive trees also forges a link
between man's world and the realm of God. These trees are the
two sons of oil, the anointed ones who stand at attention (ʿmd
ʿl) by the Lord of the whole earth. As noted by F. M. Cross,
the term ʿmd ʿl is technical language which refers to the
divine council setting. 1 Kgs 22:19 and Ugaritica V, Text 2
also employ ʿmd ʿl to describe an image from the divine council, the heavenly monarch accompanied by his courtiers. The
triadic set-up in 1 Kgs 22, in particular, parallels the triadic structure of Zechariah's image.[45] These two attending
figures, however, have a more specific identity.

As noted above, some scholars have been reticent to accept
vss. 11, 13-14 as original to the vision. While not suggesting
that these vss. are from the hand of a later redactor, C. C.
Torrey does believe them to have been nuanced in meaning
through other additions and changes in the passage.[46] Torrey
does not identify the two figures as Joshua and Zerubbabel, but
as a less historical reference to the coming of two messiahs.[47]
Torrey seeks evidence for a tradition of two messiahs in Daniel,
2 Baruch, 4 Ezra, Enoch, and in Rabbinic materials. The Qumran
discoveries, of course, would have provided grist for his mill.
In any event, he views Zechariah's reference to the two
anointed as a precursor to these later appearances and considers Zechariah 1-8 as a whole, "a prophetical work of apocalyptic

45. See F. M. Cross, *Canaanite Myth*, p. 37 and p. 37, n.
147.

46. "The Messiah Son of Ephraim," *JBL* 66 (1947), 253-277.

47. "The Messiah," 276; cf. Hanson, *The Dawn*, pp. 255-256.

nature." He thus rejects more historical and political interpretations of the figures. In fact, Torrey would consider all
more historical references in Zechariah 1-8 to be the work of a
later redactor.

While Torrey's larger work on the messiahs is interesting,
we cannot accept his characterization of Zechariah 1-8 as an
apocalyptic work, nor his source critical suggestions. The two
anointed figures of Zechariah 4 are no doubt precursors of the
two meta-historical messianic figures which will play a role in
later mythologies about the coming of the kingdom. Yet these
precursors in Zechariah are historical: The power of the
Davidic king is now balanced by that of the leader of cult, the
high priest.[48] The high priority given to cult and ritual by
this image of the anointed ones is undeniably clear.

The presence of these two figures in the triadic, divine
attendant pose is significant, especially given that the identity of these figures must have been a thinly veiled mystery to
Zechariah's audience. Human beings are placed in a council
scene and are described as those who accompany the Lord. This
image and description has prompted Wellhausen and others to
view the menorah as a place-holder or symbol for the divine
monarch, Yahweh.[49] Such a view, however, is too literal, missing the transcendent subtleties of the image. The human rulers,
with a semi-divine status, are shown to surround a cult object
which is a means of reaching God, of serving him, and of assur-
ing his visitation among them. As the eyes of the Lord sent
from the divine council rove the land to see if its people are
deserving of Yahweh's presence and favor, the anointed, by
their actions, petition him from earth.

In this way, man and God are put in contact via temple and
cult. Each of the symbols of Zechariah's vision (lamps and
trees) and each of the stated interpretations (eyes and anointed
ones) has been shown to partake of both sides of the other-
worldly/this worldly dichotomy. Each has a number of layers of
meaning, and all of these multi-vocal symbols are held in tension by a central, real-life cult object, the temple menorah. In

---

48. Cf. C. Jeremias, *Die Nachtgesichte*, pp. 146, 148.

49. See notes 15-17 above. See also C. Jeremias, *Die
Nachtgesichte*, p. 181.

his complex use of symbols, Zechariah partakes of a true mythology. He would have his religion, its cult, beliefs, and values
parallel and support his social structure, a theocracy run by
the appointed representatives of God. All of this is represented in short-hand by the multi-leveled meanings of his visionary image. It can be no coincidence that this vision, so representative of the world-view which emphasizes temple and cult,
has been set at the center of the vision cycle as a whole.[50]

Zech 2:1-4

(1   ואשא את עיני וארא
     והנה ארבע קרנות

(2   ואמר אל המלאך הדבר בי
     מה אלה[a]
     ויאמר אלי
     אלה הקרנות אשר זרו
     את יהודה[b] ואת ישראל[b] [c] ⟨ ⟩

(3   ויראני YHWH ארבעה חרשים

(4   ואמר
     מה אלה באים לעשות
     ויאמר[d] אלי[e] ⟨ ⟩

[f]⟨אלה הקרנות אשר
זרו את יהודה
[f]⟨כפי איש[g] לא נשא ראשו

[h]באו אלה[i] להחדות אותם
להחריד[i] את קרנות הגוים
הנשאים קרן אל ארץ יהודה לזרותה

1)   And I raised my eyes and saw,
     and behold four horns.

2)   And I said to the angel who was
          speaking with me,
               "What are these?"
     And he said to me,
               "These are the horns which
                    scattered Judah and Israel."

3)   Then Yahweh showed me four artisans.

---

50. See also K. Seybold, *Bilder*, pp. 34-35. Note that
Seybold refers to the menorah vision as "IV."

4) And I said,

"What are these coming to do?"

And he said to me,

<"These are the horns which
scattered Judah such that (?)   <   >
no man raised his head.">

"These have come to sharpen
them in order to make tremble
the horns of the nations who
have 'lifted horn' against the
land of Judah to scatter it."

[a]G adds κυριε, ʾǎdōnî. With most scholars we follow the
shorter reading in MT, against Chary.

[b]Mitchell, Wellhausen, and Horst regard the mention of
Israel in G and MT as a gloss. They note that vs. 4 (MT) which
repeats vs. 2b (for reasons to be discussed below) does not
include the reference to Israel. Moreover, the pairing of
Judah and Israel occurs in only one other location in Zechariah,
at 8:13. In contrast, Chary and Rignell keep the reference to
Israel, regarding the terms for the two houses as equivalents
or synonyms. We too keep the reference to Israel, following
G's syntax, τον Ιουδαν και τον Ισραηλ, which is preferable to
that of MT, את יהודה את ישראל. On the other hand, the terms
may be more than mere synonyms in this passage which refers to
the scattering of the peoples and in 8:13 which refers to their
restoration. In his idealism, Zechariah may have regarded the
return from Babylonian exile as the beginning of a larger, all-
encompassing ingathering of all the people, those who were
exiled from the land of the north and those who were exiled
from the land of the south.

[c]With Mitchell, Wellhausen and Horst omit wîrûšālāim, following G (A-Q W) = G[Zi] against MT and B-S-V. The expansion may
be a result of the frequent pairing of Judah and Jerusalem elsewhere in Zechariah (1:12; 2:16; 8:15). Chary and Rignell
retain Jerusalem and regard it, like Israel, an equivalent for
Judah.

[d]With G (A-Q W), Ziegler's choice for the Old Greek reading, against MT. So Mitchell, Chary.

[e]Om. lēʾmōr, following G as above.

^f^This phrase, which appears to re-answer the question in vs. 2, poses a number of problems. Is *'ēlleh-zērû* merely the result of scribal error? What does one do with the seeming expansion of this large dittography *kĕpî - rō'šô*? With Rothstein, Sellin, and others we must agree that there is no way to comfortably integrate the phrase, f⟨ ⟩f, into the vision as a whole. The phrase is probably best regarded as a dittography from vs. 2 plus an additional explanatory gloss.

We should pause to mention the interesting G reading for this seemingly inappropriate answer to the question about the artisans. G reads,

ταυτα τα κερατα τα διασκορπισαντα τον Ιουδαν και τον
Ισραηλ κατεαξαν

The Greek is not stylistically nice. Most scholars translate the phrase, και τον Ισραηλ κατεαξαν, "and Israel they broke," regarding it as a parallel to "who scattered Judah," τα διασκορπισαντα τον Ιουδαν. κατεαξαν, *šibbĕrû*, may be the main verb of the sentence, though it comes at the end. One might then translate the whole, "These have shattered the horns which scattered Judah and Israel."

In this way, instead of a scribal error, which repeats the answer about the horns, G may provide a variant response for the question about the *hārāšîm*. "What have these come to do? These have shattered...." An answer which employs the vb. "to come" is to be preferred. It is possible, however, that G reflects a variant answer to the question about the *hārāšîm*.

^g^Horst and a number of other scholars after Wellhausen emend to *kĕpî 'ăšer*, "so that." Wellhausen bases his suggestion on Mal 2:9. Rignell and Chary believe that the expression *kĕpî 'îš* makes sense and translate "in such proportion that..." So also BDB. Both suggestions present difficulties. One senses that a meaning of "so that" is required, but no neat solution presents itself.

^h^Most scholars agree that the *waw* conversive must be emended, whether one attempts to integrate the phrase *'ēlleh-rō'šô* into the vision or not. We emend to *bā'û* and that way eliminate only the first two letters of the MT reading.

^i^Numerous emendations have been suggested for MT *lĕhahărîd*, "to make tremble." Marti suggests *lĕhahărîb*, "to lay waste,"

Haupt ("The Visions of Zechariah," *JBL* 32 [1913], 107-122)
lĕhakrît, "to cut off," Horst *lĕhôrîd*, "to bring down." Mitchell regards MT *lĕhaḥărîd 'ōtām* as a gloss to *lĕyaddôt* etc. and
omits it. Rothstein and Sellin accept MT as it stands and
believe *'ōtām* to refer to the enemies of Israel. H. Gunkel
(*Schöpfung und Chaos in Urzeit und Endzeit* [Göttingen: Vandenhoeck, 1895], p. 122, n.3) accepts G του οξυναι, "to sharpen,"
lĕhāḥēd. He emends *'ōtām* to *'ittîm*, "cutting instruments (usually translated "ploughshares")." In this way Gunkel sees
ploughmen *(ḥārāsîm)* coming to sharpen the simple pointed instruments which served as ploughshares. Sellin follows Gunkel's
suggestion.

We accept the G του οξυναι, though the emendation of *'ōtām*
seems unnecessary. We do not, however, opt for *lĕhāḥēd (ḥdd)*
as the reading behind του οξυναι, but for the hiph. infin. of
its biform *ḥdh* (see Prov 27:17). Frank Moore Cross pointed out
the possibility of this reading to the author, noting that the
unusual vb. *ydd* does not mean "cast out/down" in the sense
which the vs. requires. *lĕyaddôt* may be a corruption for
lĕhaḥădôt. We suggest that the vs. has undergone other changes.
lĕhaḥărîd, which looks like *lĕhaḥădôt* and even more like the
biform *lĕhāḥēd*, has dropped out of G and has been displaced in
MT. The vs. originally read, "These have come to sharpen them
(the horns) in order to make tremble the horns of the nations
...." The masc. suffix of *'ōtām* creates no problem of agreement with fem. *qĕrānôt*. The masc. suffix is often used in
place of the fem. suffix, particularly in the 3rd plu., in the
late books of OT (Joüon, *Grammaire*, 149b).

Our solution to the problem may be a bit too ingenius, but
no simple solution works. As the garbled text of G indicates,
the reading has undergone much disruption in transmission. We
suggest that MT reflects not one error, but a series of errors
involving simple cases of misreading, haplography, and displacement.

Pattern of Content Elements		*Rubrics*
2:1	Indication of vision	ראשא את עיני וארא
2:1	Description	והנה
2:2	Question of seer to interpreter	ואמר...מה אלה

2:2	Answer/explanation	ויאמר אלי...
2:3	Indication of vision/description	וירא ני YHWH...
2:4	Question of seer to interpreter	ואמר מה אלה...
2:4	Answer/explanation	ויאמר אלי...

Vision II of Zechariah evidences a simplification of the two-question pattern found only in vision V. The prophet sees, he describes the seen objects, he asks for an interpretation, and an explanation is provided. This simple pattern of steps, which is found once in vss. 1, 2 and again in vss. 3, 4, is the essence of a divinatory situation. A clear transition has been made from the stylized form in which God is both questioner and explainer of the symbolic objects to one in which the prophet himself asks for enlightenment. The presence of an intermediary is another common feature of this divinatory scene.[51] Again we emphasize that the concept of revelation via interpretation lies behind this version of the form.

The introductory rubrics in vision II are fairly standard for Zechariah. Some have been common in the form since the visions of Amos and Jeremiah, the use of the verb *r'h* in the indication of the vision and of *hinnēh* before the description. *Hinnēh*, we note, is not found before the description of the second symbol, the artisans. The formalized question, *mâ 'ēlleh*, is appropriate to the motif introduced in vision V, the question of the seer to the interpreter. As expected, forms of *'mr* are used in this dialogue pattern as in others. The exceedingly lengthy rubrics which introduce speakers in vision V have been dropped in favor of somewhat simpler versions.

This basic set of motif steps and framing rubrics will be a recognizable core in the remaining visions of the formal tradition. Zech 2:1-4 is an important signpost to the directions in which the form will go, but we do not mean to oversimplify. The core of elements will remain rather stable from now on, but within that basic framework, much transition and flexible growth continues.

---

51. Note that in 2 Baruch 39:1-40:4, 4 Ezra 12:10-36, and 13:21-53, God is the interpreter.

Use of language and style

An analysis of the use of language in Zechariah vision II
continues to point to a growing literary tradition. The visions
of Zechariah continually recall those of precursors, but show
interesting new twists.

In contrast with previous passages, Zech 2:1-4 has not
been laid out as if it conformed to certain norms of balance in
line length. Instead, it has been set up as a dialogue. Like
vision V, vision II presents great difficulties to anyone who
would divide its long thought lines into manageable prosodic
units. Vs. 2 with its lengthy introductory rubric, followed by
a very brief question, and vs. 4 with its interlocking infinitive of purpose *(lĕhaḥărîd...)*[52] and subordinate clause *(han-
nōšĕ'îm...)* are confirmations that we are dealing with prose,

Worth noting, however, is the repeated use of the symbol
term *qeren*, "horn." The horn is found in the motif of initial
description and in the reply motif of vs. 2. Such repetition,
of course, has been an important characteristic of the symbolic
vision form, though its use as a method of structuring the narrative was greatly lessened in Zechariah visions VI and V.
Here too repetition of key terms at key junctures in the pattern is not a consistently employed technique. When the seer
asks about the *ḥārāšîm*, he is anwered with the demonstrative
pronoun, "These have come...." The symbol term *ḥārāšîm* is not
re-used in the explanation motif. The *qeren* term is found
again, however, two times within the complex explanation of the
ḥārāšîm. Such a repetition is not an example of traditional
economy. Indeed the term *qeren* is not found in the motif of
the seer's question to the interpreter. There the demonstrative pronoun is used. The term is not used to link together
motifs in the style of stage I. Instead this piling up of
horns in vs. 4 recalls a key image of the vision at its end,
even in the midst of an explanation of another symbol image.
This use of repetition allows the horn to become the lasting,
pervasive, and most dominant symbol of the vision, the *ḥārāšîm*
only subordinate to it. What then is the meaning of this all-
important image?

---

52. See text-critical note "i."

Symbolic usage

The horn is a mythologically rich symbol in OT. At first
glance it appears to be simply a metaphor of strength and power.
See, for example, Deut 33:17, 2 Sam 22:3 = Ps 18:3. An increase of one's power is thus *lĕhārîm qeren*, literally "to
raise horn." See 1 Sam 2:1, Lam 2:17, and Ps 75:11. A reduction of might, a humiliation or personal defeat, is to have
one's horn "cut off," as in Lam 2:3, Ps 75:11, and Jer 48:25, or
"thrust into the dust," as in Job 16:15. Most scholars have
interpreted the horns in Zechariah 2 to be such symbols of
might.[53] The expression *hannōšě'îm qeren* can thus be understood to mean, "raise their might..." and *lĕhahărîd 'et qarnōt
...,*[54] "to make to tremble the power-source...."

The image of the horn's power must come from the observation of horned animals in combat. The horns of such animals
are their chief source of power, their weapons. P. D. Miller
has shown that horned animals such as bulls or rams were favorite metaphors for young warriors throughout the Near East.[55]
Hence Deut 33:17, cited above, which pictures Joseph as a wild
bull who defeats his enemies with his horns. More important to
the passage from Zechariah 2 is the application of horned
animal imagery to deity warriors. El's epithet, "Bull," sig-
nifies his warrior status[56] and might be compared with the epithet *'ăbîr ya'ăqōb*, "the Bull of Jacob," applied to Yahweh.[57]
UT 76:II:21-22, addressed to Anat, reads, *qrn db'atk btlt 'nt/*

---

53. Mitchell, *A Commentary*, p. 132; Sellin, *Das Zwölfprophetenbuch*, p. 486; Horst, *Die zwölf kleinen Propheten*, pp.
222-223; Jeremias, *Die Nachtgesichte*, p. 163.

54. See our reading in text-critical note "i."

55. "Animal Names as Designations in Ugaritic and Hebrew,"
Ugarit-Forschungen 2 (Neukirchen-Vluyn: Butzon & Bercker Kevelaer, 1970), 177. See also his "El the Warrior," *HTR* 60 (1967),
esp. 418-423.

56. See Miller, "El the Warrior," 418-419, and Cross,
Canaanite Myth, p. 15.

57. See Gen 49:24; Is 1:24; 49:26; 60:16; and Ps 132:2,
5.

qrn db'atk,[58]   "the horns of thy strength O virgin Anat, the
horns of thy strength...."   Miller also points to horned representations of Baal and other deities.[59]

In Babylonian as well as Canaanite iconography, the deities
are depicted wearing a horned cap or crown. With reference to
the Mesopotamian evidence, E. Douglas Van Buren writes "It (the
horned crown) was above all a symbol of divinity and lord-
ship."[60]   Van Buren establishes a typology for the horned caps,
tracing the development from earlier and simpler examples to
more complex caps which held two or more pairs of horns.[61]   The
four-horned crowns, of course, have relevance to our study of
Zechariah's image. Van Buren emphasizes the sacred quality of
the horns, noting that in general the horned cap was considered
"the prerogative of the gods only, and might not be worn by
mortals."[62]   One exception to this norm was the New Year's
festival when the priest-king assumed the role of bridegroom in
ceremonies of sacred marriage; then the horned cap was donned
by the monarch. The cap was "exhibited as a symbol in temples
...set upon a base or 'seat'...."[63]   The horns or representations of them in the crown were in fact considered a "seat" of
the deities' power.

> A proof of utter destruction wrought in a temple by the
> foe was the fact that even in the case of those gods who
> still stood in their places..."their crowns have been
> thrown to the ground."[64]

Othmar Keel discusses these horned caps with special

---

58.   On the term *db'at* see F. M. Cross, "Ugaritic DB'AT
and Hebrew Cognates," *VT* 2 (1952), 162-164.

59.   See ANEP Nos. 490, 491, and 493. See also Ug V, 1.1.
20, *b'l.qrnm w dnb*, "Baal/Lord with two horns and a tail," mentioned briefly by Miller, "El the Warrior," 419, n.28.

60.   "Concerning the Horned Cap of the Mesopotamian Gods,"
Or 12 (1943), 318.

61.   "Concerning the Horned Cap," 320.

62.   "Concerning the Horned Cap," 324.

63.   "Concerning the Horned Cap," 325

64.   "Concerning the Horned Cap," 323 and n.6.

reference to 1 Kgs 22:11.[65] Providing additional evidence to
that of Van Buren, Keel concludes that the horns which are prepared by Zedekiah are actually a horned crown. Ahab is encour-
aged to assume the power of the deity upon himself, to gain for
himself the power of the gods via sympathetic association with
the horns.[66] Keel includes in the discussion one of the
Megiddo ivories, which Loud dates to 1350-1150 B.C.[67] The
center figure of the piece wears four horns.

We agree with Keel's view of the horns as magically,
divinely potent instruments of victory. The horns are no mere
metaphor for strength.[68] Coins which pictured Alexander with
horns, in the role of son of Ammon the horned Egyptian deity,
served to emphasize the monarch's divinity and his invincibil-
ity - important messages for his subjects.[69]

The active power of horns emerges in Mic 4:13:

כי קרנך אשים ברזל
ופרסתיך אשים נחושה
והדקות עמים רבים

> For your horn I will make iron
> Your hoofs bronze
> You will pulverize many peoples.

The daughter of Zion here is personified as a warrior deity in
the character type of Anat. The horns are a potent weapon, the
accoutrement of the mythological divine warrior, as real horns
are the power-source of mundane rams and bulls.[70] It is

---

65. *Wirkmächtige Siegeszeichen im Alten Testament* (Göttingen: Vandenhoeck and Ruprecht, 1974), pp. 123-146.

66. *Wirkmächtige*, p. 142.

67. Gordon Loud, *The Megiddo Ivories* (University of Chi-
cago Oriental Institute Publication 52; Chicago: University of
Chicago, 1939), p. 10. See his Pl. 22, No. 125. In Keel, see
Fig. 59.

68. *Wirkmächtige*, p. 129

69. See John Porteous, *Coins* (London: Octopus Books,
1973), p. 18.

70. Note that "horn" is used in parallelism with *māgēn*,
"shield," in 2 Sam 22:3 = Ps. 18:3. In our opinion the offen-
sive weapon is paired with the defensive shield.

difficult to know whether such descriptions picture the deity
as a human who wears a horned crown or as a real animal figure
with horns. Both could be true synonymously in the multi-
vocal metaphor of myth. The divine power of the horns is so
potent that it even applies to detached horns set on a base in
the Mesopotamian temple. The latter is an important concept to
keep in mind in analyzing Zech 2:1-4.

The horns in Zechariah 2 are to be understood in the same
sacred divine warrior context. Whether Yahweh is pictured as
the 'ăbîr ya'ăqōb by the author or whether the horns are envisioned in a more detached way, it is clear that the notion of
the power of the divine warrior, the bull, is behind the image,
just as this notion is behind the presence of horns in the
Mesopotamian temple.[71]

What then is the role of the ḥārāšîm? How do these artisans blend with the symbol of the horns? The passage from Mic
4:13 again comes to mind. The image of the Lord's making
Zion's horns of iron is not so different from the image of
artisans sharpening the horns of the divine warrior. In each
case, the horns are being made more lethal, more invincible in
their power to pierce the enemy. The image of the artificer
who prepares the deity for battle is well known from Greek and
Near Eastern sources. Hephaestus, the great smith of the under-
world, prepares arms for Achilles.[72] Similarly, Kôtar, the
architect of Baal's palace, fashions weapons for Baal before
his combat with Yamm.[73] Such an explanation of the role of the
ḥārāšîm is preferable to the interpretation which regards the
ḥārāšîm as the primary destroyer symbols of the vision.[74] The

71. Note W. F. Albright's reconstruction of Hab 3:4 in
"The Psalm of Habakkuk," *Studies in Old Testament Prophecy*, ed.
H. H. Rowley (Edinburgh: T & T Clark, 1946), 1-18. While Professor Albright's overall reconstruction is too radical to
accept, one is sympathetic to his understanding of the *qarnayim*
as "horns."

72. *Iliad*, Bk. 18, ll. 462ff.

73. See CTA 4.5.103ff. for Kôtar as builder of the palace
and CTA 2.4.7ff. for Kôtar as preparer of weapons for Baal.

74. See Mitchell, *Commentary*, pp. 133-134; Sellin, *Das*

ḥārāšîm in Zechariah 2 are based once again on courtly roles,
adapted to the mythic realm. As the human monarch has his
artificers, so Yahweh.

Admittedly, no OT passage describes Yahweh to have *ḥārāšîm*
as servants. On the other hand, in Prov 8:30 wisdom is personified as the *'āmôn* of Yahweh. The term *'āmôn* is roughly
equivalent to *ḥārāš*, as evidenced by lists of exiles in Jeremiah and 2 Kings. In Jer 52:15, the *'āmôn* are listed as a
class, the artisans, who are carried into exile by Nebuchadnezzar. The artisans of the court are referred to as the *ḥārāš*
in other lists of exiles at 2 Kgs 24:16 and Jer 24:1. It is
possible that in Zechariah 2 as in Prov 8:30, the Lord is seen
to have artisans at his service.

The multiple number of the *ḥārāšîm* is determined by the
number of horns. Four is a number which implies wholeness and
perfection, but more importantly the number four may be used to
indicate the double-power of the deity.[75] Apsu has four eyes
and four ears.[76] Organs of which the earthly creature has two,
the deity has four. Sanchuniathon seems to describe El as having more than one pair of eyes as well.[77] The power and the
perception of the deity is doubled. Hence the double and even
triple pairs of horns in the Mesopotamian and Canaanite iconography discussed above.

The symbols of horns and artificers create a theme which
relates to Zech 1:14, 15. God is now zealous for Israel and
will avenge himself on the nations whom he had allowed to
defeat Israel. Yahweh had turned his power, his horns, against
Israel to scatter them, but now he will turn his cosmic power
against the enemy nations.

Zwölfprophetenbuch, pp. 486-487; and Rignell, *Die Nachtgesichte*,
p. 64.

75. A number of scholars have suggested that the number
four stands for the four directions of the compass. See D.
Buzy, "Les Symboles," 149-153, for a review of the scholarship.

76. *Enūma Eliš*, I, 95.

77. See K. Mras, ed., *Eusebius Werke*, VIII, part I, *Die
Praeparatio evangelica* (Berlin: Akademie, 1954), I 10, 36.

One more issue must be dealt with before concluding the
study of Zechariah vision II and its symbols.

In each of the cases studied thus far an equation has been
set between the symbol and its explanation such that the image
is said to represent something other than itself. In Zechariah
vision II, however, the horns are not interpreted to be other
than they appear. Rather, this appearance is more closely
identified. The horns are not used in a neat word-play or
metaphor to reveal what the future holds. In fact, these horns
are said to be the very ones which participated in history,
which scattered Judah and Israel. The catalyst on the mythic
plane and the historical results are equal parts of reality.
In Am 7:7-9, the wording is such that a metaphor is created:
God is placing a plumb-line in the midst of his people Israel.
That is, he is judging them; such is the meaning of historical
exile. In Zechariah 2:1-4, no metaphor is created. These *are*
the horns which scattered.... In this way the symbols themselves become the cosmic instruments of God's holy war.

This phenomenon of the real-mythic symbol will also be
found in Zechariah visions I (1:7-17) and VIII (6:1-8), and is
further evidence of the living mythology employed by Zechariah.

Zech 1:7-17

7) ביום עשרים וארבעה לעשתי עשר חדש
הוא חדש שבט בשנת שתים לדריוש
היה דבר YHWH אל זכריה בן ברכיהו
בן עדוא הנביא [a] לאמר

ראיתי והנה איש רכב על סוס אדם
והוא עמד בין [b] ההדסים אשר [c] במצלה
ואחריו סוסים אדמים [d] שרקים ולבנים

9[e]) ואמר
מה אלה אדני
ויאמר אלי המלאך הדבר בי
אני אראך מה המה אלה

10) [e]< >
ויאמר
אלה אשר שלח YHWH להתהלך בארץ

(11)[f] ויען את [e]מלאך YHWH[e] העמד בין ההדסים
[f]ויאמר
התהלכנו בארץ והנה כל הארץ ישבת ושקטת

(12) ויען [e]מלאך YHWH[e] ויאמר
YHWH צבאות עד מתי אתה לא תרחם
את ירושלם ואת ערי יהודה
אשר זעמתה זה שבעים שנה

(13) ויען YHWH את המלאך הדבר בי דברים טובים
דברים נחמים

(14) ויאמר אלי המלאך הדבר בי
קרא לאמר
כה אמר YHWH צבאות
קנאתי לירושלם ולציון קנאה גדולה

(15) וקצף גדול אני קצף על הגוים השאננים
אשר אני קצפתי מעט והם עזרו לרעה

(16) לכן כה אמר YHWH
שבתי לירושלם ברחמים
ביתי יבנה בה
נאם YHWH צבאות
[g]וקו ינטה על ירושלם

(17) [k]< [h]עוד קרא לאמר
כה אמר YHWH צבאת
[i]>   < תפוצינה ערי מטוב
[j]נחם YHWH עוד את ציון
ובחר עוד בירושלם>[k]

7) On the twenty-fourth day of the eleventh month
   which is the month of Shebat, in the second year of Darius,
   the word of the Lord came to Zechariah son of Berechiah,
   son of Iddo the prophet, thus.

8) I saw and behold a man riding on a horse of red,
   and he was standing among the myrtles which were in the
      hollow (?),
   and after him were red, sorrel, and white horses.

9) And I said,
      "What are these my lord?"

And the angel who was speaking with me said,
   "I will show you what these are."

10) And he said,
    "These are the ones whom Yahweh has sent to traverse the
       earth."

11) Then the one standing among the myrtles responded to the
    angel of Yahweh and said,
     "We have traversed the earth and behold all the earth
       remains quiet."

12) And the angel of Yahweh answered,
    "Lord of Hosts, how long will you have no mercy
    on Jerusalem and the cities of Judah against
    which you have been indignant these seventy years?"

13) Then Yahweh responded to the angel who was speaking with me
    with comforting words.

14) And the angel who was speaking with me said to me,
    "Cry out saying,
    Thus says the Lord of Hosts,
    I am exceedingly zealous for Jerusalem and for Zion

15)   And I hold a great anger against the nations who have
    been at ease, against whom I had shown little anger, but
    they conspired for the sake of evil.

16)   Therefore thus says Yahweh,
    I am returning to Jerusalem with compassion,
    My house will be built in it
    Says the Lord of Hosts
    And the measuring line will be stretched out over Jeru-
       salem.

17)   Again cry out saying,
    Thus says the Lord of hosts
    My cities will overflow with good things,
    Yahweh will again comfort Zion
    And again choose Jerusalem."

[a]A few scholars have been troubled by the use of *lĕʾmōr*,
an infinitive construct which usually introduces direct dis-
course (see Joüon, 124o). Does the term here introduce the

first person subject of *rā'îtî*? Since the prophet is the
speaker and not Yahweh, Mitchell omits *hāyâ dĕbar - lē'mōr* and
proceeds directly from the date rubric to the prophet's description in vs. 8. Rothstein changes *lē'mōr rā'îtî* into *bĕmar'ōt*,
so that the word of the Lord comes in "visions of the night."
With most scholars we agree that such emendations are not
necessary. What is interesting is that the introductory rubric
has become frozen, an entity which exists on its own in tradition; it is used to indicate that a vision has taken place even
once the syntax and literal meaning of the rubric is not ideal
for the continuing syntax of the vision.

   [b]G reads των ορεων, "the mountains." Marti and Sellin
accept G. Horst, Mitchell, Rignell, and Chary accept MT. The
mythological implications of each of these readings will be
discussed later in the analysis of the symbols. From a purely
text-critical point of view, however, the MT reading is the
more difficult. G, των ορεων, reflects an intrusion from
vision VIII, Zech 6:1.

   [c]MT *mṣlh* can be vocalized in two ways: *mĕṣūlâ*, "deep" or
"hollow" from *ṣûl*; *mĕṣillâ*, "shade," from *ṣll*. The latter term
is unattested in MT, though G does seem to be reading some form
of *ṣll* with των ορεων των κατασκιων, "the mountains of the
shades/shadows." If we accept a reading based on a form of
ṣll, MT must be emended to convey the sense that the trees give
off shade; for the phrase, "Myrtles which are in the shade,"
presents conceptual difficulties. Do not the trees make the
shade? Given our acceptance of MT, *hahădassîm*, "the myrtles,"
the best choice for this reading would seem to be MT *mĕṣūlâ*,
translated "the hollow." Admittedly, however, if *mĕṣūlâ* does
mean "hollow," Zechariah 1 contains a unique usage.

   [d]G does not have *śĕruqqîm*, "sorrel" or "bay," but ψαροι,
"dappled (?)" and ποικιλοι, "spotted." These colors like the
mountains (see note "b") are intrusions from vision VIII, 6:3.
Rignell omits the reddish color, *śĕruqqîm*, believing it a gloss
for the red horses, the *'ădummîm*; he thus emphasizes two key
Biblical colors, red and white. There is, however, no strong
reason to emend MT except one's own inability to understand
what the colors represent symbolically, if indeed they are

meant to be anything other than arbitrary colors in which
horses come. For now, we simply accept MT as is.

^eAt vs. 9, problems arise in identifying the participants
in the conversation. Some corruption seems to have entered the
text; a dialogue should involve one character responding to
another as has been the case throughout the visions thus far.
Yet in this vision as it stands in MT=G, characters seem each
to speak independently, almost out of turn. See for example
vs. 9 where the interpreting angel offers to provide an answer
and then the one standing under the trees gives the answer.
Various solutions have been proposed. Sellin, Duhm, and Horst
strike 9b *wayyō'mer 'ēlay - 'ēlleh*, but as we shall see, this
phrase of the interpreting angel is very much within the narrative, elongated style of the author (see for example the pausal
questions in 4:5, 13). Sellin attempts to simplify the pattern
of speakers later by deleting *'et mal'ak - hahădassîm* in vs. 11
and by emending *mal'ak yahweh* to *hammal'ak haddōbēr bî* in vs.
12. In this way the questioner of Yahweh is the one answered
in vs. 13.

        We offer a somewhat simpler solution. First, we regard
vs. 10a as a partial dittography for vs. 11a. The introduction
of the man among the myrtles as a speaker in vs. 10 interrupts
the flow of the question/answer process. As usual, the prophet
asks the interpreting angel for information. He is the subject
of *wayyō'mar* in vs. 10, providing a response as expected within
the pattern of the form. Moreover, against most scholars we
identify the angel of Yahweh not with the man of the myrtles,
but with the interpreting angel. See note "f" below.

        ^fWe suggest that the plural vbs. *wayya'ănû* and *wayyō'mĕrû*
originally read in the singular. These vbs. have become plural
because of the influence of the first person plural vb. *hithal-
laknû*. If one emends to *wayya'an* and *wayyō'mer* and allows for
a somewhat varied syntax so that the word order is vb. - obj. -
sub., then the *'ōmēd* (who had been introduced in vs. 8)
addresses the *mal'ak = dōbēr*. In this way the man of the myrtles is the spokesman for the whole group. He thus says "We
have traversed...." In vs. 12, the *mal'ak = dōbēr* continues to
request information. As we shall see, in fact, he acts in a
prophetic intercessory role, but now he addresses not merely

members of the divine council, but the head of the council himself. A transformation has taken place. In vs. 13 the *dōbēr*
receives his comforting response and then relays a charge to
the prophet, Zechariah.

In this way the pattern of speakers is neat and unconfus-
ing and the *mal'ak yahweh = mal'ak dōbēr* plays an expected role
of intermediary and go-between throughout. All messages are
relayed through him.

Mal'ak yahweh is as general a term as *mal'ak* in OT usage
and nearly as common. There are more than fifty usages of
mal'ak yahweh outside the Book of Zechariah. There is no reason why the author of vision I could not vary the lengthy
appellation for the interpreting angel with a briefer, more
general expression. We have noted that the style in Zechariah
tends toward variation in rubric language.

[g]*qāweh* should possibly be shortened to the more usual form
of the term for "line" *qaw*, in order to improve the metrics.
The former reading is the *kětîb* reading, the latter the *qěrê*.
On the other hand, given that the poetry is late and that its
balance is not markedly improved with the shorter terms, one
might speculate that the author preferred the term *qāweh* in
order to create rhymes with *yinnāteh* and *yibbāneh*. This sort
of rhyme is common in late poetry and may be more important to
the author than balanced line length.

[h]G contains an expansion of the introduction to vs. 17
which parallels that of vs. 14. See note "k" below.

[i]We have omitted *'ôd* in this line. Even given the often
monotonous syntax of late poetry, it is unlikely that the term
'ôd would be found so many times in so short a space. Taking
into account metric considerations, we have shortened the first
line of the tricolon, thus allowing for an 8/8/8 count.

[j]G reflects a variant reading, και ελεησει, "and he shall
be merciful." We have dropped the initial *waw* in the light of
prosodic considerations.

[k]Rothstein, Nowack, and Sellin consider both vss. 16 and
17 to be redactional additions, while Rignell and Chary consider only vs. 16 to be a separate composition. We agree with
W. A. M. Beuken that vs. 16 belongs to the vision on literary
grounds (see *Haggai-Sacharja*, pp. 242-244). This vs. provides

a necessary and suitable conclusion to the pericope; for vs. 15
alone would not properly round out the piece. Vs. 15 describes
the reasons for Yahweh's turning against the nations, "they
conspired to do evil"; yet one awaits to hear the full implications of Yahweh's zealousness for Zion and anger at the nations.
Thus the *lākēn* at vs. 16 does not indicate a fissure in the
work but rather creates a link between the protasis, the accusation against the nations, and the apodosis, the positive
results for Zion in Yahweh's return.

In discussing the structure of the work, we will also find
that vss. 14-16 combine into a traditional pattern of motifs:
anger/revenge; return/procession; house-building; and fullness
and plenty.

We agree with Beuken and the others above that vs. 17 is
an addition. A redactor continued the poetry of vs. 16 with a
tricolon which further emphasizes the abundance of Zion at
Yahweh's return to its midst.

A. Jepsen considers both vss. 16 and 17 to be original to
the vision and in fact deletes the prosaizing rubrics in order
to make one poetic composition out of the vss. ("Kleine Beiträge zum Zwölfprophetenbuch III," *ZAW* 16 [1945-48], 95-114,
esp. 101, n.2.)

*Language, rubrics, motifs, and patterns: looking back and
ahead*

Vss. 7-15 of vision I, like visions V and II, are composed
in prose. Unlike visions V and II where some remnant of repetition of key motifs is found and unlike vision II, where a
doubling of the key term *qeren* exemplifies a nuanced use of the
old technique of repetition, vision I has no major reminiscenses
of the economical style which characterizes the earlier visions.
We do find some repetition of language in vss. 11, 12
(lĕhithallēk/hithallaknû), vs. 14 *(qinnē'tî/qin'â)*, and in vs.
15 *(qeṣep/qōṣēp/qāṣaptî)*. Such a re-use of language does not
serve to emphasize the symbol objects, but is a stylistic feature of the vision. In vss. 14 and 15 these repetitions have a
semi-poetic ring and combine to play on *q* sounds. Such poetic
touches are appropriate to the word of Yahweh.

Vs. 16 and the additional vs. 17 (see text-critical note
"k") which continue the word of Yahweh end the vision on a much
more clearly poetical note. Vs. 16 does not display classical
balance with a 10/6/7/10 syllable count, but the author has
employed the technique of parallelism, matching pairs of terms
and overall syntax from line to line. The additional vs. 17
has good 8/8/8 balance in the tricolon and displays parallelism.
The parallelistic pattern of these vss. is as follows:

(16	לכן כה אמר YHWH				
10	d	c	b	(a)* שבתי לירושלם ברחמים	
6		c	b	a	ביתי יבנה בה
7		(rubric)		נאם YHWH צבאות	
10		c	b	a	וקו ינטה על ירושלם
	(17	עוד קרא לאמר			
		כה אמר YHWH צבאות			
8		d	a	b	תפוצינה ערי מטוב
8		c	a	b	נחם YHWH עוד את ציון
8		c	(a)*	b	ובחר עוד בירושלם

(a)* Subject included in verb

One wonders if Zechariah and the author of vs. 17, who
continues the poem, are responding to a tradition of prophetic
predecessors who delivered the word of Yahweh in poetry.
Poetry also ends Zechariah's third vision at 2:8, 9. It is
possible that Zechariah's interest in the ancient divine warrior mythology, an interest which has emerged throughout our
study, is accompanied by an interest in composing archaic style
poetry which employs language in a fairly traditional way to
describe the saving acts of Yahweh, the warrior. We shall deal
more with Zechariah's poetry later.

The dialogue pattern, the movement from speaker to speaker
and comment to reaction, give vss. 7-15 their prosey, narrative
shape. The core motifs which we found in vision II are found
once again in this vision. These elements, which give to the
vision form the quality of a scene of divination, are starred
in the following chart. We note, however, that additional elements, supplementary to the core, are also found in vision I.
In fact, each of the visions henceforth will contain various
expansions of the structural core. For example, Daniel 7 and 8

will become much more like dramatic narratives with suitable
descriptions of the seer's emotional state. This motif, "fear
of the seer," will become common in the form. Several of the
supplementary elements which will be found in Zechariah vision
I are not at all new to us, having been introduced in the redactional layers of the visions of Jeremiah. In outlining the
pattern of this vision and the language used to present or
frame its various parts, we note both the links to past material and the indicators of future directions.

Motif/Rubric in Zech 1:7-17	Link to previous visions in content and/or language	Directions for future
vs. 7 *date-line*	anticipated by Jer 24:1 in a redactional addition to that vision	will be common: Dan 7:1; 8:1; 4 Ezra 11:1; 13:1, 2
*vs. 8 *indication of vision:* use of *hāyā dĕbar yahweh ʾel... lēʾmōr*	*dĕbar* rubric found in Jer 1:11; 1:13; form of *rʾh* found in all other previous visions; night presumed only for Zechariah visions thus far	all use a form of "to see" in appropriate language; "dream-time" if not night-time assumed
*vs. 8 *description of vision:* use of *hinnēh*	in all previously	equivalent in appropriate language in all remaining (*ʾărû* in Aramaic, *hāʾ* in Syriac)
*vs. 9 *question of seer to interpreter*	in similar language in Zechariah visions V, II, and VIII; note in pre-Zechariah V visions seer is asked about vision but does not ask himself; Zechariah vision V includes both question motifs	motif found in all remaining visions; language for introducing question changes after Zechariah
(pause-delay)	as in vision V of Zechariah (4:5, 13)	comparable narrative devices in remaining
*vs. 10 *answer of interpreter*	as in Zechariah vision II, symbol is real-mythic	answer is real-mythic in Zechariah vision VIII; relationship between

vss.	observations	X (perhaps some	symbol and inter-pretation some-what different in rest; see our dis-cussion
11-13	of divine activities; prophet drawn into them	anticipation in Zechariah vision II)	comparable inclu-sion of divine happenings in Zechariah vision VIII; in remain-ing visions hap-penings are part of initial de-scription; see our discussion
vss. 14-16 (17)	charge	found in redac-tional layer of Jer 1:15-19, vs. 17; different command language used	will be common motif in future: Dan 8:26; 2 Bar 43:1-3; 71:3-4; 4 Ezra 12:37-39; specific content of charge and language will vary within cer-tain limits

Links to the past and directions for the future are rea-sonably self-evident from the chart. While not so neat as the pattern of motifs in stage I of the symbolic vision form, the core elements certainly do provide this vision with some basis of external criteria of form. We know that certain content elements will appear in a certain order of occurrence. With Daniel and the visions of 2 Baruch and 4 Ezra, even some of the supplementary elements such as the date-line and the charge to the prophet will become reasonably consistent parts of the pat-tern. Similarly, the seemingly unnecessary delay before the meaning of the vision is revealed (4:5, 13; 1:9) will become institutionalized. In the symbolic visions of 2 Baruch and 4 Ezra the delay takes the form of the prophet's own lengthy, prayerful, and often hymnic request for revelation. The authors are lengthening the telling of the action, enjoying and drawing out the narrative wherever possible.

The rubrics which introduce speakers are common only to the Zechariah cycle, but those which introduce the vision and the initial description are consistently found in the earliest examples of the vision form and in the latest. The language

changes to Syriac or Aramaic but the semantics of "seeing" and
"behold" are identical. It is interesting that Zechariah
employs two common rubrics to introduce the vision, the one
found in Jer 1:11 and 1:13 *(hāyâ dĕbar)* and the more usual use
of a form of *rʾh*. Herein lies one hint of an eclecticism
which, in a sense, characterizes all of Zechariah's visions,
but which emerges even more clearly in these typologically latest examples.

Intertwining traditions in observations and charge

Vss. 11-17 of vision I exemplify this eclecticism and
require more explanation than is possible in a chart. In fact
this particular use of what we are calling "the observation of
divine events" is really peculiar to Zechariah visions I and
VIII. In Zechariah I and VIII, the symbols to be interpreted
at first appear rather static, not unlike the man holding the
plumb-line who appears suddenly in Amos 7. The symbol image is
interpreted in I and VIII on the real mythic level which we
have described in detail for vision II. These figures actually
are those who have been travelling about the earth, sent by
Yahweh. After the interpretation process is completed, however, the prophet observes another little scene. This scene
involves action, a verbal exchange among the divine beings,
resulting in a message being delivered to him, his charge to
the people.

Such an observation of divine events and a prophet's in-
volvement or participation in them is not unusual as the form
continues to develop. In Daniel 7, 8 and the visions in 2
Baruch and 4 Ezra such observations are typical. Yet the
divine dramatic happenings are an integral part of the interpretation process. Such scenes, in fact, provide the symbols
to be interpreted. Thus, in 2 Baruch and 4 Ezra, the prophet
sees and participates in weird visions of divine happenings -
no ordinary harvest baskets here - yet these happenings are
clearly the symbols of his dreams. The events in which he
participates are then interpreted to mean something, be it
wars among kingdoms or something else. In Zechariah vision
I, the dramatic happenings are not interpreted, but present
another example of mythic reality - this time in a dynamic

form. These divine goings on in 1:11ff. which are self-evident
and not actually part of the interpretation process are in fact
an interesting and eclectic collection of elements we usually
expect to find in forms other than the symbolic vision. In
looking more carefully at the terminology and content of these
vss., certain patterns emerge.

First, note the interpreting angel's words beginning with
ʿad mātay (vs. 12) which essentially ask Yahweh to have mercy
on his people. These petitioning words are then followed in
vss. 13ff. by a note of hope and comfort. In this pattern lie
reminiscences of a lament form, integrated nicely into the symbolic vision, right after the interpretation of the seen
objects and co-terminous with the charge motif (vss. 14ff.).
A similar nuance is found in the self-evident vision in Amos
7:5. When the prophet understands the implications of the
image of destruction, he petitions Yahweh for mercy, and the
Lord relents temporarily. This role of the petitioner also
recalls Abraham's debate with the Lord over the destruction of
Sodom (Gen 18:23-33). Again the Lord relents temporarily.
However, as noted by W. A. M. Beuken building on the work of C.
Westermann, the ʿad mātay terminology found in this vision is
idiomatic or specialized speech associated with the lament
form.[78] Zechariah is blending elements of the lament into his
vision.

Second, note the juxtaposition of a description of self-
evident divine happenings (1:11-13) with a charge motif at vs.
14 (qĕrāʾ lēʾmōr...). This combination must bring to mind the
call or initiation form exemplified by Isaiah 6 and Ezekiel 1.
In each of these two visions the prophet observes divine events
and is drawn into them; then comes the charge to speak to the
people (Is 6:9-13; Ezek 2:3ff.). Thus a second form is evoked
within this symbolic vision.[79]

In addition to the petition/comfort pattern of the lament

---

78. Beuken, *Haggai-Sacharja 1-8*, pp. 240-241; Westermann,
"Der Rolle der Klage in der Theologie des Alten Testaments,"
Forschung am Alten Testament, Gessammelte Studien II (München:
Kaiser, 1974), 250-268.

79. See also Beuken, *Haggai-Sacharja 1-8*, p. 242.

and the divine events/charge pattern of the call, Zech 1:11-16
(17) includes elements of one more traditional pattern, that of
the victory/enthronement.   In vs. 15 comes reference to the
Lord's anger, following directly upon a reference to his zealousness for Zion.   The divine warrior is aroused.   His battle
is now turned against the nations who had escaped his wrath for
a while.   In the first line of poetry of vs. 16 comes a reference to his return to Jerusalem.   This return, the aftermath of
Yahweh's victory, is a motif of post-battle procession.   Then
comes the house-building in the next colon.   Yahweh's house
will be built as is Baal's after his victory over Yamm.[80]
Finally with the last line of vs. 16 comes a reference to the
large size of the city to which Yahweh has returned.   The impli-
cation is that a measuring line *(qāweh)* will be needed to survey the size of Jerusalem, so much will the city have grown.
Vision III (2:5-9) which contains the image of a man holding a
measuring line *(ḥebel middâ)* has a similar meaning.

פרזות תשב ירושלם מרב אדם ובהמה בתוכה

> Jerusalem will remain as open regions from the
> multitude of men and animals in her midst.   (2:8)

The author of 1:17 echoes and extends this theme of growth and
abundance: "My cities will overflow from good."   As in Prov
5:16, *puṣ* should be understood in the sense of abundant overflowing rather than in the more common usage, "to scatter."[81]

     These elements: 1) anger/zealousness (the emotions of
holy war);   2) return (procession);   3) temple-building;   4)
fullness/abundance, recall those of the cosmogonic victory-
enthronement pattern.[82]   This pattern which is grounded in

---

80.   CTA 4.6.36ff.

81.   Rignell attempts a translation which accommodates the
more usual meaning of *puṣ*:   "When my cities are yet 'scattered
from (deprived of ?)' prosperity, I shall again...." *Die Nachtgesichte*, p. 54.

82.   For a good outline of this pattern as found in Near
Eastern epic materials, see Paul Hanson, "Zechariah 9 and the
Recapitulation of an Ancient Ritual Pattern," *JBL* 92 (1973),
54-55.

ancient Near Eastern myths about the young god's victory over
chaos becomes an important vehicle to describe Yahweh's role as
divine warrior in defense of historical Israel. The pattern
applied to exodus and conquest again becomes relevant in the
hopeful oracles of post-exilic prophecy, as shown by F. M.
Cross for the poetry of Deutero-Isaiah and by Paul Hanson for
Zechariah 9.[83] In vision I, the author also places the hopes
for restoration in the ancient mythic terms. He too employs a
poetic medium in vs. 16, but includes these traditional reminiscences within the form of the symbolic vision. Therein lies
an extremely creative process.

With the evocation of the victory/enthronement pattern,
the lament form, and the call form, Zechariah combines three
threads of literary tradition into the cloth of the symbolic
vision form. As we have noted, this new blend occurs not
within the core elements of the interpretation process itself
(vss. 7-10), but within the additional motifs of observation of
divine events and charge (vss. 11-16(17)). Indeed one might
say that these two motifs, especially that of the observations,
are not as yet fully integrated into the form. The same applies
to vision VIII where the observation of divine events again
will be tacked on to the end of the vision, after the symbol
objects have been interpreted. In Daniel 7, 8 and the remaining visions of our study, the divine events will have become
the stuff to be interpreted, fully integrated into the recognizably divinatory interpretation pattern.

As we have seen throughout, Zechariah is an innovator, an
experimenter, constantly attempting variations on the tried and
true older traditions. Of particular interest is his use of
dramatic happenings instead of static symbols, a usage which
allows him more vivid and alive narrations. The mythology
comes alive as the prophet is seen to interact with the visionary images. As anticipated by Zechariah vision II, the prophet
is being taken more and more into the divine confidence, now by
means of real-mythic events. In Daniel, through his dream, the
prophet will find himself in the council itself. Such a use of

83. See Cross, *Canaanite Myth*, pp. 99-104; Hanson, "Zechariah 9."

dramatic events differs from that of Ezekiel 37, in which Yahweh has the prophet participate in Boschian sign acts which
while certainly unusual and supra-mundane do not imply the
observation of instruments and functionaries of the divine government at their daily tasks. In Ezekiel 1, Ezekiel does
employ real-mythic happenings in which the prophet sees council
activities, building perhaps on the work of Isaiah 6. Yet
Zechariah attempts a more difficult literary feat, to integrate
these elements into the symbolic medium.

     Zechariah finds himself at a time when the older direct
forms of prophecy, oracles, are in decline. The reasons for
this change or fading out of certain prophetic forms are too
complex a subject for this monograph. For our current work,
the fact alone suffices that beginning with the late sixth century, some form of slightly less direct communication with the
transcendent deity was deemed necessary and appropriate. The
symbolic vision form, now subtly suggestive of the divinatory
process, becomes Zechariah's vehicle for the interaction with
God. Zechariah's integration of exciting and dramatic happenings involving the other world into the symbolic vision form
evokes the immediacy of an experience of the divine through the
safe filter and distance provided by the interpretation of symbols.

The symbols

     What of the symbols of vision I, the description of the
heavenly beings and their surroundings? As in vision II, the
symbolic appearances are explained to be real on a mythic
plane. After the symbolic figures are identified, they themselves speak giving the observer further insight into their
role. As in all the Zechariah visions, with the possible exception of VI (5:1-4), the connection between the symbol and
its interpretation is not reached via word-plays or metaphors.
One has no feeling as in stage I that a person adept at the
pseudo-science of dream interpretation might rationally predict
what God will offer as the explanation. Mystery and a sense of
the God-sent quality of the interpretation are heightened as we
must wait until the appointed divine interpreter reveals the
identity of the images. Then one must look behind and beyond

his words to see how the explanation of the symbolic images
makes sense within the complex systems of Near Eastern and Biblical mythology.

Within the vision, only the riders themselves are treated
as symbols to be interpreted. What of the myrtles, the horses
of varied colors, and the *měṣūlâ*, "the hollow (?)"? We never
hear of them again after the motif of description (vs. 8).

Certain questions about these images cannot be solved.
The meaning of the term *měṣūlâ* remains uncertain as noted above.
Are we dealing with one horse-rider team, followed by three
riderless horses, or are we to assume that these horses carry
riders?[84] Did the passage originally contain a reference to a
chariot as in vision VIII (Zech 6:1-8)? The text may be defective. It is possible, indeed, that the author has created or
experienced a mysterious scene which cannot be fully understood.

One's understanding of these supplementary objects, of
course, depends upon the readings which one accepts. As noted
above, a number of scholars do not read MT "myrtles," but G
"mountains," an image which has strong mythological connotations in vision VIII (6:1-8).[85] The term *bên* can also be
interpreted in more than one way, as "among" or as "between."
Since vision I has no indication of the number of trees or of
a specifically symmetrical arrangement, the reading "among" is
preferable.[86]

---

84. We assume the latter and therefore refer to the
"riders" in our study, but one cannot be certain.

85. F. Horst (*Die zwölf kleinen Propheten*, p. 219) and H.
G. May ("A Key to the Interpretation of Zechariah's Visions,"
JBL 57 [1938], 174) point to the image of the sun-god who
emerges from between two mountains, a motif frequently found in
Akkadian cylinder seals. Sellin (*Das Zwölfprophetenbuch*, p.
483) notes that such magic mountains are the place where this
world meets the next. See also Duhm, "Anmerkungen zu den
zwölf Propheten. VII. Buch Sacharja I (Kapitel 1-8)," *ZAW* 31
(1911), 162-163.

86. Horst, however, reads "between the myrtles" and relates this image to the common Near Eastern motif of the deity
who stands between two trees (*Die zwölf kleinen Propheten*, p.

Reading "among the myrtles," Rignell and Chary consider
the image as a hopeful symbol of the good and peaceful life
assured the people at the restoration. Citing Is 41:19 and
55:13 Chary writes that myrtles accompany the institution of
the messianic era.[87] In the comparison passages cited by Chary
and Rignell, the coming of Yahweh and his kingdom is not suggested merely by trees but by the contrasting imagery of dry-
ness, thorns, and desert which change into water, greenery, and
vegetation. Comparable imagery accompanies Baal's return from
the land of Mot.[88] The simple image of some myrtles in the
distance really does not convey the same effect.

Scholars also comb the annals of Near Eastern mythology
and OT literature for hints of the deeper significance of
mĕṣūlâ. Rignell suggests that the term *mĕṣūlâ*, which is used
most commonly in OT to refer to the depths of the sea (Ps
107:24; Jon 2:4; Mi 7:19; Job 41:23; and especially Ex 15:5),
is employed by Zechariah to evoke the crossing of the Reed Sea.
Hence through the term *mĕṣūlâ*, the prophet equates the return
from exile with the exodus.

> מצלה lenkt die Gedanken auf die Tiefe, in der Israels
> Feinde ertranken, so dass das Volk Gottes seinen Weg unge-
> hindert fortsetzen konnte.[89]

Chary also points to the association of the term with
water, but looks to "deep water" as an indication of the other
world. Quoting Albright's translation of CTA 4.4.21-22, Chary
notes that El, head of the Canaanite pantheon, was said to
dwell "at the source(s) of the (two) rivers, in the midst of
the fountains of the two deeps."[90] The term for "deeps" in CTA
4.4.22 is not a form of *ṣwl*, but reads *tihāmatêmi*, a cognate
for the Biblical *tĕhōmōt*. Nevertheless, evidently more concerned with the concept than the terminology, Chary finds in

---

219). Cf. the discussion of Zech 4:3 above.

87. *Die Nachtgesichte*, p. 24; *Aggée-Zacharie, Malachie*,
p. 58.

88. See CTA 6.3.6-7, 12-13.

89. *Die Nachtgesichte*, p. 26.

90. W. F. Albright, *Archaeology and the Religion of Israel*
(Baltimore: Johns Hopkins, 1942), p. 72 and pp. 194-195, n.7.

the *mĕṣūlâ* of Zechariah 1 "une imagerie mythologique qui était
connue des contemporains du prophète."[91]

In criticism of Chary and Rignell's suggestions, we note
that the Biblical passages cited by them clearly involve
aquatic contexts, whereas that of Zechariah 1 does not. For
example, Exod 15:5 exhibits poetic parallelism between *tĕhōmōt*
and *mĕṣūlâ*. The narrative context of the poem is the crossing
of the Reed Sea. Does the single term *mĕṣūlâ* used in the context of riders and myrtles necessarily evoke the image of the
sea?

Finally, we come to the horses and their colors. Again
the readings and emendations which one accepts affect one's
interpretation of the symbols. Scholars who emend the passage
so that it lists four horses on the pattern of Zech 6:2, 3 see
the horses as symbols for the four directions of heaven[92] or as
allusions to planets.[93] A discussion of these suggestions will
be more appropriate to the study of Zech 6:1-8 where the four-
horse pattern is original to the vision. In any event, there
is no reason to assume that the red-sorrel-white reading of MT
is incorrect in vision I (see text-critical note "d").

Rignell emphasizes the red-white color contrast and agrees
with medieval commentators such as Rashi that red, the color of
blood, is a sign of anger and battle, whereas white is associated with victory, peace, and more positive events. The contrast between red and white for Rignell is ultimately a contrast between punishment and grace.[94] Such suggestions are not
supported by an analysis of the actual usages of these colors
in OT. Red commonly indicates humanness and earthiness throughout OT, as we shall discuss in some detail in our next study.
White, on the other hand, is less consistently attached to some
specific value or connotation. While "whitening" is synonymous
with purifying in Is 1:18, it is the color of impurity, used to

---

91. *Aggée-Zacharie, Malachi*, p. 57. So recently C. Jeremias, *Die Nachtgesichte*, pp. 114-115.

92. See for example, Sellin, *Das Zwölfprophetenbuch*, p.
483.

93. See Horst, *Die zwölf kleinen Propheten*, p. 220.

94. *Die Nachtgesichte*, pp. 33-34.

describe skin diseases in Leviticus (13:3, 4, 10, 13, etc.).
In fact, this rather graphic use of the color white is the most
frequent in OT. To find in the color white an indication of
victory or the end of the Lord's punishment is to allegorize.[95]

Ultimately, then, after reviewing the many suggestions for
the deeper significance of the myrtles, the hollow, and the
horses' colors, we are led to the conclusion that in this vision
these objects provide props and setting for the primary symbols
on stage. The author, whose style tends increasingly toward
the narrative, provides a cameo picture, an oasis with trees
into which enter the key symbols. As noted above, this setting
may reflect the background imagery of a real dream. The riders
themselves are not representations of the planets, but just
what they are said to be within the mythological framework of
the vision. Included in this framework are notions of the
divine court and of the holy war which the warrior-king is
about to wage against the enemies of his people. In the context of the myth, the riders are identified as "those whom Yahweh has sent to traverse *(lĕhithallēk)* the land/earth." Like
the "eyes of the Lord" discussed for vision V, these horsemen
are divine emissaries, spies searching out the situation on
earth in order to report back to Yahweh.

That such an activity was considered a normal function of
certain members of the divine council is supported by Job 1:7,
where the *śāṭān*, a member of the council, reports back that he
has come, משוט בארץ ומהתהלך בה, "from ranging about the earth
and traversing it." Note the use of the hith. of *hlk*. In our
study of vision VIII, we will find further correspondence
between Zechariah 1 and the prose narrative of Job (1-2; 42:7-
17) in the terminology applied to the role of Yahweh's vassals.
While the Job narrative no doubt has a long oral history, A.
Hurwitz' excellent linguistic analysis rightly supports an

---

95. Klaus Seybold also rejects such allegorical solutions
and seeks origins for the horse/rider symbolism in the real-
life setting of the Near Eastern court. He does not go in the
direction of holy war imagery, however, and emphasizes different aspects of kingship than do we. See his *Bilder zum Tempelbau,* p. 72.

exilic or post-exilic date for the Biblical telling of this
story.[96] Hurwitz' work is based on the correspondence between
the terminology and syntax of Job and those of Proto-Zechariah,
the work of the Chronicler, and other Persian-period late
Hebrew works. This 6th century B.C. telling of the story of
the righteous sufferer shares with the contemporary visions of
Zechariah the same interest in the divine council and its
machinations. In Job, the role of "traverser of the earth,"
played by the $\acute{s}\bar{a}\underline{t}\bar{a}n$, is tied to the fate of the protagonist of
the story, Job. In Zechariah 1, the "wanderer" role is paral-
lel to that of the spies who are sent out before battles, particularly in the conquest stories. See for example, Num 13:2-
3, Josh 2:1, and 7:2; in each spies are sent ($\acute{s}l\underline{h}$ vb. used as in
Zechariah) to survey the scene before battle. The pre-battle
setting for the sending out of agents is confirmed throughout
the continuing vss. of Zechariah 1.

The agents fulfill their task by reporting that all is
static and quiet. As commentators note, the period when vision
I was composed was not a peaceful one historically.[97] The
meaning of the reporting agent's response is illustrated by Jer
48:11. Moab is described thus:

שאנן מואב מנעוריו
ושקט הוא אל שמריו

> Moab has been at ease since his youth
> Undisturbed has he been on his lees.

The enemies of God's people have been undisturbed during the
years of exile, like wine which has been allowed to mature.
But "days are coming" (Jer 48:12) when the quiet will be shattered and vengeance taken. The same image of prosperous ease
before the fall is employed in Ezek 16:49 (note the use of $\acute{s}q\underline{t}$).

When the angel beseeches Yahweh for the sake of Jerusalem
and the cities of Judah, mentioning the proverbial seventy
years of the exile (cf. Is 23:17; Jer 25:11; and 29:10), he

---

96. "The Date of the Prose-Tale of Job Linguistically
Reconsidered," *HTR* 67 (1974), 17-34.

97. See John Bright, *A History of Israel* (Philadelphia:
Westminster, 1976), pp. 369-370.

receives the response that God is now aroused against the
nations, *haśśa'ănannîm*, "who are at ease." Vengeance will take
place. The notion of an overly-confident, unexpecting enemy
thus is contained in the report provided by Yahweh's troops.

    The forces of Yahweh have prepared the way for battle by
surveying the situation. Divine emissaries appear again in
Zech 6:1-8.

Zech 6:1-8

		Test for balance
ראשב ואשא עיני ואראה	(1a	11
והנה ארבע מרכבות	(1b	8
יצאות מבין שני ᵃהרים	(1c	9
וההרים הרי נחשת	(1d	9
במרכבה הראשנה סוסים אדמים	(2a	13
ובמרכבה השנית סוסים שחרים	(2b	13
ובמרכבה השלישית סוסיט לבנים	(3a	14
ובמרכבת הרביעית סוסים ברדים ᵇ⟨ ⟩	(3b	14
ואען ואמר אל המלאך הדבר בי	(4	
מה אלה אדני		
ריען ᶜהמלאךᶜ ויאמר אלי	(5	
אלה ארבע רחות השמים ᵈ		
יוצאות ᵉמהתיצב על אדון כל הארץᵈ		
הסוסים האדמים יצאים אל ארץ מזרחᶠ	(6a	14
והסוסים השחרים יצאים אל ארץ צפון	(6b	15
והלבנים ʰיצאים אל ⁱארץ היטⁱ	(6c	12
והברדים ʰיצאים אל ארץ התימן	(6d	13
⟨ ⟩ʲויבקשו ללכת להתהלך בארץ	(7	
ריאמר		
לכו התהלכו בארץ		
ותתהלכנה בארץ		
ויזעק ᵏאתי וידבר אלי לאמר	(8a	
ראה היוצאים אל ארץ צפון	(8b	10
הניחו את רוחיˡ בארץ צפון	(8c	10

1) Again I raised my eyes and saw,
    And behold four chariots

coming forth from between two mountains,
And the mountains were mountains of bronze.

2) On the first chariot were red horses.
   On the second chariot were black horses.

3) On the third chariot were white horses,
   And on the fourth chariot were spotted horses.

4) And I said to the angel who was speaking with me,
   "What are these, my lord?"

5) And the angel responded and said to me,
   "These are the four winds,
   going forth after waiting upon the Lord of the whole
   earth."

6)   The red horses go to the land of the east,
      The black horses go to the land of the north,
      The white ones go to the land of the west,
      And the spotted ones go to the land of the south."

7) Then they requested leave to traverse the earth,
   And he said,
   "Go, traverse the earth."
   And they traversed the earth.

8) Then he shouted at me and spoke to me saying,
      "See those who go forth to the land of the north.
      They are setting down my spirit in the land of the
      north."

[a]We read with G, εκ μεσου δυο ορεων, *bên šĕnê hārîm*. So
Mitchell. MT, *bên šĕnê hehārîm* is probably the result of the
scribe's eye slipping to the next word, *wehehārîm*.

[b]MT reads, *bĕruddîm ʾămuṣṣîm*. With most scholars, including Horst, Chary, Mitchell, Marti, and Wellhausen, we omit
ʾămuṣṣîm. Mitchell suggests that *ʾămuṣṣîm* may be a corruption
of *ḥamuṣṣîm*, "scarlet" (cf. Is 63:1). Originally a marginal
gloss for *ʾădummîm*, the term is dislocated in its present position. Another possibility is that *ʾămuṣṣîm*, a term which looks
as if it should come from the vb. *ʾmṣ*, "to be strong," is actually a corruption of *ʾădummîm*. The reference to the red
horses has been misplaced in vss. 6, 7 so that all which remains
is the obscure reference to *ʾămuṣṣîm* at the beginning of vs. 7.

Having become a part of the text, this displaced corruption for
'ădummîm also creeps into the text at vs. 3 under a certain
literary pressure to establish a symmetry which prepares for
the mention of "the strong ones" in vs. 7.   G ποικιλοι ψαροι,
"spotted/dappled, speckled/dappled," may be doublet translations for bĕruddîm, "spotted." Alternatively, the horse colors
simply have been expanded by the addition of a color. In
either event, we have restored the shortest reading.

     ^{c}G has the longer rubric, ο αγγελος ο λαλων εν εμοι. Roth-
stein, Mitchell, and Nowack accept this long reading. We prefer the shorter MT designation for the angel. So Rignell,
Sellin, and Wellhausen. As noted in the study of vision I
(Zech 1:11, 12, text-critical note "e"), there is no reason to
assume that the interpreting angel is called by the lengthiest
designation each time he is mentioned. The shorter reference
is perfectly clear here.

     ^{d}There are two ways to deal with the syntax of vs. 5. 1)
One can assume the copula and translate like G, ταυτα εστιν οι
τεσσαρες ανεμοι, "These are the four winds...." In this way
the winds are personified as a horse/chariot team, serving as
messengers to Yahweh. Chary accepts this translation, pointing
to Ps 104:4 in which the winds are personified as Yahweh's
servants.

     2) Alternatively, one can translate, "These go forth to
the four winds...." Wellhausen, Mitchell, and Nowack allow for
such a translation by placing a preposition lĕ or 'el, "to,"
before 'arba'. Several scholars point out that this translation is possible even without emendation; for no preposition is
necessary in an accusative of direction. The vb. yṣ' should be
considered in an acc. of movement relationship with its obj.
'arba' rūḥôt. See Joüon, Grammaire, 125n and 126h.

     The first translation provides somewhat smoother syntax
than the second option. The phrase, "the four winds," is often
used in OT to refer to the four directions of the compass (Dan
8:8; 11:4; Jer 49:36; and Ezek 42:16-19). In opting for the
first translation one also allows for the more mythological
nuance. Note that in Jer 49:36 the winds also seem to play a
role as Yahweh's envoy.

^eG reads εκπορευονται παραστηναι τω κυριω, *yōṣĕʾōt lĕhit-yaṣṣēb ʿal ʾădôn.* ... If one accepts that the teams are taking leave of Yahweh to head in the directions listed in vs. 6, one must accept MT *mēhityaṣṣēb,* "from/after waiting upon...."

^fMT *ʾăšer bâ* = G εν ω ησαν, is a corruption omitted by all scholars. With Nowack, Sellin, and Chary we supply the missing red horses and the easterly direction at the beginning of vs. 6. While agreeing that some textual corruption has taken place, Horst and Mitchell prefer to view the presence of *ʾămuṣṣîm* in vs. 7 as a hint that the position of the missing horses and direction should be at the end of the list rather than at the beginning. *ʾămuṣṣîm* is a miswriting of *ʾădummîm* as explained in note "b" above. Given the repetitive, traditional style of vss. 2, 3 one would expect the author to employ the same repetition pattern of colors in vs. 6.

^gWe have added a *waw* in light of the "adding" style which characterizes the repetition pattern in vss. 2, 3 and 6c, d; for these units, which are poetic in some senses, are not characterized by archaic rules of poetry. Prosaizing *waw*'s might be expected with such lengthy lines.

^hMT reads *yōṣĕʾîm,* the participle, in 6b, but *yāṣĕʾû,* the perfect, in 6c, d. G reads εξεπορευοντο, the middle imperfect, "they went out," throughout. With Mitchell, Nowack, Sellin, and Rothstein, we read the participle throughout.

ⁱMost scholars agree that *ʾel ʾaḥărêhem* stands for the west, but there are many suggestions as to the precise reading. Sellin suggests that two variants lie behind MT, *ʾel hayyām* and *ʾel ʾāḥôr.* Chary's suggestion, *ʾel ʾaḥărē hayyām,* is appealing, but there seems to be no precedent in OT in which *ʾel ʾaḥărê* means "towards," a sense required in the context. With Nowack we read *ʾel ʾereṣ hayyām,* accepting the simplest solution.

Wellhausen suggests emending to *ʾel ʾereṣ qedem,* "to the land of the east," leaving the reference to the west until vs. 7. See note "j" below.

In contrast to the others, Rignell simply follows MT = G, reading "after/behind them."

^jWe have omitted *wĕhāʾămuṣṣîm yāṣĕʾû,* considering the phrase a displaced and corrupted reference to the red horses and their direction (see "b" and "f" above). Nowack and Sellin

translate the term "the strong ones." Mitchell and Horst emend
to *ădummîm*, "reddish ones" and continue the phrase, *'el 'ereṣ
qedem*, "to the land of the east," thus accounting for the horse
and direction which seem to be missing in this portion of the
explanation motif. Cf. note "f" above.

ᵏMitchell suggests that *'ōtî* should be emended to *'ēlay*.
In Neh 9:28 and Jud 12:2 the vb. *z ʿq* is followed by the d.o.
Thus the usage seems to be acceptable, and emendation unneces-
sary.

¹MT *hēnîḥû 'et rûḥî*, "they will make my spirit to rest,"
is translated in G by ανεπαυσαν τον θυμον μου, "they will make
my anger to cease," i.e. "give rest to my anger." G may provide a nuanced translation of *rûaḥ*, for *rûaḥ* does mean anger in
a number of passages (Prov 16:32; 25:28; Jud 8:3; Eccl 7:9).
On the other hand, τον θυμον μου may be a translation for
ḥāmātî, which is used with the hiph. of *nwḥ* in several passages
in Ezekiel (5:13; 16:42; 24:13) to mean "I will sate my anger."
Thus one's translation depends not only upon which reading one
accepts, but also upon which connotation one accepts for the
hiph. of *nwḥ*. We accept MT as it stands, and will discuss the
translation below in an analysis of the overall symbol imagery.

Patterns in language and content

Motivated by the long but even repetition patterns in vss.
2, 3 and 6 we have divided the vision into thought-lines in
order to check for patterns of balance in line length. Line
length is variable. On the other hand, balance occurs in vs.
1c and 1d (9/9), in vs. 8b and 8c (10/10) as well as in vss. 2,
3 and 6. These examples of balanced throught-lines also include the repetition of terms *(hārîm/hehārîm hārê; 'ereṣ ṣāpôn/
bě'ereṣ ṣāpôn)*. While Zechariah vision VIII is primarily a
prose piece like the last three visions with which we have
worked, the author may be employing some of the old rhetorical
flourishes. (See below.)

Vss. 2, 3, a description of the chariots and horses, comprise a balanced unit with very long lines (13/13/14/14) and a
repeated word arrangement: *bammerkābâ* + ordinal number + *sûsîm*
+ color. Vs. 6, contributing to the explanation motif, then
tells of the direction taken by each group of horses. Its

pattern is thus: *hassûsîm*+ color + *yōṣĕ'îm 'el* + locus. The
second unit recalls the symbol image via mention of the horses'
colors and by repeating the list of horses in the same order.[98]
These units remind one of the description of the good and bad
fruit in Jer 24:2. In Jeremiah 24, such folksy repetition sets
the traditional style and determines the structure of the
vision as a whole. In Zechariah vision VIII, these repetition
patterns do not dominate as much. But each of these four-lined
knots of repetition are useful creators of focus and emphasis.
The reader is made to participate as tension builds, and the
impression grows as the syntax and terms are repeated. The
author thus forms a spotlight for the horse symbols and a highlight for the explanation of the horses, an explanation which
begins in vs. 5 before the repetition pattern.[99]

The vision exemplifies a few other interesting cases of
repetition. The vb. *yṣ'* is employed in the motif of initial
description (vs. 1), in the explanation motif (vss. 5, 6), and
in the observation of divine events (vs. 8). Could this repetition of language be a reminiscence of the economical style,
essential in the structure of the visions of stage I of our
form? Note also the phrase *wĕhehārîm hārê nĕḥōšet* in vs. 1,
reminiscent of the catchy *ûpānāyw mippĕnê ṣāpônâ* in Jer 1:13.
Finally, note the re-use of forms *hlk* or *hlk + bā'āreṣ* in vs. 7
(*lāleket; lĕhithallēk bā'āreṣ; lĕkû; hithallĕkû bā'āreṣ*) and
the two occurrences of *'ereṣ ṣāpôn* in vs. 8. The piling up of
these terms does create a certain emphasis in each case, as
does the double use of *qeren* in vision II. While these two
examples from vision VIII do not involve key symbol terms nor a
technique of word association as in stage I, the author does
draw special attention to the function and ultimate goal of the
horse-chariot teams. Recall of terminology that appeared in an
earlier motif and repetition within the same motif, moreover,
remind the reader of the initial description once he has

---

98.   In order to accept this point, one must agree with
our text-critical choices; see text-critical note "f."

99.   A similar use of syntactic repetition is found in the
Tale of Aḥiqar. See S. Niditch and R. Doran, "The Success
Story of the Wise Courtier," 183-184.

reached the motif of explanation. This latter role will become
all the more important in the lengthy, complex visions of
Daniel and the rest.

The pattern of content elements in the vision is as follows:

6:1	Indication of vision	ואשב ואשה עיני ואראה
6:1-3	Description	והנה...
6:4	Question of seer to	ואען ואמר אל המלאך הדבר
	interpreter	בי מה אלה אדני
6:5-6	Reply of interpreter	ויען המלאך ויאמר אלי...
6:7-8	Observation of divine happenings	(no rubric)
(6:8	Charge ?)	

The above outline requires little additional comment and is
identical to that of vision I. Introductory rubrics are familiar to us from Zechariah's other visions; the use of r'h and
hinnēh has been well established since the visions of Amos. A
basic pattern from description to explanation has asserted
itself. The action scene in vss. 7 and 8 in which the teams
seek leave from their commander is an addendum to the question/
answer pattern, as is Zech 1:11-16(17). By a command to see,
which may be a reflex of the charge motif which we observed in
vision I and will observe again, the prophet's attention is
drawn to these horse-chariot teams' activities and to their
significance.

There are numerous points of contact in pattern of content
as well as in terminology and symbols between this vision and
vision I. Most scholars consider the two visions an inclusio.
The two have been arranged as counterpoints in a theme of
restoration and return, a theme which for Zechariah frequently
involves imagery of the warrior king and his troops.

The symbols

The warrior king-troops aspect of the restoration emerges
in a close examination of the individual symbols of vision
VIII: mountains of bronze; horses of four colors; chariots;
directions of the compass/color associations; and the land of
the north. Once again, the contextual explanation of the symbols only extends the symbolic imagery. The vision of horses

and chariots emerging from between two bronze mountains is explained in terms of role and function: "These are the four
winds of heaven going forth after waiting upon the master of
the whole earth."

The phrases, *hityaṣṣēb ʿal ʾădôn kol hāʾāreṣ* and *lĕhithallēk bāʾāreṣ*, employed in the explanation and observation motifs
respectively (vss. 5-6; 7), are technical terms which specifically refer to the divine council. Similar language is found
in Job 2:1-2 and in Zech 1:10, 11. Also note the correspondence between the first phrase and description of the *bĕnê
yiṣhar* in Zech 4:14, *hāʿōmĕdîm ʿal ʾădôn kol hāʾāreṣ*. The
horse-chariot teams like the horsemen of vision I must be considered representatives of the heavenly court, who roam the
earth in the service of Yahweh. Their place in the mythology
portrayed by the author is further reinforced and clarified by
the details of the description.

Scholars agree that the twin mountains are laden with cosmic mythic significance. Horst refers to them as "Sonnentor-
berge,"[100] "mountains of the gateway of the sun." As in his
interpretation of vision I, H. G. May goes further and sees the
entire image as a reflection of the sun god's ride with horses
and chariots through this gateway of heaven. Building on work
of Jeremias, May considers the chariot-horses-mountains image
cluster a reminiscence of the New Year's festival.[101] Chary
refers to the mountains as the entrance to the dwelling place
of the gods and points to representations of Šamaš between the
mountains, found in Babylonian seals and reliefs (ANEP 683,
685).[102] Mitchell regards them as the "ideal mountains in
front of the abode of Yahweh."[103]

Noting that the mountains are of bronze, Rothstein suggests an identification between these mythic mountains (=

---

100. *Die zwölf kleinen Propheten*, p. 236.

101. H. G. May, "A Key," 75.

102. *Aggée-Zacharie Malachie*, p. 105. See also Sellin on
"Weltberge," *Das Zwölfprophetenbuch*, p. 515. Marti suggests
that the author had in mind Mt. Zion and the Mount of Olives
(*Das Dodekapropheton*, p. 418).

103. *A Commentary*, p. 177.

pillars of the earth) with the bronze columns of the Solomonic
temple (1 Kgs 7:15).[104] Temples were, of course, considered
earthly representations or microcosms of the divine, cosmic
structure of the universe.[105] K. Seybold is quick to follow in
Rothstein's footsteps, anxious to see a hint of the "Bilder zum
Tempelbau" whenever possible in the visions of Zechariah.[106]

There is no doubt about the cosmic significance of the
mountains. They are indicators of a liminal place, a boundary
between this world and the next, and a sign post for the dwelling of the deity. The image is so well attested in the Near
East, however,[107] that it is unlikely that Zechariah need have
been specifically influenced by Babylonian notions of Šamaš.
The image of bronze mountains was culturally his as much as
that of a worshipper of Šamaš. So too the chariots with which
we will deal below. Nor does the bronze quality of the mountains necessarily imply an immediate identification with the
columns of the temple. The material of bronze or copper does
have special, often sacred, associations. It may have been
chosen as a building material in the temple, in part, because
of its special associations.[108] It was a valued metal, employed
not only in the columns of the Solomonic temple, but also in
numerous sacred instruments and fixtures of P's account of the
tabernacle (Ex 26:11, 37; 27:2ff.; 30:18; 36:18, 38, etc.) and
in various other features of the Solomonic temple (1 Kgs 7:30,
38, 45).

Even more interesting references to bronze are found in
the metaphoric descriptions of divine beings in Ezek 1:7, 40:3,
and Dan 10:6. In Ezekiel 1, the legs and soles of the living

---

104. *Die Nachtgesichte*, pp. 167-168.

105. See G. E. Wright, *et al.*, "The Significance of the
Temple in the Ancient Near East," *BA* 7 (1944), 41-88; Walter
Kornfeld, "Der Symbolismus der Tempelsaulen," *ZAW* 74 (1962),
50-57.

106. *Bilder zum Tempelbau*, p. 69.

107. See R. Clifford, *The Cosmic Mountain in Canaan and
the Old Testament* (Cambridge: Harvard University, 1972).

108. See Sellin, *Das Zwölfprophetenbuch*, p. 515; Rignell,
Die Nachtgesichte, p. 200.

beings who emerge from the midst of the fire are said to sparkle like burnished bronze. Similarly, the divine guide/sur-
veyer of Ezekiel 40 is said to have the appearance of bronze,
and of the man in Daniel 10 it is written,

ופניו כמראה ברק

ועניו כלפידי אש

וזרעתיו ומרגלתיו כעין נחשת קלל

> His face was like the appearance of lightning,
> his eyes like torches of fire,
> his arms and legs like burnished bronze.

Because of its orange-gold hue, bronze or copper is often associated with brightness and fire. *Ḥašmal*, which BDB tentatively
defines as an amalgam of gold and silver, is used in a similar
way to describe the fiery unearthly brightness which accompanies the appearance of the divine beings in Ezek 1:4, 27.
The divine beings whose bodily features are said to shine or
sparkle like bronze have taken on aspects of Yahweh as storm-
god who appears in the midst of lightning and fire. This association of theophany and fire imagery is well attested in the
mythology which OT shares with other Near Eastern cultures.[109]
Like the bronzeness of the divine beings, the bronzeness of the
cosmic mountains implies a quality of fiery, divine power,
indeed the presence of the deity.[110]

The chariot-horse teams are an equally complex image.
Mitchell and others view the chariots as a symbol for strife
and bloodshed in that they are used in battle.[111] Those who
see sun god imagery between the mountains interpret the chariot
as his means of transport (cf. 2 Kgs 23:11). So, of course,
the Greek image of the sun god, making his way across the

---

109. See F. M. Cross, *Canaanite Myth*, pp. 165-169.

110. Note Enoch 18:6, where the ends of the earth are
marked by mountains of colored stones and the presence of a
flaming fire. Mountains of metal (one of which is bronze) are
found in Enoch 52:2, 6, but are employed in a literary metaphor
which underscores the power of the Lord. Even mountains of
metal cannot withstand his onslaught.

111. *A Commentary*, p. 177.

horizon in his chariot.[112] Mitchell's concrete suggestion of
battle associations fits the context of the vision far better
than suggestions of an allusion to or reminiscence of the sun
god. We are dealing here not with the deity himself, but with
four horse-chariot teams, divine agents, each of whom is responsible for surveying a quarter of the universe.

In tracing the signification of the chariots, one should
mention Elijah's trip to heaven from earth, via the chariot of
fire and the horses of fire (2 Kgs 2:11). The chariot-horse
team serves a boundary-crossing function, linking this world to
the next in 2 Kgs 2:11 as in Zechariah 6. The horse and
chariot teams may have been imagined constantly roving the universe, as servants to Yahweh. In 2 Kings 2, these servants or
agents come for Elijah. Of course the martial potential of the
chariots allows them to re-invoke the battle theme in Zechariah
VIII, a theme built up in previous visions. In our opinion,
the actual battle is now over, however, and the chariots and
horses are not headed to holy war, but to certify Yahweh's victory by establishing his rule over the land of the north. More
on this interpretation later.

The colors of the horses in vision VIII have been treated
much like those of vision I.[113] Rignell provides a rather allegorical solution. He considers only the black, red, and white
horses to be significant and believes that each group stands
for a task: the black horses bring misfortune; the red bring
strife, war, and bloodletting; the white horses bring a reversal
to peace and good fortune.[114] The weaknesses of these suggestions were discussed in the study of vision I. Rignell is
falling prey to his own Western notions about the meaning of
these colors.

Duhm is one of the few scholars who attempt to explain the
association of certain colors with certain directions. While
he writes that the direction association for the *ămuṣṣîm
(which he translates "scheckig") is impossible to ascertain, he

---

112. See H. J. Rose, *A Handbook of Greek Mythology* (New
York: Dutton, 1959), pp. 32-33.

113. See Horst, *Die zwölf kleinen Propheten*, p. 220.

114. *Die Nachtgesichte*, p. 206.

explains that red is the color of the sun and moon as they
appear in the east, black is the color of the "lichtlosen"
north, and white is the color of the "Seenebel," the fog of the
west.[115] Duhm's ideas are speculative. We sympathize, however, with Duhm's attempt to match directions with colors
within some conceptual scheme. In traditional societies,
values of color and direction or spaciality are very important.
Given enough data on the manner in which colors and directions
are employed in the myth and ritual of a society, anthropolo-
gists are able to set up binary charts in which certain values
or concepts are found to be consistently associated with certain colors. For example, in his study of symbols in Mapuche
myth and ritual, L. Faron finds that lefthandedness is consistently associated with evil, death, night, west, north, blue
and black, whereas righthandedness is consistently associated
with good, life, day, east, south, yellow, and white.[116] We
have attempted a similar analysis of OT materials but simply
cannot come to any helpful conclusions; data is too sparse and
comes from too many differing layers of material. We may simply have to admit an inability to explain the color/direction
associations; the problem, however, is an interesting one and
one which had to be raised.

Of the four directions, the north is the chief and final
focus of the horse-chariot teams, whatever each's usual area of
provenance.[117] Interpretation of the phrase, הניחו את רוחי
בארץ צפון, is essential to the understanding of the vision. Is
the hiph. of *nwḥ* to be understood "set down" or "lay at rest"?
Is *rûaḥ* "anger" or "spirit" and if the latter does it mean simply the divine presence as in Hag 2:5 and Ps 139:7 or something
more?

Most scholars agree that "land of the north" refers to the
place of exile, land of the Babylonians. Wellhausen notes that

---

115. "Anmerkungen zu den zwölf Propheten VII. Buch
Sacharja I. (Kapitel 1-8)," 161-175, esp. 164.

116. "Symbolic Values and the Integration of Society
among the Mapuche of Chile," *Myth and Cosmos*, ed. John Middleton (New York: Natural History, 1967), 167-183.

117. See Rignell, *Die Nachtegesichte*, p. 206.

"north" could also refer to the "Mittelpunkt der persischen
Weltmacht."[118] Chary and Rignell write that the Lord's spirit
is coming to the north in order to bring salvation to the
exiles, to initiate their return to the land.[119] Sellin
emphasizes that the spirit is being set down not only to rescue
the exiled, but also to take vengeance on the Babylonians.[120]
All of the above scholars have chosen the most common denomi-
nator of translations for *hēnîḥû* and *rûaḥ*: set down my divine
presence. So also Horst.[121] Mitchell prefers the nuance of
anger for the *nwḥ*(hiph.)/*rûaḥ* combination: God will vent his
wrath. For Mitchell, the object of this wrath is Babylonia in
its second revolt against the Persians.[122]

The phrase, "land of the north," is generally employed in
OT to refer to the historical enemy Babylonia (see Jer 3:18;
6:22; 10:22; and 16:15) though Jer 10:22 like the references to
the north in Jer 1:13, 14 and Is 41:25 contains additional
nuances. In these instances, the historical and geographical
locus of Near Eastern super-powers overlaps with the mythic
locus for the dwelling place of God.[123] Thus the north is not
only the region of the enemy, but also the starting-point for
Yahweh's march to battle or the march of his instrument on
earth (cf. Ezek 38:15; 39:2), be the holy war against his own
sinful people or their enemies. Some of the same double-nuance
such that the historical location overlaps with the dwelling
place of Yahweh may be contained in the reference to the land
of the north in Zech 6:8. It is not certain, however, that
Yahweh's troops in vision VIII are headed north to prepare for
battle as implied by a number of scholars. The evidence points

---

118. *Die kleinen Propheten*, p. 184.

119. *Aggée-Zacharie*, p. 107; *Die Nachtgesichte*, p. 216.

120. *Das Zwölfprophetenbuch*, p. 516.

121. "Sie bringen meinen Geiste zur Ruhe im Land des
Nordens" (*Die zwölf kleinen Propheten*, p. 237).

122. *A Commentary*, p. 181.

123. On *yarkĕtê ṣāpōn* and *ṣāpōn*, directional terms used
to describe the dwelling place of Yahweh and/or the place of
his temple, see Cross, *Canaanite Myth*, pp. 37-38.

in another direction, as shown by a brief contrast between this
vision and Zechariah vision I.

In vision I, the prophet mentions the plight of his people
and receives a promise of rescue (1:12; 13-16(17)). In the
prediction of rescue come references to the Lord's anger and
zealousness, as well as the images of temple building and abundance. The references to wrath in particular imply preparation
for holy war. Such indications of vengeance are absent in
vision VIII; there seems to be no contextual justification to
translate *rûaḥ* as "anger." Similarly absent are clear references to the rescue and ingathering of the people, a theme
implied by other visions such as Zech 2:8, 9 (vision III),
which mentions the large number of people who will dwell in
Jerusalem and the protection of them. So one must still ask
which aspect of restoration is emphasized in vision I.

G translates the key phrase, *hēnîḥû ʾet rûḥî...*, to mean
"They are making my anger to cease." That is, "they are hal-
ting my wrath." We agree with the translator's assumption that
an abatement of wrath is presumed in this final vision, but not
with his translation. Rather, the task of Yahweh's agents is
much more positive and active than the G nuances in translation
allow. The task of the horse-chariot teams once again is to be
seen within the framework of the victory-enthronement pattern
discussed for vision I. The horse-chariot teams are bringing
the Lord's presence, in the sense of divine rule, to rest
securely over the land of Babylon. The Lord's will is being
asserted and finalized. The same nuance of divine will may
also be implied in the use of *rûaḥ* in Zech 4:6 and in Is 32:15.
In Is 32:15-20 as in Zechariah 1, the coming of the Lord's
spirit changes difficult times of anger, war, and deprivation
into times of tranquility and fullness. The divine reign
brings with it comfort, security, and overflowing richesse. In
the passage from Isaiah 32, the reign of the Lord pours down
like a shower of peace. This theme of the establishment of
Yahweh's spirit is comparable to the "manifestation of divine
reign," one of the concluding elements in the traditional pattern which describes Yahweh's victories.[124]

---

124. Normally the manifestation of divine reign is set in
more universal terms (Zech 9:10) and in terms of eternity (Ps.

Whereas vision I involves a pre-battle survey of the scene on earth, vision VIII involves a post-battle assertion of the rule of the victor. It is in these terms that the historical conquest of Babylonia would be understood. Between the inclusio formed by visions I and VIII are the other visions which include references to the holy war itself (vision II, 2:1-4; see also the hymnic material introduced by vision III, 2:10ff.) and which mention various aspects of the restoration of Yahweh to his people and his people to their land: the elimination of evil (VI, 5:3, 4; VII, 5:8-11); the election of God's representatives on earth (V, 4:14; IV - not in our form); the rebuilding of the temple and the restoration of cult (V - through the symbolism; I, 1:16).

Each of the above visions is self-inclusive in terms of structure and content. Except for IV, they can be seen in terms of the formal tradition which we have been carefully tracing. We do not suggest a plan, like that of Seybold, whereby the present ordering of all the visions of Zechariah fits a perfect conceptual scheme. In our study of Zechariah 4, however, we suggested that the position of the menorah vision at the center of the cycle may well be intentional. The arrangement of visions I and VIII at the beginning and end of the cycle also seems part of a conceptual plan. Given the rather specific correspondence in terminology and symbolism between the two visions, one might suggest that vision VIII was modeled after vision I or that they were conceived of as a pair, the beginning and end-points on the restoration continuum.

Zech 5:5-11

5) ויצא המלאך הדבר בי
ויאמר אלי

29:10; 48:15; Ex 15:18). See Hanson, "Zechariah 9," 53-58; Cross, *Canaanite Myth*, pp. 109-110. To us, however, it does seem possible to compare the image of Yahweh's spirit, in the sense of power and rule, being set down over his defeated enemy to the imagery of Ps 29:10 where Yahweh is said to be enthroned upon the flood. The latter image is of course the more immediate and overtly mythic.

שא נא עיניך

וראה ^a> < היוצאת הזאת

(6   ויאמר

מה היא

ויאמר

זאת האיפה היוצאת

ויאמר

זאת ^bעונם בכל הארץ

(7   והנה ככר עפרת נשאת

^cוהנה אשה יושבת בתוך האיפה

(8   ויאמר

זאת הרשעה

וישלך אתה אל תוך האיפה

וישלך את אבן העפרת אל פיה

(9   ואשא עיני וארא

והנה שתים נשים יוצאות

ורוח בכנפיהם

ולהנה כנפים ככנפי החסידה

ותשאנה את האיפה

בין הארץ ובין השמים

(10   ואמר אל המלאך הדבר בי

אנה המה מולכות את האיפה

(11   ויאמר אלי

לבנות לה בית בארץ שנער ^d> <

והניחה שם על מכנתה

5) And the angel who was speaking with me came forth,
   and said to me,

   "Lift your eyes,
   and see this thing which goes forth."

6) And I said,

   "What is it?"
   Then he said,

   "This is their sin in all the land."

7) And behold a lead weight was lifted.
   And behold a woman was sitting in the midst of the ephah.

8) And he said,
     "This is wickedness."
   Then he threw her into the ephah
   and thrust the lead stone against its mouth.

9) Then I lifted my eyes and saw,
   and behold two women going forth,
   and wind was in their wings,
   for they had wings like the wings of the stork.
   And they carried the ephah between the earth and the heaven.

10) And I said to the angel who was speaking with me,
       "Where are they taking the ephah?"

11) And he said to me,
         "To build a house for her in the land of Shinar.
         They will set her down there upon her resting place."

^aMT reads *mâ hayyô'ṣēt hazzō't*; we accept the shorter G
(A-Q B) which omits *mâ* = τι. Note that Ziegler's choice for G
differs from ours in this case. He bases his reading on V S,
some minuscules of L, Syr, and on Tht, which = MT.

^bMT reads *'ênām*, "their eyes." We accept G η αδικια αυτων
'ăwōnām. MT *'ênām* may be an intrusion from Zech 4:10b, which
like 5:2 contains the expression, *bĕkol hā'āreṣ*.

^cMT reads *wĕzō't 'iššâ 'aḥat* and reflects the frequent use
of *zō't* in vss. 5, 6. G preserves the correct reading.

^dG reads ετοιμασαι, *lĕhākîn*, "to prepare," a reading pref-
erable to MT *hûkan*, but not necessarily original to the vs.
lĕhākîn and *libnôt* may simply be doublets. MT may reflect a
confusion between sound alike vbs., *nwḥ* and *kwn*.

^eMT reads *wĕhunnîḥâ*, "she will be placed." We read with
G, και θησουσιν, *wĕhinnîḥûhā*, "they will set her down."

As promised in the introduction to ch. Two, we will
briefly analyze visions VII and III. While these two visions
belong to the same family as the other five visions of Zechariah
with which we have dealt, they display interesting divergences
from the developing tradition, as we see it.

	motif	*comments*
I. 5:5	Indication of vision + immediate entrance to the description motif	a form of r'h is used, but not the first person perf. or *waw* conv. impf. so that the prophet gives a retrospective of his vision experience; rather r'h is an impv., a command to see, delivered by the interpreting angel who begins to describe that which is there. note the absence of *hinnēh* to introduce the description motif.
5:6	Question of seer to interpreter	as usual, "What is it (she)?"
5:6	Answer/description Answer/explanation	a first response is on a real-mythic plane (that is, if the $y\hat{o}ṣ\bar{e}$'t is a f. s. "it" rather than a "she"); a second response explains the seen image to be other than it appears. '$\hat{e}p\hat{a}$ = their sin; this double response is unusual.[125]
II.5:7	Description	*hinnēh...wehinneh*
5:8	Explanation	note that the explanation is unsolicited. The seer does not ask, "Who is this?" The woman is said to be $riš$'$\hat{a}$, "wickedness."
5:8	Observation of inter-action between divine	note that the interpreting angel uncharacteristically takes

125. At first glance, the two responses look like variants or doublets; yet the content of both responses is necessary to understand the continuing theme of the piece. One could revise the whole vision such that the '$\hat{e}p\hat{a}$ is first mentioned in the description motif and the response motif contains only the interpretation of the '$\hat{e}p\hat{a}$, as symbol. Such a reordering of material, however, does not seem to be justified; for had the text once originally followed the rather typical ordering suggested above, one doubts that it would have been altered in transmission. That is, the regularity of the content pattern would have supported and reinforced its correct transmission through tradition. As the vision now stands, it presents a rather unusual set-up, a "more difficult reading" of sorts, and it is this reading which we believe to be original.

	beings	rather an active part in the vision, casting the female figure into the *ʾêpâ*. See the discusion of symbols below.
III. 5:9	Indication of vision	usual, first person *waw* conv. impf. of *rʾh*.
5:9	Description/observation of divine happenings	note that the description of visionary images and the observation of divine happenings are combined into one motif; in this sense the symbolic imagery seems more like that of Daniel 7 & 8 in that the dramatic events which are observed provide that about which the seer will ask in the next step of the pattern, the question motif; there are significant differences, however (see below).
5:10	Question of seer	significantly, seer asks not "What or who are these?" or "What are they doing?" but "Where are they taking the *ʾêpâ*?" See our discussion below.
5:11	Answer	appropriate to above question.

The vision motifs combine into a symbol-explanation pattern three times. The last segment (5:9-11) is closest in pattern to Zechariah visions II, VIII, and I, but the question, "Where are they taking..." may indicate a subtle departure from the truly symbolic medium, as we shall see in a moment.

All of the individual pieces of vision VII remind one of one or more of Zechariah's visions. Motifs of description, question, explanation, observation are all familiar to us, but have been juggled, nuanced, atypically combined. We can find no neat precursor to or derivation from the complex tripartite patterning of vision VII. The absence of *hinnēh* to introduce the description in segment I, the double response of the interpreter (5:6), the lack of a question motif in segment II, and the particular question asked in segment III (5:10) are all interesting and unexpected twists. The symbols, moreover, hang somewhere between the real-mythic plane and more genuinely symbolic status such that they represent something other than themselves (see our discussion of the real-mythic symbol in the study of vision II). The *ʾêpâ* is asked about and is interpreted two times, once on the real-mythic plane and once such that x = y, i.e. *'ēpâ* = *ʿāwōnām*; no one asks about the woman, but she is explained anyway such that woman = wickedness; finally, the two winged figures are taken for what they appear, real in the context of the vision.

The use of dramatic happenings observed by the prophet in this vision (segment III, vs. 9) seems a bit more advanced typologically than that of visions I and VIII. Here as in Daniel 7 and 8 the dramatic events are part of the description. On the other hand, in contrast to the visions of Daniel, the happenings are not explained, but are treated on their own terms, treated as realities and taken for what they seem rather than representations of something else. Seemingly aware of who or what the winged figures are, the seer simply asks where they are taking the grain measure. In this way, the vision subtly diverges from its symbolic relatives in form. The seer becomes less the dreamer who requires interpretation of his dream and more the visitor to the other world who describes his observations there. Though in terms of superficial structure it is like visions II, I, and VIII, conceptually this question motif places the vision somewhere between a truly symbolic vision and the "otherworldly visit" which characterizes Ezek 10-11. Enoch 54:4 and a number of the visions in 3 Baruch exhibit a similar wavering between concepts. (See our discussion of allegory below.)

In terms of language, the author has shown a marked preference for certain terms and phrases. *wĕlāhennâ kĕnāpayim kĕkanĕpê hahăsîdâ* (5:9) is another of the repetition construct chains like those in Zech 6:1 *(hārîm hārê)* and Jer 1:13 *(pānāyw mippĕnê)*, a catchy sound device. The syntax and vb. choices in vs. 6 *(wayyō'mer zō't*, 2 times) and vs. 8 *(wayyašlēḥ*, 2 times) may simply evidence a tendency to homogeneity in word usage. The constant use of *'ēpâ* is more significant. Note *hā'ēpâ* in the explanation/description (vs. 6, first segment); *bĕtōk hā'ēpâ* in the description motif of second segment (vs. 7); *'el tōk hā'ēpâ* in the observations motif of segment two (vs. 8); *hā'ēpâ* in the description/observation of the third segment (vs. 9); and finally *hā'ēpâ* in the last question motif (vs. 10).

Thus this symbol of measure, which is contextually explained to
mean "their sin (of the people)," runs throughout the vision.

The *ʾēpâ* term is not employed in as conceptually and aes-
thetically neat a plan as are repetitions of terms in stage I.
Indeed, as noted above, the motif pattern itself of vision VII
is simply not a neat one. The *ʾēpâ* symbol, however, is preva-
lent and does tend to unify the whole. It is the first symbol
which is seen and that with which the other symbolic images
interact.

The symbols in brief

The *ʾēpâ*, a grain measure, is often found in admonitions
against false measures. The wealthy are accused of selling
short, for example, in Mic 6:10 and Am 8:5. Like the measuring
devices in Am 7:7-9, Is 28:17, and 2 Kgs 21:13, the grain
weight of an *ʾēpâ*, most probably the container which holds this
weight,[126] is used here in a context of judgment, the weighing
of sins. The measure is interpreted to represent the sins
themselves, "their sin in all the land."

The female figure, which is interpreted to mean *rišʿâ*,
"wickedness," has a long pedigree in OT tradition and a long
future in post-Biblical literature. A sinful Israel is compared to a bad woman, a harlot, in Hosea 2, Jeremiah 2, 3, and
Ezekiel 16. The opposite of the female personification of wisdom is a harlotrous, evil female figure in Prov 5:3ff. A
female personification of anti-wisdom is found even more strik-
ingly in 4Q184, a Qumran composition which its earliest pub-
lisher refers to as "The Wiles of the Wicked Woman."[127] This
female personification of evil in vision VII is imagined

---

126. There is a problem in identifying the *ʾēpâ*. Is it
just a pile of grain in that amount or a container which holds
an *ʾēpâ*? The fact that the *ʾēpâ* is lifted up seems to imply
some sort of container, but one cannot be sure. Similarly, it
is not clear whether the stone is somehow placed against the
mouth of the female figure or whether a kind of stone cover is
placed on the opening of the container for the grain.

127. See J. Allegro, "The Wiles of the Wicked Woman," *PEQ*
96 (1964), 53-55.

dwelling in sins, the 'ệpậ; there she is cast, a leaden stone
placed upon its mouth. Evil itself is being imprisoned and
silenced. This image reminds one of the punishment of the
fallen-angel in Enoch 10:4-6 who is cast into a pit and covered
with rocks,[128] exiled to the land of Dudael.[129] In vision VII,
the personification of wickedness is also carried off. Šinʿār
where she is to be brought may be a name for some unknown mythical place. G, on the other hand, reads βαβυλωνος, Babylonia.
The term Šinʿār refers to Babylonia in Dan 1:2. If Šinʿār
means Babylonia in Zech 5:11, the author envisions a rather
neat way of preparing for Yahweh's return to a purified land
while taking supreme vengeance on the enemies of his people.
Wickedness, submerged in the sins of the people, is transferred
to dwell in the home of their enemies. What better form of
turning holy war against the Babylonians?[130]

Before concluding our analysis, we should emphasize the
rather literary use of symbols in this vision. Once the female
figure is explained to be a personification of wickedness and
the measure to be a measure of sin, the remainder of the vision

---

128. For a recent discussion of the rebellion-of-the-gods
theme in ancient literatures and an analysis of Šemiḥazah and
Azazel layers of the Book of Enoch see Paul D. Hanson, "Rebellion in Heaven, Azazel, and Euhemeristic Heroes in 1 Enoch 6-
11," *JBL* 96 (1977), 195-233.

129. J. T. Milik suggests a possible etymology for Dudael
and a possible geographic identification ("Problèmes de la Littérature Hénochique à la Lumière des Fragments Araméens de Qumran," *HTR* 64 [1971], 333-378, esp. 348-349).

130. Comparisons have been made between the carrying off
of the 'ệpậ and the atonement ritual which involved sending a
scapegoat into the wilderness (Leviticus 16). There is some
evidence that foreign uses of "scapegoat magic" actually involved sending the animal, symbolically laden with that which
polluted the community (be it sin or sickness), into enemy territory. See "Azazel," *The Jewish Encyclopedia*, II (1903), 366;
"Azazel," *Encyclopaedia Judaica*, III (1971), 1002. Also see
Hanson, "Rebellion," 221-225.

reads very much like an allegory. One feels more as if one
were reading a work like *Pilgrim's Progress* than a visionary
scene which smacks of the divinatory process. A comparison of
vision VII with other visions of our tradition helps to explain
why.

     In visions I and VIII the symbols and the observation
scene which follow the explanation motif are not interpreted
to be other than themselves. They are real within the mythology of the vision. In the other visions of Zechariah there are
no divine dramatic happenings. In Daniel 7 and 8 the divine
happenings, their protagonists, antagonists, and accoutrements
are the symbols and are interpreted as such, after being described in the first half of the vision. In Zechariah vision
VII, however, the symbols are interpreted to mean something
other than they appear (*'êpâ* = *'ăwōnām*; *'iššâ* = *rišʻâ*) and then
involved in dramatic happenings. The presence of non-real-
mythic symbols which are interpreted and then involved in
action gives the piece an allegorical quality not found in the
other visions. We have noted that Zechariah's visions in general have a more narrative quality than those of the simple
rhetorical style (stage I). In its particular ordering and
nuancing of motifs, vision VII partakes of a specific narrative
medium of metaphor, that of the allegory.

     In its theme of elimination of evil from the land, this
vision complements its fellows in the cycle; in content and
structure it is certainly related to the thread of tradition
which we have been following. But it presents unusual and
rather individualistic combinations of familiar motifs, nuancing them in less than traditional directions. One might say
that the author has departed from the tradition a bit more in
vision VII than in the other visions of Zechariah seen thus
far.

Zech 2:5-9

5) And I lifted my eyes and saw,   ואשא עיני ואראה   (5
    and behold a man, and in his   והנה איש ובידו חבל מדה
    hand a measuring rod.

6) And I said,   ואמר   (6
        "Where are you going?"   אנה אתה הלך

And he said,	ויאמר
"To measure Jerusalem,	למד את ירושלם
to see how much its width	לראות כמה רחבה וכמה
is and how much its length."	ארכה

7) And behold the angel who was speaking with me remained and another angel came to meet him.

והנה המלאך הדבר בי עמד[a] (7
ומלאך אחר יצא לקראתו

8) And he said to him,

ויאמר אלו[b] (8

"Run, speak to that fellow saying,

רץ דבר אל הנער הלז
לאמר

As open regions will Jerusalem remain

פרזות תשב ירושלם

From the multitude of men and animals,

מרב אדם ובהמה ⟨ ⟩[c]

And I will be to her, a wall of fire about,

ואני אהיה לה ⟨ ⟩[d]
חומת אש סביב

As the glory will I be in her midst."

⟨ ⟩ולכבוד אהיה בתוכה[e]

[a]MT reads $y\bar{o}\dot{s}\bar{e}$'. We read with G ειστηκει, '$\bar{o}m\bar{e}d$. MT reading results from the scribe's eye slipping ahead to the phrase, $\hat{u}mal$'$\bar{a}k$ '$a\dot{h}\bar{e}r$ $y\bar{o}\dot{s}\bar{e}$'.

[b]We accept shorter MT rubric. G reflects expansion, και ειπε προς αυτον λεγων.

[c]For metric reasons we suggest deleting $b\breve{e}t\hat{o}k\hat{a}$. This term, like $y\bar{o}\dot{s}\bar{e}$' above, may be the result of scribal error, for $b\breve{e}t\hat{o}k\hat{a}$ occurs again at the end of vs. 9.

[d]$n\breve{e}$'um $yahweh$ may here be a prosaizing addition.

[e]The waw may also be a prosaizing addition.

	motif		*comments*
2:5	Indication of vision		as usual
2:5	Description		*wĕhinnēh* as usual
2:6	Question		addressed directly to visionary figure and question is "Where are you going?" not "Who are you/what is this?"
2:6	Answer		appropriate to the above question

2:7-9 Observations   the seer observes the passing on
                                      of a message from Yahweh, intended
                                      for him, which actually contains
                                      the *explanation* of his vision.

The above pattern appears to be that of visions I and VIII.
A close examination of the question motif, however, has led us
to place this vision off the mainstream of the typological progression. The seer does not ask what he is seeing or what its
meaning is. He speaks directly to the visionary image, the
figure who holds the measuring line, and asks him where he is
going. Like the question motif of Zech 5:10, the "where"
question here contributes to the fading of the symbolic coloration of the pattern. A comparison with Daniel 7 makes our
point about the diminished symbolic values in vision III of
Zechariah. In Daniel 7, the seer also participates in his
vision to such an extent that he asks one of the figures within
it for information (7:16); yet in Daniel the symbolic nature of
the vision remains strong and predominant, as the visionary
interpreter apprises Daniel of a one-to-one correspondence
between aspects of the vision and their meanings. The four
beasts are the four kingdoms, and so on. In Zechariah vision
III, the prophet seems to have some recognition of the seen
images; he recognizes a man with a measuring line and addresses
him as such. He does not really ask for an interpretation of
his vision; indeed he asks his vision where it is going.

In fact, the symbolic image in Zechariah vision III differs from all the other symbolic images of Zechariah's cycle.
He is not described in any unusual way; he does not fly like
the scroll of vision VI, hover like the two winged figures of
vision VII; nor is he immediately identifiable within a sacred
context like the symbolic images of vision V. Even his task,
to measure Jerusalem, is humanly possible, if not by one man in
a day. His task contrasts sharply with the cosmic assignments
of the horsemen in vision I and the horse-chariot teams in
vision VIII. The man with measuring rod, of course, reminds
one of the man with a plumb-line in Am 7:7-9. Have we returned
to the less otherworldly symbolism of stage I? Does *ḥebel*
middâ/lāmōd 'et yĕrûšālaim qualify as word-play? We must
answer in the negative, for to measure is precisely the function

of a measuring line. There is no metaphor, no twist of meanings here. All is on a seemingly rather literal level.

The true meaning of measuring Jerusalem emerges through
contrast with the message about its measurelessness, revealed
in vss. 8-9. The meaning of the visionary image is not revealed in the answer motif, which is a direct and to-the-point
response to the question, "Where are you going?" The true significance of the man with measuring line in hand emerges in the
interaction and conversation between angels, observed by the
seer in vss. 7-9. The message to be delivered to the prophet
(hanna'ar hallāz)[131] is not a summary or elaboration of the
answer/explanation motif; it embodies the whole thrust of the
vision. Unlike the plumb-line which not only represents judgment but also helps to bring it about through sympathetic magic,
the man with the measuring line does not represent fullness;
rather, he prepares the way for a revelation about it. This
revelation about the abundance is presented in a typical "word
of Yahweh." The whole vision builds towards this message; the
explanation motif so important in other visions here becomes
only a stepping stone to the final message. Whereas the horsemen and horse-chariot teams in visions I and VIII respectively
are themselves to be participants in the cosmic events revealed
in the observations motif and thus need be identified in the
explanation motif, the man with the measuring line is not involved in that which is to come and thus is not himself identified in any more detail.

While superficially the pattern of content in vision III
seems to parallel that of visions I and VIII, the actual quality of the question, response, and observation motifs sets
vision III apart. Conceptually, this vision is more like a
sign act than a symbolic vision. That is, the man with the
measuring line serves more as a sign than as a symbol; his true
significance emerges in a traditional word of Yahweh. For
these reasons we place vision III like vision VII slightly outside the tradition formed by visions VI, V, II, I, and VIII.

---

131. Note that Jeremiah refers to himself as a na'ar in
his initiation (Jer 1:6), but this term can simply mean "fellow" or "young man" as in Jud 17:7, 11, 12; 18:3.

‖‖

Excursus

The word of Yahweh in vss. 8-9 is presented in a more
poetic medium than the dialogue prose pattern of the vision.
This preference for revealing a direct word of Yahweh in poetry
was noteworthy in stage I of the vision form and in Zechariah's
first vision. Thus vss. 8-9 which climax the question-answer
pattern of the vision display a certain parallelism in thought
and language.

פרזות תשב ירושלם (8   As open regions will Jerusalem remain

מרב אדם ובהמה (בתוכה)   From the multitude of men and beasts
                        (within it),

ואני אהיה לה (נאם YHWH) (9   And I will be for her (says the Lord)

חומת אש סביב   a wall of fire about

ולכבוד אהיה בתוכה   As the Glory will I be in her midst.

Even with the suggested emendations (in parentheses above),
the metric balance in these vss. is not ideal, but note the
parallelism between 'ănî 'ehyeh/'ehyeh; ḥômat 'ēs̆/lěkābôd; and
sābîb/bětôkâ.

Yahweh will be the wall of protection around Jerusalem, a
city to be unbound by manmade conventions, a city abundant in
men and goods. The image of fullness parallels the prediction
of cities overflowing with good things in vision I (1:7). The
parallel pair, ḥômāt 'ēs̆/kābôd has a particularly archaic ring.
The wall of fire evokes the pillar of fire, which accompanies
the travelers in the Yahwist's account of the desert trek; the
kābōd is an ancient term for Yahweh's majesty, a term adopted
by P as a technical designation for the revealed presence of
the deity.[132]

The theophanic images of fire and glory once again evoke
themes of the divine warrior. This impression of the divine
warrior is continued and reinforced by the hymnic material
which follows in vss. 10-17. A full discussion of the redaction history of Zech 2:6-17 is beyond the scope of our study of
the vision form itself, a form which ends at vs. 9 in this
pericope. Parts of vss. 10-17 may have once comprised a poetic

132. See F. M. Cross, *Canaanite Myth*, pp. 164-167, 322.

whole which has been broken up by additions and prosaizing
rubrics in the process of transmission. This hymnic material
may have been composed to continue the vision itself or may
have been a separate composition (or compositions) which a
redactor found appropriate to the message of the vision in vss.
8-9. In any event, as the chapter now stands, the conclusion
of vision III, evoking the theme of the divine warrior, serves
as an introduction to the materials which follow. These materials contain the markings of a victory-enthronement pattern,
employed in the context of rescue.

vengeance, victory, and rescue	10-11	Yahweh urges escape to his allies
	12-13	He is to swoop down upon the ene- mies of his people.
rejoicing and cele- bration	14	The rescued rejoice.
enthronement	14-16	Yahweh dwells again in the midst of his people; general in- gathering.
warcry as tagline	17	Inclusio with beginning of pat- tern: Yahweh is aroused.

This material, which fits the traditional pattern outlined
above, and vss. 8-9 of vision III underline the way in which
the restoration and return of the late 6th century B.C., like
the exodus itself, are put in terms of the ancient mythic patterns which evoke the victories of the divine warrior.

Findings from five visions in Zechariah

1. The content pattern of the vision form has become more
flexible, stretched in a narrative direction which allows for
the inclusion of additional motifs supplementary to the ques-
tion/answer core: the date rubric (1:7) and the observation of
divine happenings (1:11ff.; 6:7ff.). These motifs point in the
direction of Daniel and the post-Biblical visions.

The pause before the revelation of the meaning of the symbols in visions V (4:5, 13) and I (1:9) is further evidence
that the vision report process itself is becoming more like the
narration of a story.

Finally and most important, visions V, II, I, and VIII reveal a change in the question motif such that the seer himself
asks for an interpretation of his vision. This shift in the
question motif becomes standard for the form and lends a more
divinatory thrust to the interpretation pattern (see below).

2. The loosening and stretching out of the content pattern is paralleled by a change in the use of language in the
visions of Zechariah. The tight associative technique of stage
I of the vision form, which related the symbol to its meaning
via word-play or simile, is dropped. The economical-rhetorical
style is replaced with a more prosaic medium. All use of repetition is not abandoned, however. In vision II and more particularly in vision VIII, repetition, now devoid of hints of
dream interpretation methodology, creates emphasis and/or
achieves a literary, structural link between parts of the
vision. The repeated terms are not used in a word-play or
simile as in stage I; they do, however, serve a unifying literary function in vision VIII, a function which will be important to the structure of the baroque symbolic visions of Daniel,
2 Baruch, and 4 Ezra.

3. The symbols have become more mythologized and contrast
with the mundane symbol objects of the visions of Amos and
Jeremiah. The symbolic visions of Zechariah make special use
of themes of the divine warrior and the divine council. In
visions II, I, and VIII, the symbols have a quality which we
have described as "real-mythic." The symbol is itself in the
mythic context of the vision. A somewhat simpler relationship
between the symbol and its meaning is reasserted in Daniel 7
and 8.

4. Zechariah's extensive use of the symbolic vision form
implies a certain view of God and his relationship with man.
God is more difficult to reach. Communication with God involves
indirectness, a filter, a code. The dream quality and night
setting of the visions, the more complex and mysterious symbols,
the presence of an intermediary interpreter, and most important,
the unknowing seer's request for an interpretation point to the
transcendence of God, his conceptual distance from man. In
Zechariah's world-view, temple, cult, king, and priest are more
important than ever in that they provide a means of bridging

that gap between man and God. It is in this context that Zechariah and his group could justify the new emphasis placed on
priestly leadership.[133]

---

133. Subsequent to completing this chapter, I have come
across John J. Collins' discussion of the revelation-interpretation phenomenon (*The Apocalyptic Vision of Daniel* [HSM 16;
Missoula: Scholars, 1977], pp. 74-88). I find that some of our
thinking has moved in similar directions. Collins briefly mentions Proto-Zechariah and, in fact, employs some of the same
metaphors as do I. For example, he speaks of the interpreta-
tive process as decipherment, as a filtering process, and so on
(see pp. 75, 77 in particular). While Collins and I agree in
some areas and share some of the same language, we differ considerably in some essentials. For example, my study of the
symbolic vision form shows that Zechariah's visions are firmly
rooted in a prophetic tradition represented by visions of Amos
and Jeremiah. Collins, however, suggests that Zechariah may
have borrowed the symbolic vision from the Babylonians (p. 86).
This view, in turn, must affect his conception of Daniel's
position in the tradition. Again, Collins speaks of mantic
wisdom as a foreign phenomenon while I am interested in showing
that certain varieties of divination - namely those involving
dreams - would have been an acceptable and long-pedigreed means
of receiving divine communication in Israel itself. This means
of communication is more popular in some periods than in others.
This pattern of relative popularity is also of great interest.

Chapter Three

THE BAROQUE STAGE OF THE SYMBOLIC VISION FORM

Daniel 7

1) In the first year of [a]Belshazzar king of Babylon[a]
Daniel saw a dream ⟨   ⟩[b] while in his bed. Then he wrote down
the dream,[c] [d]the essence of it.[d] 2) [e]⟨   ⟩ I saw in my vision
[f]of the night[f] and behold the four winds of heaven were stirring up the great sea. 3) And four great[g] beasts were rising
from the sea, [h]each different from the other.[h] 4) The first
was like a lion and had [i]wings of an eagle. I watched while
its wings were plucked off and it was lifted up from the ground
and made to stand on two feet like a man and the mind of a man
was given to it. 5) And behold[j] another beast ⟨   ⟩[k] like a
bear. It was raised up on one side and three ribs were in its
mouth ⟨   ⟩[l] and thus it was told "Arise, devour much flesh."
6) [m]After this I saw and [n]behold [o]another like a leopard and
it had four bird-wings [p]on its back[p] and the beast had four
heads and dominion[q] was given to it. 7) After this I saw in
my visions of the night and [r]behold a fourth beast terrifying
[s]dreadful, and exceedingly strong.[s] It had great[t] iron teeth.
It devoured and broke into pieces, and the rest it trampled
with its feet. It was different from all the beasts which preceded it, and had ten horns. 8) As I was looking at the
horns,[u] behold another horn, a small one, rose up from among
them,[v] and three of the previous horns were uprooted before it.
Behold, in this horn were eyes like the eyes of a man and a
mouth speaking great things [w]and it made war against the holy
ones.[w]

> 9) I was looking
> until thrones were set up
> And an Ancient One sat down
> His clothing was as white as snow[x]
> And the hair of his head like clean wool[y]
> [z]His throne was [a]flames of fire[a]
> [b]Its wheels burning fire.[b]

10) ^{c}A river of fire flowed
And came forth from before him^c
A thousand thousands were serving him
And myriad myriads stood before him.
^{d}The court sat in judgment
And the books were opened.^{d}

11) I looked then because of the sound of the great words which the horn was speaking ⟨ ⟩^{e} until the beast was killed, its body destroyed and given up to the burning fire. 12) As for the rest of the beasts, their dominion was taken away, but their lives were prolonged for a season and a time. 13) I was looking in the visions of the night and behold with^f the clouds of heaven one like a man^g was coming and unto the Ancient One he came and they brought him before him.^{h} 14) And to him was given dominion and ^{i}glory and kingship.^{i} All peoples, nations, and languages^j serve him. His dominion is an eternal dominion which will not pass away, and his kingdom one which will not be destroyed. 15) As for me Daniel my spirit was anxious ^{k}in its sheath^k and the visions of my head dismayed me.^{l} 16) I approached one of the ones standing about and I sought to know for certain from him about all of this. And he told me^m and the interpretation of the dream he made known to me.

17) "As for these four great beasts ⟨ ⟩,^{n} four kingdoms^o will arise from the earth,^{p} 18) but the holy ones of the most high will receive the kingdom forever, forever and ever."

19) Then I wished to know for certain about the fourth beast who was different from all of them, ^{q}exceedingly terrifying,^{r} its teeth of iron and claws of bronze - it devoured, broke in pieces, and the rest it trampled with its feet - 20) and concerning the ten horns which were on its head and the other that arose before which fell three ⟨ ⟩^{s} - and eyes it had and a mouth speaking great things and its appearance mightier than its fellows' - 21) I was looking and this horn made war against the holy ones and prevailed over them 22) until the Ancient One came and judgment was rendered for the holy ones of the most high and the time came^t and the holy ones took possession of the kingdom. 23) ^{u}Thus he said:^{u}

"As for the fourth beast, a fourth kingdom will

be on earth which is different from [V]all kingdoms.[V]
It will [W]devour the whole earth[W] and trample it, and
break it in pieces. 24) As for the ten horns, from
that kingdom ten kings will arise, and another will
arise after them. He will be different[X] from the
former ones and three kings will he bring low. 25)
And words against the most high he will speak and the
holy ones of the most high he will wear out and he
will think to change the times and the law, and they[Y]
will[Y] be given into his hands until a time, two times,
and a half-a-time. 26) And the court will sit in
judgment and [Z]his dominion will be taken away [a]to be
destroyed and to be destroyed to the end. 27) And
the kingdom and the dominion and the greatness of the
kingdoms under [b]all heaven is to be given to the holy
ones of the most high. Their kingdom will be an
eternal kingdom and all dominions will serve and obey
them."

28) [C]Here was the end of the matter.[C] As for me Daniel, my
thoughts greatly alarmed me and I went pale, but the matter I
kept to myself.

1)   [a]G provides a slightly longer variant of the opening formula, βασιλευοντος βαλτασαρ χωρας βαβυλωνιας. The formula in G
is comparable to those at 1:1, 2:1, and 8:1 while MT parallels
that of 10:1.
       [b]With G omit וחזוי ראשי, an insertion from 4:2 or 7:15.
       [c]With shorter reading in MT. G expands, το οραμα ο ειδεν
εγαψεν.
       [d]Th omits the phrase ראש מלין אמר. G, εγραψεν εις κεφα-
λαια λογων conveys the same notion of "summarizing the essentials" found in MT ראש מלין. With G omit the superfluous אמר.
Admittedly the phrase ראש מלין is not a regular idiom found
elsewhere. Hartman suggests a new translation keeping אמר,
"thus beginning his account."
2)   [e]With Th, G omit ענה דניאל ואמר, an expansionary rubric.
       [f]With G καθ' υπνον νυκτος as in 2:19, בחזוא די ליליא.

3)   [g]G omits רברבן.

[h]G=MT. Th omits this phrase.

4)   [i]M = G[88 - S]. G[967] reads εχουσα ωσει πτερα αετου influenced by כאריה.

5)   [j]G expands και ιδου μετ᾽ αυτην.

[k]Th reads δευτερον, G, αλλο θηριον. MT is a conflation of
both variants, with חיוה אחרי תנינה.

[l]With G[967] omit expansionary בין שניה found in Th, MT, and
88-Syh. Hartman writes that the phrase "between its teeth" is
a hint that an early glossator correctly believed that ʿilʿîn
here means "fangs, tusks." Hartman bases his translation
"tusks" on a metaphorical use of the Arabic ḍalaʿ "rib" to mean
"tusk" or "large tooth" (*The Book of Daniel*, p. 205).

6)   [m]G adds και.

[n]G omits וארו a traditional transition which is to be expected in the presentation of symbols.

[o]G expands to θηριον αλλο.

[p]Th and G read υπερανω αυτης and επανω αυτου respectively,
"upon it."

[q]G reflects an interesting variant reading, και γλωσσα
εδοθη αυτω, "and language was given to it."

7)   [r]G omits וארו.

[s]G has και ο φοβος αυτου υπερφερων, "and the fear of it
was exceedingly strong."

[t]Th omits רברבן.

8)   [u]G has the possessive, εν τοις κερασιν αυτου.

[v]G adds εν τοις κερασιν.

[w]G adds και εποιει πολεμον προς τους αγιους, "And it made
war against the holy ones." In this way, the accusation
against the small horn is found not only in the seer's request
motif (7:21) but also in the description motif. (Note that MT
7:21 expands with ויכלה להון whereas G 7:21 expands differently
with και τροπουμενον αυτους, "And he made them flee." G 7:8
contains neither of these expansions of the "made war" phrase.)
Bentzen and Montgomery follow MT for vs. 8. Like Charles, we
believe MT to be defective and read with G. These words in G
provide proper negative nuancing for the first accusation in
vs. 8 concerning the speaking of great things. The phrase, ופם

ממלל רברבן = και στομα λαλουν μεγαλα, is often compared to
descriptions of the wrongdoings of Antiochus IV in 1 Macc 1:24,

ελαλησεν υπερηφανιαν μεγαλην

He spoke very arrogantly.

"Speaking arrogantly" is clearly a negatively nuanced expression whereas "a mouth speaking great things" might even be considered an expression of respect and awe. A similar contrast
might be made between Dan 7:8 and the references to speech in
Ps 12:4, 17:10, 1 Enoch 1:9, and 5:4. In Ps 12:4, *lāšôn
mĕdabberet gĕdōlōt*, "a tongue which speaks great things," is
paired with *kol siptê ḥălāqôt*, "all flattering speech." The
nuance is clear. Similarly, Ps. 17:10 employs the term *gē'ut*,
"pride," to describe a manner of speech. Finally, the two
passages from 1 Enoch associate the term "words" with a form of
σκληρος, "hard, harsh, unyielding."

και σκληρων ων ελαλησαν λογων

1 Enoch 1:9

κατελαλησατε μεγαλους και σκληρους λογους εν στοματι
ακαθαριας

1 Enoch 5:4

In all of the above, the negative meaning of the speech is made
clear. Without references to arrogance, pride, or harshness,
Dan 7:8 requires mention of Antiochus' hostility towards the
holy ones in order to properly nuance the meaning of the mouth
which speaks great things. If one has no clear indication of
the hostile actions of the little horn, there is no motivation
for the judgment scene which follows. With the mention of the
enemy's hostile treatment of the holy ones in vs. 8, however,
the *rîb* pattern follows a logical progression: 1) sin, wrong-
doing; 2) judgment scene; 3) punishment, sentencing, vengeance.

Moreover, the explanation motif in vss. 17ff. consistently
recalls the description of the vision. It is unlikely that a
detail as important as evidence of the little horn's bad treatment of the holy ones would have been omitted in the initial
description. Montgomery would have us believe that the author
waited to reveal the matter about the battle against the holy
ones until the prophet's speech (vss. 21-22) in order to create
dramatic effect (*The Book of Daniel*, p. 309). Porteous and
others solve the problem by considering vss. 21-22 an expansion

(*Daniel*, pp. 96-97). What then does one do with the reference
to "wearing out the holy ones" in vs. 25? For us, the most
successful explanation is to assume that this image of battle
against the holy ones is found both in the description (vs. 8)
and in the repetition of the description in vs. 21. It is this
aspect of the vision which is alluded to in the explanation
(vs. 25).

9) ^x_GZi χιονα λευκην = MT is based on Just. 967, 88-Syh omit
λευκην, reading simply חלג.

     ^y_GZi εριον καθαρον = עמר נקא again is based on Just. 967
88-Syh add λευκην reading כעמר נקא חור.

     ^{z}G has the article, not the pronoun: ο θρονος.

     ^{a}G reads φλοξ πυρος βαδιξουσα, שביב די נור דלק.

     ^{b}G omits this phrase.

10) ^c_GZi (967) reads και εξεπορευετο κατα προσωπον αυτου ποτα-
μος πυρος, ונפק מן קדמוהי נהר די נור.

     G breaks the parallel poetry of MT, but Charles "with some
hesitation" nevertheless deletes נפק as an explanatory gloss on
נגד.

     ^{d}G reverses the parallel phrases και βιβλοι ηνοιχθησαν
και κριτηριον εκαθισεν.

11) ^{e}G omits חזה הוית עד די and has simply και. Th omits חזה
הוית but retains εως. While there is no pressing reason to
prefer the conjunction to the preposition, we have omitted חזה
הוית as dittographic in accordance with the Greek traditions.

13) ^{f}G reads επι, על. Charles prefers this preposition to MT,
Th עם, viewing the clouds as the chariot of the supernatural
figure (p. 165). Imagery of the storm-god is achieved with
either preposition.

     ^{g}Translate with G. Vermes ("The Present State of the 'Son
of Man' Debate," *JJS* 29 [1978] 123-134).

     ^{h}G reflects a variant reading και οι παρεστηκοτες προσηγα-
γον αυτον, "And those standing by approached him/brought him."

14) ^{i}G is haplographic. The rhythmic run of nouns found in
MT is typical of the style of the author (see below).

     ^{j}G reflects expansion and syntactic variation, και παντα
τα εθην της γης κατα γενη και πασα δοξα λατρευουσα αυτω, "And
all peoples of the earth, nation by nation, and all 'glory'
will serve him." G δοξα may reflect scribal error under the

influence of ויקר earlier in v. 14.

15) [k]G reads εν τουτοις "because of this," but as noted by
Hartman 1 Qap Gen 2:10 reads wnšmty lgw ndnh, "and my spirit
within its sheath." Dan 7:15 contains a Biblical example of
the notion that the body is a vessel or container for the
spirit, a theme found in Rabbinic literature (see Gen Rab 14:7).

[l]G reads εν τω οραματι της νυκτος, perhaps under the influence of vs. 2.

16) [m]G adds αποκριθεις "truly" - a possible dittography from
earlier in the verse.

17) [n]MT ארבע אנין די is an expansionary gloss. MT which refers to the beasts as "large" and "four" may reflect conflation
of two variant readings: Th τα θηρια τα τεσσαρα and G τα θηρια
τα μεγαλα.

[o]On מלכין vocalized molkîn as "kingdoms" see H. L. Ginsberg, Studies, p. 65, n. 6, 8; p. 66, n. 12 and "'King of kings'
and 'lord of kingdoms,'" American Journal of Semitic Languages
and Literatures 57 (1940), 71-74.

[p]G reads αι απολουνται, "which will be destroyed" and con-
centrates upon the fall of the kingdoms rather than upon their
rise. MT reflects the more colloquial and original reading.

19) [q]G adds και.

[r]G adds και ιδου.

20) [s]MT and G include an explanatory gloss וקרנא דכן. This
phrase may be a dittography from vs. 21.

22) [t]G reads εδοθη perhaps reflecting the wording of vs. 12.

23) [u]G reflects some variation: και ερρεθη μοι περι, "And he
said to me concerning...."

[v]G reads πασαν την γην, "all of the earth," possibly influenced by the earlier portion of the vs. in which בארעה
appears.

[w]G omits this phrase.

24) [x]Th, G add κακοις: υπεροισει κακοις; διοισει κακοις υπερ -
"he will be more evil."

25) [y]G adds παντα, "all."

26) [z]G, Th read την εξουσιαν, την αρχην, שלטנא.

[a]G contains an interesting variant reading: και βουλευον-
ται μιαναι "he will resolve to defile."

27) [b]In G the modifier "all" refers to the kingdoms, πασων των
υπο τον ουρανον βασιλειων.

28) [c]In G this phrase comes at the end of vs. 27, and כה is
omitted, εως καταστροφης του λογου.

Patterns of Content Elements	*Rubrics/Formalized Language*
7:1	Date-line	בשנת חדא...
*7:1,2	Indication of vision/dream	חלם חזה
		חלם חזית בהזוי עם ליליא
*7:2-14	Description	וארו...
7:15	Fear of seer	...וחזרי ראשי יבהלנני
*7:16	Seer's request for inter-	יציבא אבעא מנה...
	pretation	ואמר לי ופשר מליא
		יהודענני
*7:17-18	Answer of interpreter	
*7:19-22	Question of seer to interpreter	
*7:23-27	Answer of interpreter	
7:28	Fear/keeping in heart	...רעיוני יבהלנני

A tradition shared by Daniel 7 and the visions of Zechariah emerges immediately in the pattern of content: indication of vision; description; request for interpretation; and
interpretation. The last two elements are found two times in
this vision as in Zechariah vision V. The date rubric, anticipated by the redactional layer of Jeremiah 24 and found in
Zech 1:7, makes its appearance here becoming a common feature of
the pattern. (See our chart in the study of Zechariah vision
I.) Terminology of "seeing" for the indication of the vision
and the "behold" term which introduces the description are also
fully expected.

The basic four-part pattern (starred in the outline above)
is to be distinguished from the pattern of stage I of the
vision form in which the seer does not ask to know the meaning
of the vision. The active request to understand the otherworldly symbolic appearance, found since vision V of Zechariah,
is a key element in a true scene of dream divination.

Throughout our study of the symbolic vision form we have
made a careful distinction between divinatory technique and a
divinatory pattern of events. By a technique we mean the association of like with like which establishes a connection

between that which is seen in the vision and that which is
meant by the symbols. This associative technique lies behind
the visions of stage I, helping to determine their very structure. Again we emphasize that in these visions the seer does
not request an interpretation to his vision; it is merely provided. God creates the symbols and immediately himself provides an explanation; the seer merely observes passively, a
tool in the presentation of the message of the Lord. Thus in
spite of the visions' use of divinatory technique, we do not
consider the chain of events in stage I to proceed in a divinatory fashion or to resemble a situation of dream interpretation.
After stage I, the form develops in a more narrative direction,
and this narrative comes to look more and more like a divinatory exchange between one who experiences a vision and one who
interprets it. The seer actively requests an explanation of
that which he has seen. Revelation comes via interpretation.
At the same time, however, hints of divinatory technique are
not found. The symbol does not relate to its meaning via word-
play or simile, but via deep interrelationships in the ancient
mythology of Near Eastern culture. The studies of the visions
of Zechariah attempt to uncover the roots of these interrelationships. In Daniel 7 such symbols and their meanings are
becoming a formalized language of their own. With regard to
the beasts/empires equation, in fact, one suspects that the
interpreter translates the language of symbols in a way expected by his listeners or readers. On the other hand, on
formal grounds of patterning, content of motifs, etc., the
vision remains fully symbolical with an item for item or scene
for scene revelation of correspondences between symbol and
meaning.

The use of symbols in Daniel 7 is an important subject for
discussion below. First we note how the symbolic form is
becoming more like a story. Certain additional nuances in
Daniel 7 extend the four-part pattern found in Zechariah
visions II, I, and VIII, making this scene of dream interpretation much more of a narrative event.

Narrative touches

In Zechariah vision I, night time is assumed as a setting
(1:8) and the rubric of "seeing" is in the perfect tense. This
combination of night plus a sense of the past gives Zech 1:7-17
the nuance of a dream remembered. Daniel 7 is much more explicit in dream nuance, for the narrator's introduction actually says that a dream (חלם) was seen while Daniel lay on his
bed. Moreover, we are told that Daniel writes down his dream.
Then opens Daniel's first person account in which he speaks of
his visions of the night. In this way we have a rather clear
distinction made between liminal dream-time when one communes
with the divine and normal time when one recalls what has happened that night. This sense of a dream which has been experienced subtly but significantly breaks with the prophetic visions
of stage I. In stage I, the visions come upon the seer suddenly and not necessarily during sleep. The notion of visions
occurring at night is introduced in Zechariah but becomes all
the more explicit in Daniel 7.[1]

The night/dream nuance reflects a decline in direct forms
of revelation and the blossoming of the more indirect method of
learning about the will of God through the filter of the symbolic vision.[2] The distance of a dream provides more to this
filtering effect.[3] One might say that examples of the symbolic
vision form from Amos and Jeremiah (our stage I) are more
ecstatic or direct symbolic visions, those of Zechariah less
so, and those of Daniel the least ecstatic.

---

1. MT of Daniel 8 makes no reference to dreams, i.e.
visions which occur during sleep as opposed to visions of the
day which occur to a waking person. G 8:2 includes the phrase,
εν τω οραματι του ενυπνιου μου, "in the visions of my dream."
Thus Daniel 8 may or may not have as explicit a reference to a
dream event as does Daniel 7.

2. Cf. John J. Collins, *The Apocalyptic Vision*, p. 75.

3. Some of the post-Biblical materials with which we will
deal briefly indicate that the seer sleeps on purpose by command of Yahweh's envoy, in order to receive information through
a dream. The seer in these cases is practicing a form of incubation.

The less immediate quality of the visions of Zechariah and
Daniel also fits our theory about the increasingly literary-
narrative style of the vision form. The tight, catchy rhetori-
cal/economical visions are no more. Zechariah visions V, I, and
VIII, in particular, evidence a stringing out of the dialogue
pattern with lengthy rubrics, delays before the explanation
motif (4:5, 13), and the addition of the observations motif
(1:11-13; 6:7-8). In Daniel 7, an essentially prose work,[4] the
observations of dramatic events have become part of a lengthy
visionary image (the description motif) which indeed is a story
in itself within the divinatory pattern of which it is part.

In addition to the dream/night setting, another factor
contributing to the narrative quality of the vision's basic
pattern is the fear motif. This motif is an expression of the
seer's emotional state after seeing the symbolic images (7:15)
and after hearing the interpretation (7:28).[5]

These narrative elements, the prophet's fear, the night
time setting, and the use of the date-line, are not essential
to the central core of the work, a core composed of the description of the vision and its equally lengthy interpretation.
Nevertheless, the narrative touches which frame these core elements must make us think of Daniel 2 and its older typological
relative, Genesis 41. It is to these folktales about wise
interpreters of dreams that we trace the narrative elements of
Daniel 7.

In a recent paper, the author and her husband show that
Daniel 2, Genesis 41, and The Tale of Aḥikar share a folktale
type, that of the wise hero who obtains a rise in status
because he alone is able to solve a problem posed by his
superior in status.[6] In Genesis 41 and Daniel 2 the specific

---

4. That is, except for vss. 9-10, which we will discuss
below.

5. Note that the interpretation is part of the dream.
This belief that interpretation of one's dream could take place
during the dream or during a second dream was evidently common
throughout the Near East and is part of the lore of dream divination. See Oppenheim, *The Interpretation*, pp. 208, 212.

6. Robert Doran and Susan Niditch, "The Success Story."

difficult problem is to interpret a king's dream. A comparison
between Daniel 2 and Genesis 41 reveals the difficult problem,
dream divination, to be more important in Daniel 2 as it now
stands than in Genesis 41. In Genesis 41 the main theme involves the young Joseph and his rise to become vizier over
Egypt. Dream interpretation is the means of obtaining this
reward. In Daniel 2, the story of the exile's success shares a
place with the universal and cosmically significant message of
the dream itself, a dream which depicts ages of history. In
Daniel 7, the story elements are even less significant. They
are the barest frame. The dream *is* the form, its description
and interpretation its structural pillars. The element of
fear, for example, is mere window dressing, while in Daniel 2
and Genesis 41 the dreamer's fear is the chief motivation for
finding a dream interpreter who in turn is the true protagonist
of the story, the person of lower status around whom the narrative revolves. Indeed the story of how the dream comes to be
interpreted, so central in Genesis 41 and Daniel 2, is virtually non-existent in Daniel 7. The seer asks for interpretation in half a verse and is answered directly, all within his
own vision.

     Clearly, Daniel 7 shares key motifs with Genesis 41 and
Daniel 2: the symbolic dream itself; the desire to understand
it; and the more tangential elements of fear (cf. language in
Dan 4:2 and 7:15) and the time of day. Yet these motifs have
been combined with others into two different forms: the symbolic vision form in which the dream is central and the folktale in which the dream is an important motif, but not the
basis of the form itself. In terms of patterning and nuances
of content, Daniel 7 shares much more with or is more integrally related to the visions of Zechariah than to the tale of
Daniel 2. On the other hand, Daniel 2 and Daniel 7 are both
manifestations of the reblossoming of interest in the literary
and prophetic potential of dreams and their meanings, a renewed
interest which we first observed in the late sixth century B.C.
visions of Zechariah. It must have been a very easy process
for some of the narrative touches - such as the fearful emotional state of the seer or the image of a person who dreams in
bed - to travel from the folktale about a wise interpreter of

dreams to the symbolic dream/vision form itself. Such touches
give more coloration to the personality of the seer while
allowing us a sense of setting. Thus the pattern of Daniel 7
has expanded, becoming more story-like than the visions of
Zechariah. We might diagram the developmental process thus:

> Amos-Jeremiah (economical, tight) $\longrightarrow$ Zechariah V, I,
> VIII (more strung out, more in the direction of narra-
> tive) $\longrightarrow$ Daniel 7 (recognizably narrative frame, with
> story-like elements)
>
> $\uparrow$
>
> Daniel 2
> (folktale about wise interpreter of dreams)

Our next task in the study of Daniel 7 is to explore its
style, the way in which language is used to present the motifs
outlined above.

Strings of terms and simple clauses

In contrast to the economical descriptions of Amos and
Jeremiah, the author of Daniel 7 lengthens his descriptions by
the use of synonymous terms, showing a concern for detail, and
often describing the same image in several ways. Strings of
equivalent adjectives, verbs, or nouns are common, and given
the rules of Aramaic morphology, the synonyms often rhyme, creating sound rhythm. These strings of terms build excitement
and drama, making the reader fully atuned to the imagery, making its impact all the more powerful.

vs. 7   דחילא ואימתני ותקיפא יתירא

vs. 7, 19   אכלה ומדקה ושארא ברגליה רפסה

Such phrases are interspersed with brief, often self-
contained non-enjambed clauses which at times verge on poetic
parallelism by virtue of similarity in syntax and language.

a) vs. 2 subj. + part. + obj.   ארבע רוחי שמיא מגיחן לימא
רבא

vs. 3 subj. + part. + prep. ph.   וארבע חירן רברבן סלקן מן
ימא...

b) vs. 4 perf. pass. vb. + prep. ph.   ...ונטילת מן ארעא

prep. ph. + perf. pass. vb.   ועל רגלין כאנש הקימת

ולבב אנש יהיב לה   subj. + perf. pass. vb. +
                                    prep. ph. (poss.)

ושנין די פרזל לה רברבן...   c) vs. 7 subj. + prep. ph. (poss.) +
                                    pred. adj.

וקרנין עשר לה   subj. + prep. ph. (poss.)

קטילת חיותא...   d) vs. 11 perf. pass. vb. + subj.

והובד גשמה   perf. pass. vb. + subj.

ויהיבת ליקדת אשא   perf. pass. vb. (subj.
                                    understood) + prep. ph.

The above combinations of phrases are not poetic; for the
seemingly or potentially parallel phrases can be separated from
one another by other prosaic phrases as in "c" above; in all
cases the phrases are part of longer, fully prosaic sentence
structures created by coordinating conjunctions. These simple
phrases of like syntax, however, do give the piece a certain
rhythm, as the vision is revealed bit by bit.

The above features, word chains and simple (often self-
contained) clausal constructions, recur throughout the vision
and help to explain the almost poetry of vss. 13 and 14 and
23-27. A number of scholars have seen poetry not only in vss.
9-10, which we too consider genuinely poetic, but also in the
description of the man's presentation to the Ancient (13-14)
and in the expansion of the fourth beast (23-27). Porteous[7]
and Bentzen[8] consider all three segments to be poetic, while
Delcor[9] defines only vss. 9-10, 13-14 as poetry. Other scholars including Rost[10] and Dequeker[11] write that 9, 10, 13 and

---

7. Actually, Porteous uses the term "rhythmical," but he
sets these three segments in a stylistic group apart from the
rest of the vision. We believe that vss. 13-14, 23-17 share a
rhythmical prose style with the rest of the vision. See Porteous' *Daniel: A Commentary* (London: SCM, 1965), p. 96.

8. A. Bentzen, *Daniel* (HAT 19; Tübingen: Mohr, 1937), p.
29.

9. M. Delcor, "Les Sources du Chapitre VII de Daniel," *VT*
18 (1968), 291.

10. L. Rost, "Zur Deutung des Menschensohnes in Daniel
7," *Gott und die Götter* (Festscrift for E. Fascher; Berlin:

14 once belonged to a more ancient poetic whole.

        With the possible exception of vs. 14, vss. 13, 23-27 are
merely further contributors to the rhythmic prose style discussed above. Take for example vs. 13.

                    וארו עם ענני שמיא

                    כבר אנש אתה הוה

Certainly these phrases each have the same number of units and
hence it is easy to find a balanced accent pattern. We even
have rhyme in the last two units of each line on $\bar{e}$ and $\bar{a}$, but
do we have an adherence to poetics? There is no parallelism
as in classical style poetry, nor the economy of language of
the rhetorical style found in the visions of stage I. All one
can say is that we have two equally brief phrases. In this
case, even the syntax of each phrase is not the same; nor indeed is each of the phrases self-contained. The subject of the
supposed bicolon does not come until the second line. These
two phrases or lines in turn are grammatically enjambed to the
next brief phrase, עד עתיק יומיא מטה, which this time is syntactically like and rhyming with כבר אנש אתה הוה, the second
line of the supposed bicolon above. Yet how does the phrase,
וקדמוהי הקרבוהי, relate to its partner in the bicolon arranged
by Kittel and accepted as valid by Bentzen and the rest? This
phrase, קדמוהי הקרבוהי, is simply another brief, self-contained
phrase which allows the image to unroll in small individual
pieces of description. Such is the narrative style of the
author.

        Vs. 14 is parallelistic a b c / c a b; a b c / A c. Again
we notice the chains of synonyms, שלטן ויקר ומלכו; עממיא אמיא
ולשניא, which are a trait of this author's prose style, but
admittedly also a common feature of late poetry.[12] It is fully
possible that in this vs. the author has eased into poetry.
His own medium, filled with synonyms and parallel syntactic
constructions, might easily break into more fully traditional

Evengelische Verlagsanstalt, 1958), 41-43.

        11. L. Dequeker, "Daniel VII et les Saints du Très-Haut,"
Eph. Theo. Lov. 36 (1960), 361.

        12. See our discussion of the theories of P. Hanson and
A. Ehlen in studies of Jer 1:13-19 and Zech 5:1-4 respectively.

phrases as it does in vs. 14b and again at the end of vs. 27.
These usages, however, melt into the essentially prose, if
rhythmic-prose, style of the work. One vs. or half-vs. does
not an ancient reconstructable poem make.

Vss. 23-27 provide further evidence of this rhythmic prose
style. Note the chains in vss. 23, 26, and 27.

ותאכל כל ארעה ותדושנה ותדקנה	vs. 23
... להשמדה ולהובדה	vs. 26
...ומלכותה ושלטנא ורבותא	vs. 27

Simple repeated syntactic constructions are found in vs. 24,

עשרה מלכין יקמון	subj. + vb. *(QWM)*
ואחרן יקום אחריהן	subj. + vb. *(QWM)* + prep. ph.

or better in vs. 25.

ומלין לצד עליא ימלל	d. o. + vb.
ולקדישי עליונין יבלא	d. o. + vb.
ויסבר להשניה זמנין ודת	vb. + d. o.[13]

In the case of vs. 25 in particular, the language seems on
the verge of poetry. "Most high one" and "holy ones of the
most high" are parallel terms for those against whom the fourth
kingdom acts; "speaking against," "wearing out," and "thinking
to change" might also be considered parallel members. More
accurately, however, vs. 25 reflects a building up of images
through simple self-contained clauses which are joined by conjunctions; the syntax of the first two lines is alike while the
third contains a chiastic reversal of vb. and obj. The style
has a simple, dramatic effect, but is not poetic. The unaccept-
ability of viewing vs. 24b as a poetic bicolon emerges best in
translation:

And he will be different from the former ones
Three kings will he bring low.

---

13. Note that syntactically the first phrase of our example from vs. 25 is composed of the vb. ימלל, the direct obj.
מלין, and the prep. ph., לצד עליא. Yet semantically, the
"action phrase" of the line is ימלל מלין לצד, "he will speak
words against," and the obj. of this action is עליא, "the most
high." It is this semantic relationship between the components
of the line which we wish to stress.

Poetry has conceptual as well as structural requirements. What is the concept behind these syntactically alike clauses which links them into poetry? These simple phrases create the effect of a riddle which is being revealed, but are not lines of poetry. Thus we find no evidence of poetic composition in vs. 13, 23-27. Nor can vss. 13-14 be regarded as a continuation of that which we consider to be a poetic snippet in vss. 9-10. Even if vs. 14 can be called poetic, its chain, adding style, has more in common with the rest of Daniel's vision than with the more classical use of balance and parallel pairs in vss. 9 and 10.

Sources and style

We will deal with the poetry in vss. 9-10 in a moment, but first we wish to draw one more conclusion from the fairly consistent style we have found in Daniel 7. Ginsberg,[14] Noth,[15] Dequeker,[16] Jepsen,[17] and Hölscher,[18] all propose source theories for the chapter. The thrust of the above scholars' views is that the reference to the little horn in vs. 8 is from a later source; so too its interpretation and later references to it.[19] All of the above scholars except Ginsberg consider the

---

14. H. L. Ginsberg, *Studies in Daniel* (New York: Jewish Theological Seminary, 1948), pp. 11-23; "The Composition of the Book of Daniel," *VT* 4 (1954), 264, 268.

15. M. Noth, "Zur Komposition des Buches Daniel," *Th. St. und Kr.* 98/99 (1926), 143-163, esp. 144-153.

16. "Daniel VII," 364.

17. A. Jepsen, "Bemerkungen zum Danielbuch," *VT* 11 (1961), 391. Jepsen would date the core of the chapter to some period after Alexander's death, but before Maccabean times.

18. G. Hölscher, "Die Entstehung des Buches Daniel," *Th. St. und Kr.* 92 (1919), 119-123; he views the core as pre-Maccabean.

19. In addition to following Hölscher's suggestions about the secondary origins of the "horn" references, Noth suggests that vss. 9, 10, 13, and 14 were secondarily added to the original vision image, which consisted only of the beasts portion (vss. 2, 4, 5, 6, 7). He would date this "original" layer to

earlier source which does not include the reference to the
little horn to be pre-Antiochan. Ginsberg would place the
"non-little-horn" source in the time of Antiochus IV, but
before the persecutions of 167-6. Against the above group of
scholars and with Montgomery,[20] Delcor,[21] Charles,[22] Rowley,[23]
Porteous,[24] and recently Collins,[25] we agree to the essential
integrity and unity of the chapter. The arguments of the
scholars who believe in the unity of the chapter is further
supported by our stylistic analysis - at least vis à vis vss.
24-25, which are often considered part of a secondary source.

Ginsberg's second layer, for example, includes vss. 8,
11a, 20a-22, and 24b-25. Dequeker includes all of vss. 20 and

---

Alexandrian times! For a good critique of Noth's views, see
Porteous, *Daniel*, p. 97.

20. Montgomery seems to hedge on the unity issue (*A Critical and Exegetical Commentary on The Book of Daniel* [New York:
Scribner, 1927], cf. pp. 95 and 282), never really saying where
he stands. Within his commentary of the text itself, however,
he treats the suspicious vss., such as vs. 8 which refers to
the horn, as an integral and essential part of the vision, and
so we like Delcor (*Le Livre*, p. 141) assume Montgomery to be in
the pro-unity camp.

21. *Le Livre de Daniel* (Paris: Gabalda, 1971), pp. 141-
143.

22. R. H. Charles, *A Critical and Exegetical Commentary
on the Book of Daniel* (Oxford: Clarendon, 1929), pp. xxxvii-
xxxviii.

23. H. M. Rowley, "The Composition of the Book of Daniel,"
VT 5 (1955), 272-276; "The Unity of the Book of Daniel," *The
Servant of the Lord and Other Essays* (Oxford: Blackwell, 1965),
266-269.

24. N. Porteous, *Daniel*, pp. 96-97. Porteous, however,
considers vss. 21-22 to be a minor interpolation.

25. John J. Collins, "The Son of Man and the Saints of
the Most High in the Book of Daniel," *JBL* (1974), 53. See his
n. 23 for a detailed outline of the pro-unity and anti-unity
points of view; Collins' opinions are reproduced and expanded
in his *Apocalyptic Vision*, pp. 127-132.

24 as well in this source while Hölscher includes also the end
of vs. 7. Yet we have noted that vss. 24-25 are good examples
of the "brief clause" style of the author, while the end of vs.
7 is a complement in syntax to an earlier portion of the verse.
While an argument based on stylistics alone is obviously not
definitive proof for the unity of the chapter, it is interesting that some of scholars' "questionable" verses seem fully in
line with stylistic trends in other portions of the vision,
portions which these scholars would claim to be an earlier
layer or source. The continuity in style between vss. 13-14
and the rest of the vision also supports our case against
scholars who claim that vss. 9-10 and 13-14 once formed a
poetic whole.

Vss. 9-10, poetry and the anthological style

While we believe that vss. 9-10 have always been an integral part of the vision, we suggest that these vss. describing
the Ancient might have been snipped from another composition
which had its own integrity of form. The author of Daniel 7
simply employed these verses in his own work. Vs. 9a (- עד די
יתב)   and the end of vs. 10 (דינא - פתיחו) may be transitions
which the author set at the beginning and end of the borrowed
segment in order to have it blend into the context of the
vision; for these two transitionary bits display the brief syntax pattern parallels discussed above, while not displaying the
true poetic parallelism of the rest of vss. 9 and 10.

לבושה כתלג חור
ושער ראשה כעמר נקא
כרסיה שביבין די נור
גלגלוהי נור דלק
נהר די נור נגד
ונפק מן קדמוהי
אלף אלפין ישמשונה
ורבו רבון קדמוהי יקומון

The style of this description differs significantly from
that of the remainder of the chapter. In particular we contrast the use of parallel pairs - לבושה / שער ראשה; תלג חור /
עמר נקא; כרסיה / גלגלוהי - with the strings of synonyms in vs.

14. In our discussion of the redactional layers of Jeremiah 1,
we noted that good Hebrew archaic or archaizing poetry is characterized by a flexibly formulaic use of language. Images created should be fresh while traditional. Strings of synonyms,
stock phrases, repetitions in syntax, rhyme, and very long
lines are the marks of late, "neo-classical" poetry.

Given the decent balance between cola, which average in
the 8 syllable range,[26] the use of parallel pairs, and the
vivid and fresh yet fully traditional imagery, one must call
this piece from Daniel 7 an example of good archaic-style
poetry in Aramaic. Then one is led to questions of authorship
and original language. Could the author of Daniel 7 have composed this piece of poetry? Given the difference in style
between vss. 9-10 and the rest of the composition, we doubt
that the same author is responsible for both, though the presence of good parallelism in vss. 9-10 does not itself necessarily imply that they were composed long before the rest of
Daniel 7 or in a language other than Aramaic. A number of the
Aramaic incantation texts discussed by Montgomery and more recently by Isbell display a very traditional-style use of parallelism and formulaic expression, and these works are centuries later than Daniel 7.[27]

On the other hand, certain features of Dan 7:9-10 stand
out as extremely archaic. The term ʿattîq yômîn is suggestive
of the epithet applied to El in Ugaritica V, malku ʾabū šanîma,
"king, father of years."[28] As we shall discuss in more detail
later, the image of the white-haired elder figure is similarly
suggestive of the head of the Canaanite pantheon. The combination of archaic imagery, epithet, and poetics might lead one to
hypothesize that the author of Daniel is quoting from much

---

26. By averaging we are applying the technique suggested
by David N. Freedman, "The Structure of Job 3," *Biblica* 49
(1968), 503-508.

27. J. A. Montgomery, *Aramaic Incantation Texts from
Nippur* (Philadelphia: Univ. of Penn., 1913); C. D. Isbell,
Corpus of the Aramaic Incantation Bowls (Missoula: Scholars,
1975).

28. See F. M. Cross, *Canaanite Myth*, p. 16.

older Phoenician material. Comparisons with the work of Philo
of Byblos come to mind. Philo, a first century scholar whose
work is preserved by Eusebius, actually claims to use sources
from the Phoenician Sanchuniathon.[29] In the case of Daniel 7
as in the case of Philo's work, it is impossible to assert that
the author quotes directly from ancient materials. It seems
more likely that such materials were preserved in and mediated
through more recent sources. Nevertheless the ultimate antiq-
uity of elements contained in Daniel 7 cannot be doubted.

While the epithet ʿattîq yômîn and the image of the white
haired figure have no specific parallels in OT, the streams of
fire, the thrones, and the attending myriads, also as old as
Canaanite images of the divine court, are found elsewhere in
OT. The image cluster of wheels, shining fire, and thrones
evokes Ezek 1:16ff. and 10. One also thinks of the somewhat
simpler imagery of the initiation scene in Isaiah 6. The use
of this image cluster in 1 Enoch 14:18-22 is even more relevant
to our discussion of Daniel 7.

In Enoch, the description of the enthroned deity is part
of a heavenly tour genre, a genre of literature also found in
the Slavonic Enoch and in 3 Baruch.[30] Charles dates 1 Enoch
14:18-22 to pre-Maccabean times.[31] Vss. 18-20 appear to be
found at Qumran (4QEn[c] I viii).[32] What is most interesting
about this fragment, once reconstructed from the Greek into the
Aramaic, is the similarity of single terms and longer expressions used to describe the enthroned deity to those of Daniel
7:9-10. The wheels ([גלגלוהי]) are present with the throne
([כרסיא]); also found are the streams of fire (שבלין ד]י נור[

---

29. *Praeparatio evangelica*, I 9, 21. See the discussion
of L. R. Clapham, "Sanchuniathon: The First Two Cycles" (unpub-
lished doctoral dissertation, Harvard University, 1969), pp.
2-6.

30. See also 2 Cor 12:1-4 for an allusion to the heavenly
tour.

31. *A critical and Exegetical Commentary*, p. 183.

32. J. T. Milik, *The Books of Enoch* (Oxford: Clarendon,
1976), p. 199, Pl. 13. Milik dates the script of the fragment
to the late Herodian period.

versus נור די שביבין די נור/נהר in Daniel) and the comparison
between the deity's clothing and white snow (ת[לגא מן וחור
versus כתלג חור in Daniel). The Greek version of Enoch goes on
to mention the "myriads, myriads standing before him," κυκλω
μυριαδες μυριαδες εστηκασιν ενωπιον αυτου (vs. 22) which corre-
spond to MT Dan 7:10 רבו רבון קדמוהי יקומין and to G Dan 7:10,
μυριαι μυριαδες παρειστηκεισαν αυτω. While this passage from
the Greek version of Enoch, employed by Milik in his extensive
reconstruction, is set in a narrator's first person prose
account, many of the familiar formula patterns of the poem from
Daniel 7 are discernible.[33] The phrase, שבלין די נור, is a
good oral-traditional variant of שביבין די נור or of נהר די נור;
חור מן תלגא is a flexible variant of כתלג חור.

Enoch 14:18-22 and Dan 7:9-10 suggest that there were certain accepted ways to describe the enthroned deity in the second century B.C. Such descriptions probably would have been
especially common in the heavenly tour genre. Enoch 14:18-22
is a prosaized version of one of these enthronement scenes.
Dan 7:9-10 is a poetic account which may have been snipped from
a larger work, one which employed more ancient materials, translated into the Aramaic. The important point is that both share
not only the traditional imagery which we can trace back to
descriptions of the Canaanite El, but also a flexibly traditional means of expressing this imagery.

If our suspicions are correct that Daniel borrowed a
poetic description from another work, then we have an interesting insight into his style. Like the Qumran covenanters who
often quote from other sources or the Chronicler who combined
two psalms and inserted them into his account of the celebra-
tion before the ark in 1 Chronicles 16 (1 Chron 16:8-22 = Ps
105:1-15; 1 Chron 16:23-33 = Ps 96:1-13), the author of Daniel
7 is adopting an anthological style. He is not merely re-
using older traditions, adapting them and creating new syntheses relevant for his own time, as is true of Zechariah, but he
is incorporating in whole cloth another author's expression of

---

33. On formula patterns see A. B. Lord, *The Singer*, p.
44. For an application of Professor Lord's theories see S.
Niditch and R. Doran, "The Success Story."

those traditions. This is a further indication of the self-
conscious, planned, and in this sense, literary style of the
author.

Repetition: unity of form

Finally we turn to the topic of repetition as employed in
this version of the symbolic vision form. Repetition of key
symbol terms to create metaphor or sound-play is essential to
structural integrity in the visions of stage I. As discussed,
this technique is a reminiscence of dream interpretation methodology. Saying that *qāyiṣ* means *qēṣ* creates a sympathetic-
magical relationship which helps the "end" to come about. In
the visions of Zechariah, this particular technique virtually
disappears, even while the motif of the seer's request for
interpretation makes the vision scene seem more like an act of
divination than the visions of stage I. (See our introduction
for some possible explanations of this paradox.) In some of
the visions of Zechariah, a term used to describe the symbol is
occasionally mentioned in a later motif (the interpreter's
reply in II, 2:2; V, 4:10b or the seer's question in V, 4:11),
but such repetitions play the purely literary function of linking motif to motif. This technique is used more effectively
and consistently in the last vision of Zechariah. Here we find
it again in Daniel 7.

The fourth beast of the description motif (vss. 7-8) is
recalled virtually verbatim when Daniel asks for more detailed
information about that symbol in vss. 19-22. A number of terms
used to describe the visionary image or its recapitulation in
the question motif are then intertwined into the explanation
motif.

Interpretation		Symbolic Image	
תשנא מן כל מלכותא	vs. 23	משניה מן כל חיותא	vs. 7
ותדקנה	23	ומדקה ומדקה	7 19
מלין...ימלל	25	פם ימלל פם ימלל	8 20
ומלכותה ושלטנא ורבותא...	ולה יהיב שלטן ויקר ומלכו 27		14
יהיבת לעם קדישי עליונין		דינא יהיב לקדישי עליונין	22

As noted by Porteous, the fourth beast, the one which
deals with the author's own actual time period, is the one
which concerns him most.[34] Thus it is the most fully described
beast and its description the most fully repeated. Of course
the mention of the four beasts in the explanation at vs. 23,
and of the ten horns when they are explained in vs. 24 serve
as subject headings which also tend to unify the piece. A
simple demonstrative pronoun plus the copula would not do as an
introduction to the explanation of the symbols in this lengthy
and complex vision. Each piece of the puzzle must be recalled
by a title, as repetition of the symbol terms becomes essential
to the literary unity of the work.

*Symbols: Near Eastern background and the use of symbols in
    Daniel 7*

The symbols of Daniel 7 have had a more thorough scholarly
examination than those of any of the visions with which we have
worked thus far. Recent articles by A. Caquot, the commentary
by N. Porteous, and the monograph by J. Collins give rather
detailed reviews of major approaches.[35] For this reason we
will not go over old ground and will feel free to deal with the
symbols in terms of the main interests of this monograph.

Unlike the static symbols of Zechariah vision V, which are
related to one another thematically but which are essentially
self-contained, the symbols of Daniel 7 interrelate in a narrative drama, all within the vision form itself. As noted in our
last two studies of Zechariah, the horse-rider and horse-
chariot scenes of visions I and VIII respectively are transitionary to this more dramatic variety of symbolic imagery.
Whereas the action scenes involving the horse symbols seem to
be tacked on to the end of visions I and VIII of Zechariah, the
symbolic action in Daniel becomes that about which the seer
inquires, that is, the symbolic stuff of the description motif.

---

34. *Daniel*, p. 106.
35. A. Caquot, "Les Quatre Bêtes et le Fils d'Homme
(Daniel 7)," *Semitica* 17 (1967), 50-62; Porteous, *Daniel*, pp.
98-102; Collins, *The Apocalyptic Vision*.

Thus in Daniel 7, the symbolic imagery must be dealt with somewhat more synthetically than, for example, the lamps, menorah, and trees of Zechariah vision V. Once again, however, it will suit our purposes to think in terms of two sides of an equation, x, the given description = y, the explanation of that seen image as provided within the vision.

As noted by many scholars, the image cluster of beasts, sea, destruction of beasts, elevation of a younger figure by an elder is reminiscent of the ancient Near Eastern myths which describe the destruction of chaos and the rise in status of the victorious young deity. Earlier scholars such as Gunkel, followed by E. Heaton, tended to compare Daniel 7 to the Babylonian *Enūma Eliš*. This creation myth deals with the defeat of Tiamat, a beast-producing female sea deity, by the young god Marduk.[36] More recent lines of scholarship point to the parallels between Daniel 7 and the El/Baal/Yam Canaanite version of this mythic type.[37] With Cross and Collins, we find the suggestions of Emerton most compelling.[38] Specific details of the imagery in Daniel 7, the white haired appearance of the elder figure and the association of clouds with the son figure, point in particular to scenes of El and Baal. Such imagery, of course, was applied to Yahweh at an early time.[39]

---

36. Gunkel, *Schöpfung und Chaos in Endzeit und Urzeit* (Göttingen: Vandenhoeck & Ruprecht, 1895), pp. 323-335; Ellis W. Heaton, *The Book of Daniel* (London: SCM, 1956), pp. 171-175.

37. A. Bentzen, *King and Messiah* (London: Lutterworth, 1955), p. 75; *Daniel*, p. 33; L. Rost, "Zur Deutung," 42-43; J. A. Emerton, "The Origin of the Son of Man Imagery," *JTS* N.S. 9 (1958), 225-242; John J. Collins, *The Apocalyptic Vision*, pp. 95-106.

38. Cross, *Canaanite Myth*, p. 17 and p. 17, n.345; and Collins, "The Son," 51, 53.

39. We disagree with Emerton's suggestion that Yahweh may have been subservient to El Elyon in a brief period after David's conquest. In this way, Emerton would explain how the Baal figure in Daniel 7, whose imagery is much like that associated with Yahweh in OT, is subservient to the elder El figure (240-241). With Cross we agree that both El and Baal imagery

The author of Daniel 7 has adapted these themes, the defeat of chaos and the enthronement, to his own purposes. As
noted by Collins and Porteous, the all-important battle-conflict
element is absent in Daniel 7.[40] The destruction of the beasts
is not the result of the warlike efforts of the figure who
appears with the clouds, but a result of the judgment scene,
suggested by the set thrones and open book of the divine court.
In fact the pattern, 1) presentation of wrong-doing (7:8), 2)
scene of judgment (7:10), 3) punishment (7:11), is subtly suggestive of the prophetic lawsuit form. We agree with G. E.
Wright's view of the $r\hat{\imath}b$ form as one which combines aspects of
secular treaties with mythological concepts of the heavenly
council.[41] In this way we consider the author of Daniel 7 to
be participating in the renaissance of ancient creation myths
while employing the mythological traditions of the divine court,
so important in the works of the classical prophets. Thus like
the author or school of authors responsible for the visions of
Zechariah, the author of Daniel 7 innovates but constantly
links himself to the older tried and true traditions, creating
new syntheses appropriate to his message.

---

and terminology were attributed to Yahweh in pre-monarchic
times (*Canaanite Myth*, pp. 46-75, 89-90, 113-190). The author
of Daniel has adapted these traditions to his own purposes.
One need not like J. Morgenstern be fixated on the fact that
each image complex which is applied to the elder and the
younger figures in Daniel 7 also belongs to Yahweh in various
OT contexts ("The 'Son of Man' of Daniel 7 13 f. A New Interpretation," *JBL* 80 [1961], 65-77).

    40. See *The Apocalyptic Vision*, p. 105, and *Daniel*, p.
99. A distant reflection of the battle theme may be found in
the battle against the holy ones (our reconstructed vs. 8b) and
in their subsequent victory. On the other hand, the son figure
in the passage does not seem to engage in a battle which brings
about a victory against the forces of evil.

    41. "The Lawsuit of God: A Form-critical Study of Deuter-
onomy 32," *Israel's Prophetic Heritage*, eds. B. W. Anderson and
W. Harrelson (New York: Harper, 1962), 26-67.

Thus we view the background of the symbolic imagery of
Daniel 7. What of the other side of the equation? In the context of the vision, the four beasts are interpreted to be four
kingdoms. Scholars generally agree that the kingdoms meant are
Babylonia, Media, Persia, and Greece, the same group which is
meant in Daniel 2:36ff. where Nebuchadnezzar, king of Babylon,
is told that his kingdom is the first about which the dream
symbols speak.[42] The list minus Babylonia is also found in
Daniel 8:20, 21. The ten horns are rulers (probably successive
rulers) of the period following Alexander's death.[43] The little horn which becomes great is Antiochus Epiphanes. We note
that the horn(s) is not used in the highly mythologized manner
of Zechariah vision II, where it emphasizes the divine warrior
theme. In Daniel 7, the horn, a symbol of strength and domi-
nance, refers to political powers.

A. Caquot traces the association between the eagle-winged
lion, the bear, and the leopard and the Babylonian, Median, and
Greek kingdoms respecively to Babylonian astrological texts and
their descriptions of signs of the zodiac.[44] His associations
are too imprecise, requiring too many exceptions and allowing
for too many accommodations. With the mainstream of scholars
from Montgomery on, we would compare the list of four beasts to
the four metals of the creature in the vision of Daniel 2. In
each vision we find,

> the progressive degeneration of the kingdoms of this world:
> from gold to iron the basest of metals, from the eagle-
> winged lion, typifying the kings of beasts and birds, down
> through the meaner bear and leopard to a nameless monster,
> whose business is destruction.[45]

---

42. See H. H. Rowley, *Darius the Mede and the Four World
Empires in the Book of Daniel* (Cardiff: Univ. of Wales, 1959),
pp. 98-120.

43. See Porteous, *Daniel*, pp. 106-107, for a review of
scholarship.

44. A. Caquot, "Sur les Quatre Bêtes de Daniel VII,"
Semitica 5 (1955), 5-13; Caquot is followed by Delcor, *Le Livre*,
pp. 144-147.

45. J. A. Montgomery, *Book of Daniel*, p. 283.

The emphasis of symbols in both of these visions is on four
successive kingdoms.

The winged lion is familiar to us from the art of Assyria-
Babylonia. Both the eagle and the lion are associated with
Babylonia in OT (Jer 50:44; Ezek 17:3). Moreover, the reference to the mind of a man which is given to the beast (Dan 7:4)
must be an allusion to the tradition associated with Nebuchadnezzar, the Babylonian king, in Daniel 4.

The associations of the bear with Media and the leopard
with Persia are less easily explained. Scholars point to the
swiftness of the leopard or panther and the speed associated
with the forces of the Persians. As suggested by Porteous for
the fourth beast, it is more likely that these images were
selected and adapted to fit the particular interests of the
author, a writer of the time of the Maccabean revolt against
Antiochus IV.[46] This suggestion is a significant one; for in
agreeing with Porteous we are saying that Daniel's use of symbols is quite planned. The meaning or interpretation exists in
the mind of the author before he creates his visionary image.
The process is quite self-conscious. As regards the author's
view of the events of the past and the present, that is, up to
his own times, we believe the above description of the self-
conscious use of symbols in Daniel 7 to be accurate. The mysterious symbols of Daniel 7 through vs. 8 are more conscious
products of the mind than those of the visions of Zechariah or
of the visions of stage I. Even the meaning of the three ribs
in the bear's mouth (7:5) and the identity of the three horns
overthrown by the little horn (7:8), topics which scholars have
debated for years, probably held a see-through historical meaning for the circle whom Daniel addressed.

We should also emphasize that the author is adopting the
fiction that he is looking into the future as a seer who lives
in the time of Belshazzar, king of Babylon, a fiction which
must have been understood by his readers.[47] The same fiction
will be found in examples of the symbolic vision form in 4 Ezra

---

46. *Daniel*, p. 106.

47. See John J. Collins, *The Sibylline Oracles of Egyptian Judaism* (Missoula: Scholars, 1972), p. 9.

and 2 Baruch. This device allows the author to maintain the
use of a symbolic form of prophecy - to retain use of the
revelation-interpretation phenomenon with its implicit insist-
ence on the all-knowingness of God and the ingorance of the
prophet. Paradoxically, however, a major part of his interest
is to provide an overview of history, of that which is already
known to have happened. These events of the past provide a
larger cosmic setting in which to place his view of the future.
Such a device of predating one's work by centuries is another
aspect of the literary, even artificial, style of the author's
use of the symbolic vision form, a usage quite different from
that of his precursors.

This fiction of the past as well as the basic agreement of
scholars on the identity of the four beasts, the ten horns, and
the little horn underline the see-through and literary quality
of the use of symbols in Daniel 7:1-8. The same cannot be said
of the portion of the vision beginning with the appearance of
the Ancient in vs. 9. We will leave this portion of the vision
which refers to future events for a later discussion. Suffice
it to say that with Dequeker and Porteous we agree that a different quality enters the vision at the time when Daniel finds
himself within the divine council, observing its activities.[48]
First, however, we must examine more closely this readily perceived identification between the four beasts and the four
empires. The notion of four successive kingdoms, the last of
which will be overthrown and replaced by a final and eternal
idyllic kingdom, has its own integrity in Near Eastern tradition. Daniel 7 shares the use of this theme with a number of
local cultures and with the redactor of Daniel 2.

We might state that we do not believe the vision of Daniel
7 to be based on that of Daniel 2 or vice versa.[49] The core
narrative of Daniel 2 may be much earlier than the final version. Like the Book of Esther, it is another of the exile's
tales of success in a foreign court.[50] Even in its earliest
stage of redaction, it is fully possible that the wise man's

48. Dequeker, "Daniel VII," 362; Porteous, *Daniel*, p. 107.
49. Contrast Collins, *The Apocalyptic Vision*, pp. 158-159.
50. See S. Niditch and R. Doran, "The Success Story."

problem in Daniel 2 was to interpret a dream. Such a feat,
allowing for the help of God, would have been as fully acceptable an activity for a Jewish hero of the post-exilic period as
for the young Joseph of the Elohist's account in Genesis 41.
We recall our discussion of the declining use of dreams and
visions as a literary motif and credible prophetic activity in
the period of classical prophecy and its resurgence in the
post-exilic period. The dream motif employed by the Elohist,
like the ancient Near Eastern myths about the defeat of chaos,
are used with a new freedom and blossom after the exile.[51] The
night visions of Zechariah and the story about Daniel evidence
this renewed interest in dream visions.

On the other hand, the specific dream now included in
Daniel 2 as the "difficult task motif" must be later than the
story which surrounds it - that is, if our suspicions about an
early date for the core of Daniel 2 are correct. The dream in
Daniel 2 is a closer contemporary to the dream in Daniel 7;
both contain the theme of the four kingdoms. Different symbols
are used in each to represent Babylonia, Media, Persia, and
Greece. In our view, the version of the kingdoms theme in
Daniel 7 is later than that of Daniel 2.

A handle for the approximate date of the dream in Daniel 2
is provided by the symbol of mixed clay and iron feet (2:32).
These symbols are interpreted within the vision to mean that
during the rule of the fourth kingdom "they will mix with one
another in marriage but they will not hold together just as
iron does not mix with clay" (2:42-43). With Porteous, Delcor,
and most, we believe that these verses refer to one or more of
the marriages between members of the Ptolemaic and Seleucid
royal families, attempts by the leaders of these dynasties to
re-unify part of the old Alexandrian empire.[52] The first of
these marriages between Berenice Syra, the daughter of Ptolemy
Philadelphus II, and Antiochus II took place ca. 252 B.C.; the
last such marriage was between Cleopatra I, daughter of

---

51. For some possible explanations of this phenomenon,
see our introduction.

52. Porteous, *Daniel*, pp. 49-50; Delcor, *Le Livre*, p. 85;
Collins, *The Apocalyptic Vision*, pp. 45-46.

Antiochus III, and Ptolemy V in 193 B.C. These dates would
seem to provide termini ad quo and ad quem. There is little
doubt that the dream in Daniel 2 is not so late as the time of
Antiochus IV; for we have no reference in this dream to particular persecutions or hardships imposed by him. There is none of
the rancor reserved for the reference to his rule in the vision
of Daniel 7. As Collins notes of the dream in Daniel 2, "The
dream implied ultimate destruction of Gentile rule, but this
was not emphasized."[53] In other words, the polemic is on the
order of a general doom prediction. For the third century or
second century B.C. reader, this vision implied the ultimate
defeat of foreign overlords. The present kingdom would pass
away as did those which preceded it.

In contrast to the vision of Daniel 2, the vision of
Daniel 7 employs the four kingdoms theme to present a vitupera-
tive polemic against the dregs of the last kingdom, the little
horn which arises from the fourth and most horrible beast. The
little horn prevails against the holy ones, but will itself be
destroyed.

Questions still remain about the background of this kingdoms theme which is used so effectively by each of the above
authors. A. Caquot, John J. Collins, and many others have
shown that the four kingdoms pattern was a relatively common
literary phenomenon. For example, the *Bahman Yasht*, a work
which also employs metals as symbols for the four ages (indeed
the same order of metals as in Daniel 2) is a Persian example
or representative of the four kingdom scheme.[54] Collins notes

---

53. John J. Collins, "The Court Tales in Daniel and the
Development of Apocalyptic," *JBL* 94 (1975), 229.

54. A. Caquot, "Les Quatre Bêtes," 39-50. John J. Collins, *The Sibylline Oracles*, pp. 9-14. For further bibliography see Collins, ch. 1, n.85, and also J. Lebram, "Die Welt-
reiche in der judischen Apokalyptik," *ZAW* 76 (1964), 328-331.
Collins writes that the similarities between the *Bahman Yasht*
and the vision in Daniel may indicate that they go back to a
common source (*The Sibylline Oracles*, p. 11). We do not believe
a common origin is necessary to explain the close similarities.
Also contrast Collins, *The Apocalyptic Vision*, pp. 41, 43.

that the four kingdom pattern is found in Herodotus and even
earlier in Hesiod, while Caquot takes note of the theme of four
ages or *yugas* in Indian mythology. In our opinion, neither the
author of Daniel 7 nor the redactor responsible for the inclusion of the four kingdoms theme in Daniel 2 need have borrowed
it from some particular source, so widespread was it. Each of
these authors has adapted this view of history to his own
message.

     Thus we suggest that the dream which includes the four
kingdoms schema was inserted into the narrative pattern of
Daniel 2 sometime in the late third or early second century
B.C. For the author of Daniel 7, this dream complete with
kingdoms theme was integrally involved in the intial composition process. The use of the kingdoms theme in Daniel 7 re-
turns us to a discussion of symbols as language. The complex
symbols in Daniel have become like a language, one which is
readily translatable into a comprehensive cosmology of four
empires. In other words, four metals in descending values,
found in Daniel 2 and the *Bahman Yasht*, or the four beasts of
descending nobility, found in Daniel 7, would have immediately
evoked the four empires theme. We would not, however, call
Daniel 7 an allegory; for formally it is a neat symbolic
vision.[55] Questions are asked about the seen images and appropriate interpretations are given (cf. comments on Zechariah
vision III).

     The correspondence between the beasts and the empires is,
in fact, somewhat more precise than the correspondence between
the image of the Ancient, the judgment scene, and the enthronement scene and their explanation which comes first in the one
cryptic line at vs. 18. Is the symbol language of these later
images less immediately intelligible? Are we dealing with less
of a comprehensible language? With these questions we return
to our observation concerning the differing quality of the symbols which refer to the period before and during the author's
own time versus those which refer to a future time.

     The meaning of the holy ones of the most high - the given
interpretation of the son figure - is most important in this

---

     55. Contrast Collins, *The Apocalyptic Vision*, pp. 95ff.

context.[56] A number of scholars, including Procksch, Noth, and
Dequeker, suggest that the term "holy ones" originally referred
to heavenly beings or angels in the earliest layer of this
passage,[57] as does the term "holy ones" elsewhere in OT.[58]
These scholars believe that the text was later reworked in
order to have the term *qaddîšîm* apply to the persecuted Jews.
Vss. 21, 22, and 25 which contain this nuance would thus seem
to evidence the hand of a later redactor. Coppens believes
that "holy ones of the most high" refers to heavenly beings
throughout the chapter.[59]

The more popular view regards the *qaddîšîn* as a term for
the faithful among the people.[60] Bentzen goes further and suggests that the notion of a corporate, primal man lies behind
the son figure who is the representative of the people.[61] In
any event, for this second group of scholars, son = holy ones =
people. Their suggestion seems to fit the context of the passage better than the identification of holy ones with angels,
especially given our preference for regarding the chapter as a
unity. On the other hand, the relationship between symbol and
meaning is still not entirely clear and differs significantly
from the precise one to one correspondences between beasts and
kingdoms. The equation between son and holy ones has some of
the same quality as the imagery of Zechariah visions V and VI,
in which both sides of the symbol/meaning equation were rather

---

56. For a good review of current theories see Caquot,
"Les Quatre Bêtes," 66.

57. O. Procksch, "Der Menschensohn als Gottessohn," *Christentum und Wissenschaft* 3 (1927), 429; M. Noth, "Die Heiligen
des Höchsten," *Gesammelte Studien zum Alten Testament* (Vol. 1;
München: Kaiser, 1966), 274-290; Dequeker, "Daniel VII," 390-392.

58. See Collins, "The Son of Man," 52. Note that Ps
34:10 is an exception. For use of the term to mean "angels"
see Ps 89:6, 8; Job 5:1; 15:15; Zech 14:5.

59. J. Coppens, "La Vision Danielique du Fils d'Homme,"
VT 19 (1969), 181-182.

60. See, for example, Montgomery, *Book of Daniel*, p. 307;
Porteous, *Daniel*, p. 112; Delcor, "Les Sources," 305.

61. *King and Messiah*, pp. 75, 109, n.5.

mysterious and otherworldly. What is the significance of this
mysterious symbol scene in Daniel 7 for future events on earth?
What is this rule which is forever and shall not pass away?

It is very tempting to interpret the holy ones simply as
God's faithful on earth and to compare this prediction about an
eternal kingdom to the promise to David in Ps 89.[62] Vss. 18
and 27 certainly translate the son figure into something more
than an individual. We agree with Delcor and others that the
son figure does not represent a messiah of the Davidic line.
We cannot agree, however, that the enthronement scene represents the victories of a historical Israel and her king.[63] In
this, Daniel 7 differs from Zechariah visions IV and V in which
specific historical figures are pictured in an enthronement or
elevation scene which is set in the divine council. If the
message in Daniel 7 is about political, historical victory, it
does not include reference to an individual king; but rather,
as Cross notes, it is an interesting democratization of the
political structure such that rule is given not to one person,
but to the people represented by the figure of the son.[64] Yet,
is a political view of a new earthly kingdom that which the
author has in mind? So believe Delcor, Caquot, and Porteous.[65]
Are we dealing with the same historical time-line upon which
ruled the four kingdoms, represented by the beasts?

The image of an unending kingdom which belongs to the holy
ones contrasts sharply with the set-up of the world portrayed
by the symbols of Zechariah vision V. In the latter, a relationship with God is mediated through cultic and political
institutions on earth. Even in the visions of Zechariah in
which the symbols are interpreted to be themselves - to be real
on the mythic plane - one senses no major break with the mythopoeic world-view of the Biblical prophets. Divine influences,
even heavenly beings, dip down into the human realm, affecting

---

62. Note D. Hillers, *Covenant: The History of a Biblical
Idea* (Baltimore: Johns Hopkins, 1969), pp. 116-117.

63. Delcor, "Les Sources," 305.

64. *Canaanite Myth*, p. 17.

65. Delcor, "Les Sources," 305; Caquot, "Les Quatre
Bêtes," 69; Porteous, *Daniel*, p. 112.

the whole course of history on earth, but ultimately the divine
beings or instruments return to their own realm. Ritual and
myth is the means by which the two realms, the earthly and the
divine, are kept in touch. King and priest, appointees of the
Lord, and divinely sanctioned social and political institutions
remain the means by which the human realm is governed. In
Daniel 7, one is not so sure that normal, political, worldly
institutions remain intact.[66] The notion in Daniel 7 of a
kingdom which will last forever is akin to the image in Daniel
2 of the mountain which comes to fill the whole earth (2:35).
In Daniel 2, this "stone not cut by human hand" which becomes a
great mountain is also interpreted to mean that God will set up
a kingdom which will last forever. What is the nature of this
eternal government? We have already noted the seeming absence
of a single appointed head of state.

It is probable that the author of Daniel 7 regarded the
Maccabean revolt as a momentous event which would change the
nature of political institutions; the nature of this new gov-
ernance was yet unknown. On the other hand one senses in this
vision as in the vision of Daniel 2 - which we believe to be
pre-Maccabean - that the authors had something more in mind
than a new democratized government. It is more likely that the
author of Daniel 7 regarded the revolt as the eschatological
event which would usher in dramatically new times, a kingdom
which could not be destroyed, which would be eternal. The
exact nature of this kingdom is not outlined.[67] As discussed
above, the meaning of the enthronement of the son figure

66. We agree in this with many points made by Collins,
The Apocalyptic Vision, pp. 166, 174-175.

67. While the earliest Qumran covenanters may have shared
this rather undefined and non-hierarchical view of the kingdom
to come, evidence of the Community Rule in particular emphasizes the structured, hierarchical world-view which arose among
the covenanters, one which contrasts sharply with the lack of
definition in Daniel 7. Such differences may of course be
attributed to differences in genre, but see Murphy-O'Conner,
"La Genèse Littéraire de la Règle de la Communauté," *RB* 76
(1969), 528-549.

remains couched in mystery. As noted by Dequeker, the image of
the Ancient and the son seems "plus profondemont réligieux"
than the image of the beasts which "est plutôt d'inspiration
historique."[68] Porteous too notices a difference between the
image cluster in vss. 1-8 and 9ff. and writes that with vs. 9
the author begins to relate a truly "ecstatic" experience.[69]

It is clear that, while the beasts represent historical
events, the appearance of the Ancient moves the vision into
metahistory. Hence the halo of mystery. The seer's confusion
and the secrecy at the end of this vision and at the end of ch.
8 is no mere literary artifice, but underlines the mystery which
the future holds. The rise and fall of worldly kingdoms is to
be replaced with something else, but the nature of this thing
is as yet unclear. For this reason, the symbolic drama involving the Ancient and the son and the interpretation of it is
less see-through than the succession of beasts which connotes
the passage of human kingdoms.

John J. Collins suggests that the "holy ones" refer to
human and angelic beings at the same time. Pointing to 1 QM
17:6-8, the Qumranite War Scroll, Collins notes that the Qumran
covenanters envisioned an "intermingling of angels and men in
the course of the (eschatological) battle." He writes, "if the
term 'holy ones' in the Book of Daniel contains any reference
to the Jewish people,...it is only in virtue of their association with the 'holy ones,' the angelic host led by Michael
which fights for Israel in the heavens."[70] Though we are not
entirely convinced by Collins' identification of the son as
Michael, we do appreciate his explanation of the holy ones, an
explanation which accounts both for the usual angelic meaning
of "holy ones" and for the term's seeming reference to the persecuted people within the context of the passage.

---

68.   "Daniel VII," 362.

69.   *Daniel*, p. 107.

70.   "The Son of Man," 62-63. On the identification of
the son as Michael see the critique offered by Z. Zevit, "The
Structure and Individual Elements of Daniel 7," *ZAW* 80 (1968),
393-395.

We also approve of Collins' approach to the judgment and enthronement scenes of Daniel 7 as eschatologically charged events. Again, these scenes are quite different from the observation of divine events in visions I and VIII of Zechariah or from the non-symbolic vision IV. In these visions of Zechariah one has no indication that normal, everyday history is coming to a close or that the kingdom of Zerubbabel and Joshua is everlasting.

Daniel 7 contains an interesting dichotomy: in vss. 1-8 the mythic beings represent characters and forces in history; in vss. 9ff., the equally mythic symbolism points to a time beyond the rise and fall of ordinary world empires. We have noted that one basic pattern lies behind the symbolism of the work as a whole, that of creation and victory over chaos. As Frank Moore Cross has discussed with reference to use of the creation story in OT, this pattern is essentially one of theogany followed by cosmogony.[71] First comes the creation of divine beings who are often listed in pairs of natural phenomena such as heaven/earth; night/day; dry land/sea.[72] These are the old gods. Beasts such as those brought forth by Tiamat (*Enūma Eliš* III, 36) and the cyclops born to Earth (*Theogony*, 1. 139) are also part of this theogonic (pre-cosmogonic) time of creation. At this point in creation, there is no neatly defined hierarchy among the gods, no clear order or reality as we know it on earth. All is without differentiation. When the younger, more active deities born to the old gods rebel, destroying their elders or rendering them impotent, a new order is established. A cosmogonic process takes place, a process of ordering. Clear hierarchies are established among the gods (*Enūma Eliš* V, 1) and the young deity who conquered the older god is enthroned as head of the pantheon. The world is

---

71. "The 'Olden Gods' in Ancient Near Eastern Creation Myths," *Magnalia Dei: The Mighty Acts of God. Essays on the Bible and Archaeology in Memory of G. Ernest Wright*, eds. F. M. Cross, W. E. Lemke, and P. D. Miller (New York: Doubleday, 1976), pp. 329-338.

72. For example, see *Theogony*, 11. 104-125; *Enūma Eliš*, I, 1ff.

organized and ordered, the moon set in its place by night, the
sun by day (*Enūma Eliš* V, 12; Gen 1:17), the calendar is created (*Enūma Eliš* V, 14f.), and man's place on earth is established and defined (*Enūma Eliš* VI, 33, 34). Cosmogony is not
merely a process of creation, but also a process of ordering.[73]

In Daniel 7, the mention of sea and the beasts which come
forth from the sea evokes theogony. The appearance of the
Ancient, the destruction of the beasts, and the enthronement of
the younger figure are elements of cosmogony; a new order is
established, an eternal kingdom which shall not be destroyed.

Let us put together the two threads of our discussion.
The beasts section of the vision symbolizes history. This is
the theogonic portion of the larger creation pattern. The
Ancient, the destruction of the beast, and the enthronement of
the son figure point to metahistory; this is the cosmogonic
part of the larger mythic pattern. We suggest that the author
of Daniel 7 believes that all ordinary history is the time of
chaos, without meaningful form. It is only through destruction
of the earthly empires that order and a meaningful reality are
established. All history has been prepared for this time. All
history has been a meaningless succession. Interestingly, in
the *Enūma Eliš* and other true creation myths, cosmogony means
the establishment of normal time, complete with its cycles of
seasons; in Daniel, cosmogony implies an end of the cycles of
history and a quantum leap to permanence, foreverness.

The same pattern of theogony and cosmogony, implicit in
Daniel 7, is found in more elaborate and extreme form in Enoch
6-11, where reality is described as a time of chaos, of destruc-
tive beasts which consume the world or mankind itself (Dan 7:23;
Enoch 7:4, 5). Enoch 9:3-10:16 includes a judgment pattern.
The destroyers are to be destroyed, the seed of Noah, the
chosen, blessed (Enoch 10:17ff.). The saved will then participate in a new idyllic order (Enoch 10:18ff.).

This treatment of history as a prelude or earlier portion
on the larger time-line of the cosmos is a feature of a number
of the baroque examples of the symbolic vision form whose

---

73. See T. Jacobsen, *The Treasures of Darkness* (New Haven:
Yale, 1976), p. 191.

symbols depict a retrospective of the past as well as a prediction about a much improved future. Such a retrospective of the past and view of the future is found, for example, in 4 Ezra 11-12, an example of our form which was no doubt composed with Daniel 7 in mind (see 4 Ezra 12:11). In its monster-eagle from the sea, 4 Ezra 11-12 shares some of Daniel 7's theogonic motifs, though the former does not so fully evoke the whole theogonic-cosmogonic complex. 4 Ezra 11-12 and the vision of the forest in 2 Baruch 36 do share with Daniel 7 the theme of successive empires; the worst empire in 4 Ezra and 2 Baruch becomes Rome. This empire will fade as a new age is established.

In its use of symbols to depict past history as a time of trouble amid rising and falling empires, and in its conviction that these empires will be replaced with a new eternal idyllic kingdom, Daniel 7 marks thematic trends for later versions of the symbolic vision form. This form, exemplified by Daniel 7, is now expansive and literary and is marked by story-telling motifs such as the fear of the seer and his dream-state. Employing a prose style with an interlude of poetry which is probably borrowed from another source, the author assumes the fiction of true prophecy. He actually lives during the reign of the final worldly empire which he predicts. The symbolic vision form has become a medium of the apocalypticist. His symbols are grounded in the fund of ancient Near Eastern mythology. The meaning of these symbols concerning the past a and present is a language readily translatable into the theme of successive empires, a theme well understood by his own circle. The nature of that which is to follow the final empire, however, remains as mysterious as the mythic symbols themselves. The interpretation of those symbols, provided within the vision form, helps little to understand; for the seer himself does not think he knows the full truth.

Daniel 8

In many ways, the study of Daniel 7 culminates our work in the development of the symbolic vision form in OT. We have shown how the vision form has been carried to baroque yet eloquent proportions in the hands of a sensitive author and how

literary forethought and self-conscious creation of symbols now
play a role. The distance between the mundane world of the
seer and the otherworldly setting into which he is drawn is
underlined, as the symbolic vision form serves as a medium
which joins divine and human realms. The use of this vision
form by an author with a special - even transcendent - view of
a future kingdom to be established on earth will be found further in 2 Baruch and 4 Ezra.

Before turning to the post-Biblical relatives in form of
Daniel 7 we have yet to deal with Daniel 8. Daniel 8 is another example of the baroque, narrative stage of the symbolic
vision, but one which does not concern itself with the meta-
historical continuation of the cosmic time-line. Many scholars
feel, in fact, that ch. 8 comes as an aesthetic anticlimax to
Daniel 7.[74] Their reasons for this negative evaluation of the
piece will emerge in the analysis below.

1) In the third year of the reign of King[a] Belshazzar a vision
[b]appeared to me,[b] Daniel, after that which appeared to me at
the first. 2) And I saw in the vision [c]of my dream[c] and I was
in Susa the capital which is in the province of Elam and I was
at [d]the river Ulai.[d] 3) I raised my eyes and saw and behold[e]
a ram[f] standing before the river and [g]he had two horns and the
horns were high,[g] but one was higher than the other and the
higher one was growing [h]afterwards.[h] 4) I saw the ram pushing
westward, and northward, and southward, and none of the beasts
could withstand him and there was no one who could rescue from
his power; he did according to his will and became mighty. 5)
As I was taking (this) in behold a he-goat came from the west

---

74. Porteous, *Daniel*, 119; Montgomery, *The Book of Daniel*,
p. 325. The question of original language in Daniel 7 and 8
and the change to Hebrew in ch. 8 are not issues of concern
here. John J. Collins' arguments in favor of assuming the
author or authors to have composed in the languages in which
their work now appears are convincing and thorough. We share
Collins' assumptions concerning the original languages of chs.
7 and 8 and need not go over the same ground (*The Apocalyptic
Vision*, pp. 15-19).

across the face of the whole earth, not touching the ground,
and the goat had a conspicuous[j] horn between its eyes. 6) And
he came to the ram with two horns which I had seen standing
before the river, and he ran towards him with [k]fierce anger.[k]
7) I saw him approach the ram; he was enraged against him and
struck [l]the ram[l] and broke his two horns and the ram had no
strength to withstand [m]him;[m] he threw him to the ground and
trampled him and no one could save the ram [n]from his power.[n]
8) And the he-goat became exceedingly mighty but when he was
at his strongest, the great horn was broken and four others[o]
rose in its place towards the four winds of heaven. 9) And
from one of them came forth a small[p] horn which grew exceedingly[q] toward the south, toward the east, and toward [r]the
glorious land.[r] 10) It magnified itself over the host of
heaven and threw (some) down from the host ⟨ ⟩[s] and trampled
them. 11) And [t]it magnified itself[t] even up to the prince of
the host and because of it [v]the continual offering was removed[uv]
and [w]the place of his sanctuary cast down.[w] [x]. 12) [y]And it
set sin[y] upon the continual offering, and threw truth to the
ground and did and succeeded. 13) Then I heard a holy one
speak and one holy one said to the fellow who was speaking,

>"For how long is the vision concerning the ⟨removed⟩[z]
>continual offering and the appalling sin ⟨which is set
>up⟩[a] and the sanctuary ⟨which is thrown down⟩[b] and the
>trampled host?"

14) And he said to him,[c]

>"For two thousand and three hundred evenings and
>mornings and then the sanctuary will be righted."

15) When I Daniel had seen the vision,[d] I requested comprehen-
sion and behold one standing before me with the appearance of a
man. 16) And I heard the voice of a man in the midst of the
Ulai[e] and he called[f] and said,

>"Gabriel, make this man understand the vision."

17) He came[g] near to where I was standing and at his coming I
was terrified and fell upon my face and he said to me,

>"Understand, O man, that [h]the vision is for the time of
>the end."

18) And as he spoke with me, I fell into a deep sleep with my
face to the ground; then he touched me and stood me on my feet.

19) He said[i]

"Behold I am letting you know that which will be at the
end of the indignation,[j] for it is for [k]the appointed
time of the end.[k] 20) The ram which you saw which had
two horns is the kings[l] of Media and Persia. 21) The
he-goat[m] is the king of Greece and the large horn
between his eyes is the first king. 22) That it
broke[n] and four[o] arose in its place means that four
kingdoms[p] will arise from his nation[q] and not through
their[r] power. 23) And at the end of their dominion
[s]when their sins are completed[s] there will arise a king
strong of countenance and understanding riddles. 24)
His power shall be mighty ⟨ ⟩,[t] he will speak[u] wondrous
things and succeed and do; he will destroy the mighty
ones and the nation of holy ones. 25) And against
⟨the holy ones⟩[v] is his cleverness. Craft will succeed
in his hand. In his heart he will magnify himself,
when least suspected (i.e. in quiet) he will destroy
many, [w]and against the prince of princes[w] he will arise
[x]but by no human hand will he be broken.[x] 26) The
vision of the evening and the morning which has been
told is true. And you,[y] seal up[z] the vision for it
applies to many days hence."

27) I Daniel [a]was exhausted[a] and was ill for days.[b] Then I
arose and did the king's business, but I was appalled by the
vision and did not understand it.

1)   [a]G omits המלך while MT, Th have the longer designation.

       [b]MT reads חזון נראה אלי while G reads ορασιν ην ειδον, "a
vision which I saw."

2)   [c]MT appears to be a conflation of two variant readings,
ואראה בחזון and ויהי בראתי. G expands thus: εν τω οραματι του
ενυπνιου μου while Th omits all except ואראה, και ειδον. We
have opted for G which conveys most clearly the sense of a
dream experience.

       [d]Hartman suggests the reading ʾăbûl, "gate" with G, τη
πυλη, and in accordance with the Akkadian cognate abullu,
"gateway." See also Charles. The traditional translation of
ʾûbal, "river" is based on the root יבל meaning "conduct."

ʾÛbal is thus related to Hebrew yābāl (Is 30:23; 44:4) and
yûbāl (Jer 17:8) as well as to the Akkadian abâlu.

3)   [e]G omits והנה.

[f]G adds μεγαν, גדל.

[g]G is briefer και ειχε κερατα υψηλα.

[h]It is not entirely clear what is meant by באחרנה, "after-
wards," "at the last." G places the term at the beginning of
vs. 4 to have it mean "after these things," μετα δε ταυτα.

5)   [i]G omits כל.

[j]MT reads חזות. G has the less difficult reading εν,
"one."

6)   [k]MT has the more difficult reading בחמת כחו while G has
simply εν θυμω οργης, באחרון אף (cf. G Jonah 3:9).

7)   [l]G omits the object את האיל and reads και επαταξε και
συνετριψε τα δυο κερατα αυτου, "and he struck and broke his two
horns."

[m]G reads του τραγου, "the he-goat."

[n]G reads απο του τραγου, "from the he-goat."

8)   [o]MT ותעלנה חזות ארבע seems to reflect some corruption, a
confusion between חזות (vs. 5) and אחרות (G: ετερα τεσσαρα).
G adds κερατα reading "four other horns," but the shorter cor-
rected reading in MT is clear without the addition. Th reads
κερατα τεσσαρα, "four horns."

9)   [p]MT מצעירה should probably be read צעירה, "small" (cf.
Gen 19:20). G ισχυρον, עצומה reflects confusion with vs. 8
above.

[q]G reads και κατισχυσε και επαταξεν "And it grew strong
and struck...."

[r]G βορραν, צפון, reflects a less difficult reading and a
possible confusion with צבי. Th την δυναμιν, צבא, reflects a
misreading with an eye-slip to vs. 10, עד צבא השמים. The term
ṣĕbî refers to the land of Israel as in Ezek 20:6, 15; Jer 3:19.

[s]MT adds ומן הכבים, "and from the stars." With Hartman
we agree that the phrase "from the stars" was originally a
gloss for "the host of heaven" which has now been included in
the text and joined to it via the word "and."

11) [t]MT has the masculine form. The blurring of genders in
the presence of a dual feminine noun is not uncommon (Joüon,
150d). This text also may reflect a confusion between the

gender of the symbol (small horn) and that of the interpretation (a king [8:23]). G reflects an interesting but curious
variant reading, ρυσηται την αιχμαλωσιν, "he redeemed the cap-
tivity." There may be some confusion between הגדיל and a form
of גאל, "to redeem." Nevertheless, the reading is difficult to
explain. G reflects a good deal of variation and expansion at
this point (see below).

^uRead *hūram* instead of MT *hūraym*.

^vG reads τα ορη τα απ᾽ αιωνος ερραχθη, הרי התמיד השלכו
"the eternal mountains were cast down."

^wG reads και εξηρθη ο τοπος αυτον και θυσια, והרמו
מכונו (?) ותמיד.

^xG is expansive at this point continuing, και εθηκεν αυτην
εως χαμαι [επι την γην] και ευωδωθη και εγενηθη και το αγιον
ερημωθησεται. Charles believes the phrase και - ερημωθησεται
to contain some indication of original reading at the end of
vs. 11, but his suggestions are speculative (*A Critical and
Exegetical Commentary*, pp. 206-207).

12) ^yMT is corrupt. G reads και εγενηθσαν επι τη θυσια αι
αμαρτιαι. "And sins happened upon the continual sacrifice."
By translating in line with Deut 21:8, "to set," by vocalizing
wětintēn (cf. Aramaic 2:16), by reading פשע instead of בפשע,
and by omitting וצבא one is able to leave the horn as subject
of the phrase but follow the sense of G: ותנתן על התמיד פשע.

13) ^zWith G η αρθεισα and in line with vs. 11.

^aMT reads *tēt* the infinitive while G reads η δοθεισα, the
participle. We are reading participial modifiers throughout
vs. 13, hence *nittān*.

^bThe host is trampled but the sanctuary thrown down in
line with vs. 11. We are assuming that קדש originally had a
participial modifier.

14) ^cWith G, Th αυτω.

15) ^dG omits החזון.

16) ^eG reads ανα μεσον του Ωλαμ.

^fG contains a lengthy expansion: ανα αναβοησας ο ανθρωπος
ειπεν επι το προσταγμα εκεινο η ορασις, "And calling out the
man said upon that command: the vision."

^gG expands, και ηλθε και εστη, "And he came and stood."

^hG reads τουτο το οραμα, החזון הזה.

19) [i]G adds μοι, אלי.

[j]G adds τοις υιοις του λαου, לבני העם.

[k]G reflects a more expanded version of the formula, εις ωρας καιρου συντελειας, עד מועד עת קץ (cf. G 11:35).

20) [l]G, Th reflect the singular, βασιλευς.

21) [m]MT reflects two variants for he goat צפיר and שעיר. G with τραγος των αιγων reflects צפיר העזים (v. 5).

22) [n]G reflects a plural participle συντριβεντα through confusion with other nearby plural verb and noun forms.

[o]G adds κερατα, "horns."

[p]G reads βασιλεις, "kings."

[q]MT reads $miggôy$, "from the nation." Charles, Montgomery and most follow G του εθνους αυτου, "his people." MT may reflect an Aramaism $miggawwô$, "from its midst." (See Hartman, *Daniel*, p. 228).

[r]With G read the plural, την ισχυν αυτων.

23) [s]Read with G πληρουμενων των αμαρτιων αυτων, "when their sins are completed," against MT כהתם הפשעים, "when sinners have reached their fullest."

24) [t]MT adds ולא בכחו an intrusion from vs. 22. This phrase is omitted in G.

[u]MT ונפלאות ישחית makes no sense. ישחית is probably an intrusion from later in the vs. G, και θαυμαστως φθερει, "And he will destroy marvellously" reflects the same error. The similarities between 8:24 and 11:36 lead one to suspect that the original phrase was ונפלאות ידבר (cf. ידבר נפלאות in 11:36). See also Hartman, *Daniel*, pp. 228-229.

25) [v]MT ועל שכלו is haplographic. With G we restore to επι τους αγιους το διανοημα αυτου "and against the holy ones is his cleverness."

[w]G has the variant, επι απωλειας ανδρων στησεται, "upon the destruction of men he will stand."

[x]The Greek traditions provide interesting variants: G, και ποιησει συναγωγην χειρος και αποδωσεται, "And he will a gathering (אספה) of a hand and be given over (?)." Th, και ως ωα χειρι συντριψει "And like eggs in hand he will break."

26) [y]G reads και νυν, ועתה.

[z]G reflects the passive participle πεφραγμενον, "sealed up."

27) [a]MT נהייתי is omitted in G.
     [b]G adds πολλας, "many."

Patterns, rubrics, and narrative nuances

8:1	Date-line	...בשנת שלוש ל
8:1-3	Indication of dream/vision	...חזון נראה אלי ואשא עיני ואראה
8:3-14	Description	...והנה
8:15	Seer's request for interpretation	ואבקשה בינה
8:16-26	Answer of interpreter	

   (8:17-18 trance of seer upon seeing interpreter and fear)

8:26	Charge to seer	
8:27	Fear/sickness of seer	

   The motif pattern of Daniel 8 conforms to the divinatory
sequence with the expected rubric of "seeing" to indicate a
vision experience and the "behold" term to introduce the description. Note that the version of the rubric employed in
vs. 3 is the one so frequently employed by Zechariah, *wā'eśśā'*
ʿênay wā'er'eh. The prophet sees, requests knowledge, and his
dream is interpreted. Of interest is the specific name given
the intermediary interpreter. Daniel 8 reflects a developed
angelology whereby members of the divine council are assigned
specific names. As in Daniel 7, subject headings are used in
the interpretation motif in order to link each symbol with its
meaning.

   האיל אשר ראית (8:20) ...והקרן (8:21), והצפיר and so on.
Repetition thus serves as a unifying literary device.

   As in Daniel 7, this basic pattern is filled out by narrative touches which describe the setting (vss. 1-2) and the
seer's feelings (vss. 17, 27). Vss. 1 and 2 seem to have been
disrupted in transmission, and contain some translation problems.[75] Does *'ûbal* in vs. 1, for example, mean gate (G, πυλη)
or river as in the forms *yûbal* (Jer 17:8) and *yiblê* (Is 30:25,
44:4)? We opt for the latter reading; the prophet is placed in
a setting similar to that of Ezekiel, who sees a vision by the
river Chebar (Ezek 1:1). Admittedly a gateway or a stream

---

   75. On these difficulties see the discussion in Montgomery, *The Book*, pp. 325-328, and text-critical notes 1a-2d.

provide equally good "boundary" places where one might experience communication with divine beings. In any event, with vss.
1-2 the author takes pains to set the vision, to frame it as
one would frame a story, with time, place, and situation.
As noted earlier, the night-time or dream-time aspect is
not emphasized in the introductory rubrics of ch. 8, though G
vs. 2 does mention του ενυπνιου μου, *ḥălōmî*. On the other
hand, vs. 18 includes an interesting reference to sleep.

ובדברו עמי נרדמתי על פני
ארצה ויגע בי ויעמידני
על עמדי

> And as he spoke with me, I fell into a deep
> sleep with my face to the ground; then he
> touched me and stood me on my feet.

This swoon of the prophet is another of the narrative and
dramatic touches in the account of the vision experience. One
is reminded of Zechariah vision V (4:1), where the prophet says
that he was aroused like a man is awakened from sleep. In
Zechariah this arousal introduces the vision experience. Here
the prophet falls into sleep after having seen the visionary
image, when the interpreter of the vision first addresses him.
The falling upon one's face is reminiscent of Ezekiel's physical response to the vision in Ezek 1:2. Ezekiel is told to
arise and is not given an interpretation of his vision (Ezekiel
1 is not an example of the symbolic vision form) but a charge.
Such descriptions of falling upon one's face are stylized expressions of man's reaction when confronted with a powerful
image of the divine. The use of the vb. *rdm*, however, adds
additional nuancing.
A noun from the vb. *rdm*, *tardēmâ*, "deep sleep," is employed
in a number of liminal contexts. In Job 4:13 we again find the
juxtaposition of deep sleep and visions.

בשעפים מחזינות לילה
בנפל תרדמה על אנשים

> In disquieting thoughts from visions in the
> night when deep sleep falls upon men

This term for deep sleep is applied to Adam's state when the

Lord removes his rib in order to fashion Eve (Gen 1:21). Yahweh is also responsible for induced sleep called *tardēmat Yahweh* in 1 Sam 26:12. This sleep overcomes David's enemies so
that he can take the water jar and spear of Saul and prove that
the power of God is with him.

The image of the prophet's faint into deep sleep increases
the aura of mystery about the vision but also underlines the
association between sleep and the closer presence of the divine.
Such a sleep like death is not humanly controllable. The otherworldly, even eerie quality of the vision increases.

Style, use of language

Ch. 8 does not employ chains of synonymous terms as does
ch. 7, but does include several examples of the "brief clause"
style. At vs. 8:4 is a series of briefer and briefer synthetically parallel descriptions of the victory of the ram.

וכל החיות לא יעמדו לפניו
ואין מציל מידו
ועשה כרצנו
והגדיל

The syntax of the above clauses is not alike, but this upside-
down pyramid of language does build a tension of thoughts in a
dramatic yet deliberate fashion.

Vs. 7 reflects more the kind of "brief clause" style we
found in ch. 7, as the attack of the he-goat against the ram is
described.

ויתמרמר אליו	vb. + prep. + obj.
ויך את האיל	vb. + obj.
וישבר את שתי קרניו	vb. + obj.
ולא היה כח באיל לעמד לפניו	(change in syntax)
וישליכהו ארצה	vb. + obj. + prep. ph. of direc- tion
וירמסהו	vb. + obj.
ולא היה מציל לאיל מידו	(change in syntax-refrain)

This description, punctuated by the two lines of commentary
which serve as refrains, suggests the tension-building drama of
battle.

A similar sense of violence and hostility is created by
the staccato description of the little horn's actions or the
effects of its actions in 8:11.

הרם התמיד   pass. vb. + subj.

והשלך מכון מקדשו   pass. vb. + subj.

and 8:12

ותשלך אמת ארצה ועשתה והצליחה   vb. + obj. + prep. ph. of direc-
tion/vb./vb.

Vss. 23-25 also reflect a style which is more rhythmic
than ordinary prose, if only by virtue of the brief and self-
contained qualities of the phrases which pile one upon the next.
Some parallelism in content is found between these phrases
while the total effect, as in the explanation motif of ch. 7,
is that of a riddle which lists a number of hints.

Note the parallelism of thought in the following:

עז פנים	strong of countenance,	
ומבין חידות	understanding riddles	8:23
והשחית עצומים	He will destroy the might ones,	
ועם קדשים	and the nation of holy ones.	8:24
ועל [קדשים (G)] שכלו	And against the holy ones is his cleverness.	
והצליח מרמה בידו	Craft will succeed in his hand.	
ובלבבו יגדיל	In his heart he will magnify himself;	
ובשלוה ישחית רבים	in quiet he will destroy many.	8:25

End rhyme is also found in the first two examples from vs. 24
above. The description of the final king ends on two brief
phrases which create an antithesis between the king's most
hubristic act and his punishment.

ועל שר שרים יעמד
ובאפת יד ישבר

Thus, like the author of Daniel 7, the author of Daniel 8
adopts a narrative style designed to underline mystery and tension. Information is provided bit by bit. However, the author
of Daniel 8 does not rely on syntax repetitions as much as the
author of Daniel 7, nor does he create almost formulaic refrains

through the repetition of phrases and terms as does the author
of Daniel 7. On these stylistic grounds, the same author cannot be responsible for Daniel 7 and 8.

One cannot agree with scholars who suggest that one
author is responsible for the whole book of Daniel,[76] nor with
those who suggest that Daniel 7-12 may come from the hands of
one author.[77] While larger questions about unity in the book
of Daniel are beyond the scope of this study, our analysis of
language and style in Daniel 7 and 8 convince us that these
cannot be from the same hand. The two writers simply use language differently.

Moreover, as we shall see, the author of Daniel 8 does not
employ the rich ancient mythic traditions in the integrated and
complex manner of Daniel 7; his is a less elaborate and more
functional use of imagery, for he is concerned with portraying
only real, historical time. A more elaborate picture with a
more complete cosmology is left for later chs. which are not
part of our form. We have fewer doubts about the individual
authorship of Daniel 8-12.

Because Daniel 8 deals only with history, concentrating on
the period of Antiochus IV, our task in analyzing the symbols
is made much easier. Like the beasts in ch. 7, the ram and he-
goat in Daniel 8 are see-through in meaning, indeed even more
see-through than the symbols connoting historical events and
characters in ch. 7.

Symbolic usage

Within the context of the vision, the two-horned ram is
identified to be the kings of Media and Persia. The he-goat is
the king of Greece, the large horn, the "first king." The four
horns are four kingdoms which arise after him, and finally after

---

76. See, for example, H. H. Rowley, "The Unity of the
Book of Daniel," *The Servant of the Lord and Other Essays on
the Old Testament* (Oxford: Blackwell, 1965), pp. 249-280; S. R.
Driver, *The Book of Daniel* (Cambridge: Cambridge University,
1900), lxv-lxvii.

77. See Montgomery, *The Book of Daniel*, pp. 95-96; Collins, *The Apocalyptic Vision*, pp. 18, 21.

their reign arises the little horn (vss. 9-14), a king who is
"strong of countenance and understanding riddles" (vss. 23-25).

One need go only a short conceptual step behind the last
three references to identify the first king as Alexander the
Great, the four following kingdoms as the dominions of the
Diadochi, Macedonia-Greece, Asia Minor, Syria-Babylonia and the
East, and Egypt,[78] and the king who understands riddles as
Antiochus IV.

Scholars have proposed explanations for the background of
the animal figures in ch. 8 which sound much like the suggestions proposed for the beasts of Daniel 7. Once again they
point to the representations of rams and goats or unicorns in
Near Eastern art and literature, where such creatures are symbols of fierce strength. Also mentioned are the references to
the speed and power of the Persian and Greek forces in Is 41:3
and 1 Macc 1:1-4 respectively. Thus fierce animals = fierce
empires.[79] Bentzen and Delcor suggest astrological explanations for the animal empire associations.[80] As explained by
Porteous,

> ...Persia was thought of as under the zodiacal sign of
> Aries and Greece as sharing with Syria, the principal ter-
> ritory of the Seleucid monarchy, the zodiacal sign of
> Capricorn.[81]

The astrological explanations work a bit better for the animal
symbols of Daniel 8 than for the beasts of Daniel 7. Whatever
the background for these animal types, they have been adapted
and described specifically in order to portray certain historical figures and events. It is this manner of usage which interests us. In fact, these figures have been set in images
which are far less subtle and artistically complex than the
symbol drama of Daniel 7.

In Daniel 7, the author accommodates his message to a
whole motif pattern associated with the mythology of creation.

---

78. See Porteous, *Daniel*, p. 124.

79. For a typical discussion, see Montgomery, *The Book*,
pp. 330-331.

80. A. Bentzen, *Daniel*, p. 37; Delcor, *Le Livre*, p. 170.

81. Porteous, *Daniel*, p. 122.

In Daniel 8, however, a simpler relationship exists between the
symbols and their meanings: a fight to the death between two
horned animals means a battle between two kingdoms. Again we
emphasize the more straightforward presentation of the author
of Daniel 8. He conforms to the symbolic vision pattern in a
no-nonsense, even wooden manner.

Similarly, the little horn's activities in the description
motif (vss. 11-12) are rather thinly veiled references to the
historical actions of Antiochus IV as portrayed also in 1 Maccabees. It is clear that we are deling with a reference, however exaggerated, to Antiochus' disruption of cult and defile-
ment of the altar (see 1 Macc 4:38, 45ff.). The *mĕkôn miqdāšô*
is a technical and highly visible term for the temple. The
little horn is thus described as attacking divine territory
itself. The stars imagery in vss. 10-11 is the only mythologically laden theme employed by the author and describes the
hubristic behavior of Antiochus.

Is 14:13 comes to mind immediately.

ואתה אמרת בלבבך

השמים אעלה

ממעל לכוכבי אל

ארים כסאי

ואשב בהר מועד

בירכתי צפון

  And you said in your heart,
  "To heaven I will ascend,
  Over the *stars of El*
  I will raise up my *throne*
  I will sit on the *mountain of the council*
  In the *far places of the north*."

Isaiah's attack upon the king of Babylon is filled with archaic
terms for divine provenance (in italics above) - terms applied
to aspects and areas of El's dominion in Ugaritic materials.[82]
Cross notes that the expression *kôkăbê 'El* appears in the Pyrgi
Inscription in the form of *hkkbm 'l* and that it refers to the
northern stars, the heavenly hosts of Yahweh as divine warrior.[83]

The heavenly host, the stars, are not merely made subservient in Daniel 8:10-11 but are made to fall to the ground

where they are trampled down. The rebellious king also rises
up against *šar haṣṣābā'*, another archaic term for the commander
of the heavenly host. The expression *šar ṣĕbā' yahweh* is found
in Josh 5:14 when, as noted by Cross, Joshua is confronted by
"his cosmic counterpart."[84] The stars are portrayed as the
armed forces of Yahweh in the equally early conquest tradition
of Judg 5:20. Thus Daniel like Isaiah is using very early
terminology, very early motifs. The combination of motifs
which depict a rebellion by lower powers against the heavenly
forces is also found in non-Biblical materials.

In connection with her work in Revelations 12, Adela Yarbro
Collins has collected a number of relevant texts which contain
the rebellion theme.[85] Rev 12:4 like Dan 8:10-11 employs the
stars motif within the rebellion theme. The red dragon sweeps
down a third of the stars of heaven with his tail and casts
them to the ground. Collins points to the Babylonian myths of
Labbu and Zu.[86] The former contains a reference to a sweep of
the villain's tail, a tantalizing link to the Revelation text,
but neither of the above mythic texts preserves a reference to
stars. The Greek accounts of Zeus's battle with Typhon who
attempted to usurp Zeus's power are even more to the point.
The story is preserved in Hesiod's *Theogony* (820-869), an
account which does not include the stars motif. The stars
motif, however, is found in Nonnos' *Dionysiaca* (1.163-164, 180-
181), a late 5th century A.D. work which may well preserve more
ancient traditions. In this account Typhon is said to drag
down some of the stars. While the rebellion theme with the
attack-on-stars motif has not been found in the Ugaritic corpus,
one would assume that the same myth was common in the Hebrews'

---

82. On *yarkĕtê ṣāpôn* see Cross, *Canaanite Myth*, p. 38; on
the expression "mountain of the council" see Cross, *Canaanite
Myth*, pp. 36-37, and CTA 2.1.19-21.

83. See *Canaanite Myth*, p. 45 and n.4 on that page.

84. See Cross, *Canaanite Myth*, p. 70.

85. *The Combat Myth in the Book of Revelation* (HTR Diss.
Ser. 9; Missoula: Scholars, 1975), pp. 76-83.

86. The texts can be found in A. Heidel, *The Babylonian
Genesis* (Chicago: University of Chicago, 1951), pp. 141-147.

ancient Near Eastern environment. This myth is preserved in
Isaiah 14 and applied to a historical figure and is employed
again in Daniel to refer to Antiochus. The attack upon earthly
cult and sanctuary is thus put in terms of the rebellion against
the dominion of the deity and his forces, the stars. Once
again, historical events are put in terms of mythic events.

The interpretation of the little horn (vss. 23-25) describes a king figure in the riddle-like, brief phrases discussed above. Persecutions are alluded to (vs. 24) and there
is further mention of the direct assault on the divine. The
reference to *śar haśśārîm*, in fact, seems to extend the hostility beyond the commander of Yahweh's forces to Yahweh himself.
Interesting in the description of Antiochus and his evil deeds
is the emphasis placed on stealth and cleverness as well as
physical force. Commentators point to the descriptions of Antiochus' double-dealing or that of his agent in 1 Macc 1:29ff.[87]
There is no doubt that Antiochus was regarded as an ignoble
sneak as well as an oppressor. Cleverness or wisdom used for
evil purposes and physical power or strength are also the characteristics of the character-type of the tyrant, as described
by Plato, Polybius, Lucian, and other Greek writers.[88] This
literary type has a historical basis in the rulers who first
arose in the Greek cities along the Aegean coast from the sev-
enth century B.C. on.[89] The tyrant as negatively viewed by the
above Greek writers was a demagogic figure who rose to power by

87. See, for example, Montgomery, *The Book*, p. 351.

88. Plato, *The Republic*, 9.3.573-575; Polybius 6:3ff.;
Lucian, *The Downward Journey or the Tyrant*, LCL 2.

89. A. Andrewes, *The Greek Tyrants* (London: Anchor, 1956),
pp. 31-42. See also M. Smith, *Palestinian Parties and Politics
That Shaped the Old Testament* (New York: Columbua University,
1971), pp. 136-144. Smith applies the tyrant typology to Nehemiah. In a paper dealing with Josephus' account of the Tobiads,
Joseph and his son Hyrcanus, we have shown that the tyrant
typology also lies behind Josephus' characterization of these
two men. See "Father and Son Folktale Patterns and Tyrant
Typologies in Ant 12.160-222," forthcoming in JJS (1981).

violence or deceit, employing false promises, treachery, and
backstabbing. Plato writes in Book 9 of *The Republic*,

>...for the sake of a blooming new-found *bel ami*, not
>necessary to his life, he would rain blows upon the aged
>father past his prime, closest of his kin....
>...if they themselves want something, they themselves fawn
>and shrink from no contortion or abasement in protest of
>their friendship, though, once the object gained, they
>sing another tune....
>...must they not run wild and look to see who has aught
>that can be taken from him by deceit or violence?[90]

A. Andrewes notes that the tyrant relied on private mercenary
troops, often resorting to acts of violence against his subjects. Lucian's satire of the tyrant, *The Downward Journey or
the Tyrant*, also emphasizes the violent use of power by the
tyrant and his overwhelming pride. This combination of deceit-
ful cleverness, ability to use great physical power, and hubristic pride, found in the picture of Antiochus, not only reflects
historical realities of his rule as perceived by the writer,
but also falls into the stylized and typological description of
the tyrant shared by the non-Jewish writers above. By the second century B.C. this type no doubt would have been well known
and recognized by the circle for whom the author of Daniel 8
wrote.

The only hint of a time beyond the rule of this tyrant is
the half-line, וּבְאֶפֶס יָד יִשָּׁבֵר, literally, "With nothing of a
hand, i.e. no human hand, he shall be broken." This phrase has
the same nuance as Daniel 2:34, דִּי לָא בִידַיִן. Except for these
few words, the author has chosen to concentrate on his own
times. Throughout, his symbols have been conscious creations
describing the course of history leading up to and including
the current empire. His "symbolic" description of that final
reign dips into a fund of accusations against the historical
Antiochus, thinly veiled propaganda which parallels accounts in
1 Maccabees. In cosmological scope this vision is narrower
than Daniel 7 and the post-Biblical works which we will mention

---

90. 9.3.574 C, 576 A, and 573 E (LCL translation).

in a final overview. Of special interest have been the author's
use of the rebellion-attack-against-the-stars theme and the
type cast portrayal of Antiochus as tyrant. We would like to
discuss one more distinguishing feature of Daniel 8.

The scene which begins at vs. 13 must remind us of the
visions of Zechariah. The formulaic lament question, ʿad mātay,
"how long," is addressed by one of the otherworldly figures in
the vision to another (Dan 8:13). This questioning is observed
by the seer, as in Zech 1:12. Secondly, the command to one of
the heavenly beings to say something to the seer includes the
unusual demonstrative hallāz in referring to the seer, as in
Zech 2:8. The use of these terms in a situation identical to
those portrayed by Zechariah is significant and, in our opinion,
not coincidental. Is the author of Daniel 8 consciously copying his predecessor in the symbolic vision tradition or is he
less consciously falling into a traditional means of expression,
into traditional idiom? In these cases, we believe that the
author of Daniel 8 is consciously modeling his work on the work
of Zechariah; for while the ʿad mātay formula itself is a common one in OT, only Zechariah uses it in this particular vision
scene situation, depicting a conversation between two divine
beings which is overheard by the seer. Similarly, only Zechariah employs the unusual demonstrative in exactly this situation. Unlike the symbolic vision pattern itself, these two
particular usages of language do not seem to be shared by a
lengthy tradition; they are included in Zechariah's own creative and often distinctive presentation of the form. The
author of Daniel 8 (and none after him as far as we can tell)
has adopted a few of these distinctive features found in Zechariah, thereby giving his vision additional credibility and
pedigree. This self-conscious modeling of a vision on earlier
works becomes more and more common in post-Biblical examples of
the vision form.

Daniel 8 joins Daniel 7 as an example of the baroque, narrative stage of the symbolic vision form. The divinatory pattern is found as are the narrative touches which make the pattern more of a drama. The trance-like state described in vs.
17, in fact, adds to the divinatory setting of the piece. On
aesthetic grounds, one is less impressed with the style of

Daniel 8 than with the style of Daniel 7. The former does exhibit some of the same stylistic features as Daniel 7, features
which help to create a sense of building tension and drama.
Daniel 8 differs in thematic scope from Daniel 7 in that the
message does not reach much beyond the historical present of
the author. Of course, the same "fiction of the past" is
assumed in this vision as in Daniel 8, as the author writes in
the time of Belshazzar.

Post-Biblical Examples

Visions of many varieties are so popular and so numerous
in evidence from the period following Daniel that some should
be mentioned which carry on the symbolic vision form tradition,
the particular interest of this study. Given this variety of
visions, the formal picture becomes extremely complex in the
post-Biblical period. The four visions below from 2 Baruch and
4 Ezra continue the thread from Daniel rather precisely. The
motif pattern of these pieces is identical to that of Daniel 7
and 8, complete with similar narrative touches. In fact, these
four visions tend to carry certain features of Daniel's visions
even further. Increased emphasis is placed on the dream background; some extremely long explanation motifs are found while
the question of the seer to the interpreter becomes a prophetic
soliloquy, a true prayer by a supplicant.

In view of the length and complexity of these four works,
we will not attempt to deal with stylistics or to discuss the
symbols in detail. However, provided below is a schematic outline of the pattern of content found in each; underlined are
rubrics and formulaic expressions which have asserted themselves
in the tradition. We will comment briefly on the extensions,
exaggerations, and elaborations of certain parts of the divinatory pattern, as found in the following post-Biblical works.[91]

---

91. Texts employed are published in A. M. Ceriani, *Monumenta sacra et profana ex Codicibus praesertim Bibliothecae
Ambrosianae Opera Collegii Doctorum ejusdem* (Vol. 5; Mediolani,
1868).

	2 Baruch 36-43	2 Baruch 53-76	4 Ezra 11:1-12:39	4 Ezra 13:1-53
date	x	x	11:1	whw̆ʾ mn btr šbʿʾ yumyn 13:1
dream status	36:1 ...ʾmkt tmn whzyt blly̆ʾ hzw̆ʾ	53:1 ʾmkt tmn whzyt hzw̆ʾ	whw̆ʾ blly̆ʾ tnyʾ 11:1 hzyt hzw̆ʾ	whzyt hzw̆ʾ blly̆ʾ
description	36:2-37 wh̆ʾ...	53:1-11 wh̆ʾ...	11:1-12:3 wh̆ʾ...	13:2-13 wh̆ʾ...
awake/fear	37 wʾnʾ dyn ʾttʿyrt	53:12 wʾnʾ mn dḥlt̆ʾ ʾttʿyrt	12:3-6 ...ʾnʾ dyn mn swgṭʾ dzwʿt̆ʾ wmn dḥlt̆ʾ rbt̆ʾ ʾttʿyrt	13:13 ...wʾnʾ dyn mn swgṭʾ dzwʿt̆ʾ ʾttʿyrt
question of seer/prayer	38:1-4 (38:1) wṣlyt wʾmrt ...(38:3) ʾwdʿyny hkyl pwšqh dḥn̆ʾ hzw̆ʾ	54:1-22 (54:1) wbʿyt mn hylty̆ʾ wʾmrt...	12:7-9 (12:7)...wʾnʾ bqwšt̆ʾ bʿwty sigt qdm rbwt̆ʾ dprswpk... (12:8) wʾwdʿyny ly lʿbdk pwšqh wpwršnh dḥnʾ hnʾ dḥzyt	13:13-20 (13:13) wbʿyt mn mrymr wʾmrt... (13:15) whš̆ʾ gly ly twb pwšqh dḥzw̆ʾ hn̆ʾ
interpretation	39:1-40:4 (39:1) ...hnw pwšqh dḥzw̆ʾ dḥzyt (39:2) ʾyk dḥzyt ʾb....	55:74 ...(56:2) wmwdʿw ʾwdʿk hyltn̆ʾ (56:3) ...ʾyknh gyr dḥzyt ʿnn̆ʾ...	12:10-36 (12:10) ...hnw pwšqh dḥzw̆ʾ dḥzyt (12:11) nšrʾ dḥzyt...	13:21-53 (13:21) ...ʾp pwšqh dḥzwk ʾmr lk ʾp ʿl ʾylyn dmllt ʿglh lk... (13:25) pwšqh dyn

	2 Baruch 36-43	2 Baruch 53-76	4 Ezra 11:1-12:39	4 Ezra 13:1-53
interpre-tation	(40:4) *hnw ḥzwk whnw pwšqh*	(71:2) *hnw ḥzw' dḥzyt whnw pwšqh*	x	*dḥzwk hnw mṭl dḥzyt gbr'...* (13:53) *hnw pwšqt dḥzw' dḥzyt*
closing charge	43 (43:1) *'nt dyn brwk' twn lbk...* (43:3) *wpqd l'mk...*	76:3-4 (76:4) *...zl w'lpyhy l'm'...*	12:37-39 (12:37) *ktwb hky l bspr' hlyn klhyn dḥzyt sym 'nym bdwkt' dksy'* (12:38) *w'lp 'nyn lḥkymwhy d'mk...*	

Notes

Date

The visions in 4 Ezra come after incubation (10:60; 12:51).
The seer is actually told to sleep in order to receive a vision.
His motivation for sleeping is the hope for divine revelation.[92]

In the two visions from 4 Ezra, the date-line does not set
the vision in a king's reign, time of the month, etc., but in
relation to the other vision experiences of the seer as nar-
rated in the larger vision cycle. Nevertheless, the introductory date-line does serve the function of telling when the
dream-vision occurred.

Dream status

In all four visions, the dream nuance is made clear. Night
(*lēlyâʾ*) is mentioned in three of the four. The vb. *dmk*, "to
sleep," is used in the visions from 2 Baruch. Dream-night-
sleep-time is the liminal time, as in Daniel 7. The incubation
element mentioned above strengthens the divinatory thrust of
the narrative, adding to the "filtering" effect of the symbolic
vision discussed earlier. Visions do not suddenly happen; one
must create the appropriate numinous, otherworldly conditions
to commune with the divine.

Note the use of variant rubric patterns, all of which include *ḥzyt ḥzwʾ*, "I saw a vision."

Description

All four visions employ the "behold" term to introduce the

---

92. E. L. Ehrlich considers 1 Kgs 3:5-15, Genesis 15, Gen
28:10-29, and other OT passages in which a Biblical character
receives divine revelations after "lying down" at a holy place
examples of incubation. While the notions of sleep, holy
place, and revelation are clearly related in the tradition, it
is not clear in these OT passages that the people go to certain
places and lie down specifically in order to receive knowledge
of God. The motivation is lacking in the stories. In the
visions of 4 Ezra, however, the motivation is clear; incubation
is present. See Ehrlich's *Der Traum im Alten Testament* (Berlin:
Töpelmann, 1953), pp. 13-55.

description motif. All descriptions are quite long and intricate.

4 Ezra 13:2-13 is filled with heavily mythological elements. The stirring sea and winds evoke the creation complex while the one like a man who is accompanied by fire and storm has the attributes of the divine warrior.

Creation motifs of sea and monster are also found in 4 Ezra 11:1-12:3, which includes the schema of four kingdoms. Note the parallelistic constructions which begin at 11:41. The author seems to lapse into a kind of poetry in 11:41-45. Could this mixing of poetic interludes with the prose now be a regular stylistic feature of the form?

The waves and forest of 2 Bar 36:2-37 are nature motifs if not exactly recognizable elements of the creation cluster. The kingdoms pattern is found here as well.

2 Bar 53:1-11 does not employ a kingdoms pattern, but is concerned with reviewing past history from OT and with dividing that history into certain periods of good and bad. The black and white waters imagery does evoke the order versus chaos theme of creation. While no specific figure is mentioned in connection with the time of the consummation, the theophany attribute of lightning is present towards the end of the description (vs. 9).

The overview above shows that nature-creation imagery continues to be important in the visions which follow Daniel 7. Water and the opposition between order and chaos are emphasized in all. The visions from 4 Ezra have motifs which are more specifically reminiscent of the visions of Daniel. The kingdoms pattern is found in two of the above, while a retrospective of the past is found in a third. Thus certain rather interesting aspects of imagery and theme seem to continue into post-Biblical examples; aspects of content become as expected as the more structural elements of form with which we have dealt. As noted for Daniel, vision imagery becomes a language.

Awaking and/or fearing

Note the similarity of the expressions for waking and fearing after experiencing a vision. These expressions might well be called formulaic, being "a group of words which is

regularly employed...to express a given idea."[93] Variations
such as those between 2 Bar 53:12, 4 Ezra 12:3 and 13:13 are
allowable in any flexible formula pattern as discussed in some
of our previous studies.[94]   2 Baruch 37 employs a much simpli-
fied version of the pattern.

Question/prayer

Note that a form of b^{ς} is employed in three of the four
visions (cf. Dan 7:16 *(bqš)* and Dan 8:15). A form of $ṣly$ is
found in 2 Bar 38:1. All of these terms convey the nuance of
prayerful petition.

A causative form of yd^{ς} is found in the petitions of 4
Ezra 12:8 and 2 Bar 38:3, as in Dan 7:16. In Dan 8:15, the
seer requests $bînâ$, "wisdom, intelligence." These terms for
knowledge or knowing are interesting indicators of new thematic
directions for the vision form. If one examines the lengthened
requests of the seers in these four visions, one finds that
they have much in common with the didactic psalms of OT (such
as Psalms 1, 112, 32) and with the first of the Qumran hodayot
(1 QHod 1),[95] all of which have affinities with the genre which
S. Mowinckel defines as "learned psalmography."[96]   The long and
poetic prayer of 2 Bar 54:1-22 is the fullest example of this
"wisdom" phenomenon. The following themes are found; note comparisons with the Qumran hymn.

---

93. For a definition of the formula see A. B. Lord, *The
Singer of Tales*, p. 30. For our purposes the metrical element
is not applicable.

94. See A. B. Lord, *The Singer*, p. 44; also see our discussion of poetics and formulaic composition in the study of
Jeremiah 1:13-19 and of Daniel 7.

95. The text used is J. Licht, מגילת ההודיות (Jerusalem:
Bialik, 1957), pp. 56-64.

96. See S. Mowinckel, "Psalms and Wisdom," *Wisdom in
Israel and the Ancient Near East*, eds. M. Noth and D. Winton
Thomas (Leiden: Brill, 1955), 205-224, esp. 214. See also W.
S. Towner, "The Poetic Passages of Daniel 1-6," *CBQ* 31 (1969),
317-326.

	2 Baruch 54	1 Q Hod 1
God's great acts in creation	1-3	9-20
God's unique and unsurpassed wisdom	1-2	6-9
The special relationship between God and the wise-good	4-7	21-27
The humility of the petitioner	9	22-23
The contrast between the sinners and the faithful to whom the petitioner belongs	14-22	27, 35-38

While not all of the above elements are found in the
prayerful request motifs of the other three post-Biblical
visions, the final theme mentioned above of contrast between
the wise, good, faithful folk and the foolish sinners is found
in each. As in the didactic psalms mentioned above, the seer
counts himself among the former group. Thus in 4 Ezra 12:7-9
the seer prays, "If I am more blessed before you than the many
..." interpret my vision for me. In 4 Ezra 13:13-20 he speaks
of the fearful times to be experienced by the survivors of the
end-time, but he considers them better off than those who will
not survive; again the contrast between saved and not saved is
underlined. 2 Bar 38:1-4 does not mention the enemies of God
specifically but instead emphasizes his friends, "You always
enlighten those who are led by understanding...your wisdom is
right guidance...from my (earliest) days I departed not from
your wisdom." Thus the positive side of the wisdom theme is
presented.

In this way a kind of didactic psalm (the lengthiest of
which is found in 2 Baruch 54) extends the question motif,
which is a brief line in the visions of our form which precede
these post-Biblical examples. On the one hand, such an extension of the questioning process can be seen to create tension
and increased drama before the answer is revealed. On the
other hand, it is probably more correct to note that these
prayers tend to anticipate the interpretation of the vision
which will also emphasize the good-saved vs. bad-cursed theme.
The question motif thus becomes further indication of the
planned, self-conscious, literary quality of the vision. The
author provides foreshadowing in order to prepare the reader
for his central message.

Interpretation

Note the item for item repetition which links each symbol with its interpretation. Answer motifs are lengthy, the interpretation of the vision in 2 Bar 55:4-74:4 exceedingly long. Before providing the lengthy interpretation the author has the words of the interpreter recall good vs. bad wisdom theme, the lot of the bessed vs. the lot of the cursed (2 Bar 55:4-8).

In three of the four visions God himself plays the role of dream interpreter. This convention may be an attempt to portray Ezra and Baruch as old-style prophetic figures such as Amos or Jeremiah. 2 Bar 55:4-74:4, however, like the visions of Daniel and Zechariah, has an interceding angelic figure. The figure is named Ramiel as the figure in Daniel is called Gabriel, but interestingly, in 2 Baruch 55:3, this figure is said to be the angel specifically in charge of dream interpretation. The roles of members of the divine council would appear to be well developed in the angelology of the times.

Note the use of opening and closing rubrics which are variants of the same pattern. A similar rubric is found in Gen 40:12 and 40:18 as Joseph is about to explain the dreams of the butler and the baker respectively. It is entirely possible that the post-Biblical writers are employing the idiom of Elohist. They may be introducing interpretations of visions as is done in OT narrative, thereby giving their idiom a certain pedigree. This rubric found at 2 Bar 71:2 comes not at the very beginning of the interpretation motif or at the very end, but right before the most important interpretation which the seer is to receive. The rubric thus becomes a means of creating emphasis.

Charge

R. H. Charles views 2 Baruch 75-76 as a later addition.[97] We are not convinced that these chapters are secondary. Even if Charles is correct, however, the redactor has filled out the dream vision in a fully traditional way. We recall the use of a charge in Zech 1:14 and Dan 8:26. A charge is also found in 4 Ezra 12:37-39 where there is no doubt about its originality.

---

97. *Apocrypha and Pseudepigrapha*, p. 519.

In 4 Ezra 12:37, as in Daniel 8:26, the prophet is told to seal
up the vision. In all three of the post-Biblical visions which
include the charge motif, the prophet is instructed to speak
with his people. Two of the visions employ the vb. '*lp*, "to
teach," while 2 Baruch 43 has the term *pqd*, "to command."

Conclusion

    This brief schematic analysis has revealed great continu-
ity between these four visions and the baroque stage of the
symbolic vision form represented by Daniel 7 and 8. The pattern of content is identical, while the post-Biblical works
lengthen and emphasize certain motifs more than do the visions
of Daniel. We have noted certain similarities in imagery
between the four apocryphal visions and Daniel 7. Themes of
creation and chaos again play a role while the four kingdoms
schema is found in two of the works. Of new interest is the
wisdom theme which emerges in the lengthened, prayerful question motif. S. Mowinckel places the thanksgiving hymn which
follows Daniel's receiving an answer to his prayers in Dan
2:20-23 among his "learned psalms."[98] With him we agree that
this poetic prayer is not original to the folktale in Daniel 2.
It is possible that the redacted form of Daniel 2 (which included the prayer) or more likely the existence and popularity
of such wisdom hymns in the inter-testamental period influenced
these late authors of symbolic visions. 2 Baruch 53-76 includes such a hymn not only as the question/prayer motif, but
also in the seer's expression of thanksgiving in chapter 75.
The similarity of this usage to that of Daniel 2:20-23 should
not be overlooked.

    Finally in terms of the use of language in the four visions
two interesting phenomena have emerged: 1) the presence of
poetic interludes in essentially prose works; 2) the formula or
rubric variants shared by the works and underlined above.

---

98. "Psalms and Wisdom," 217.

CONCLUSIONS

The study of the symbolic vision form has revealed great
continuity in one interesting strand of Biblical tradition.
This form of divine revelation does not spring up suddenly in
post-exilic times, but has earlier deep roots in OT. Ths simple symbolic visions of Amos and Jeremiah are precursors to the
more complex works of Zechariah and Daniel. The question/
answer pattern, the factor of symbolic usage, and certain key
features of terminology remain consistent threads throughout.
At the same time the basic form adapts to meet prophets' changing thematic needs.

1. In Am 7:7-9, 8:1-3, Jer 1:11-12, and 1:13-14, the
vision form creates a warning prediction of judgmental doom
addressed to the covenant-breaking people. In Jeremiah 24, the
form, now equipped with contrasting symbol images, actually
serves as a propaganda document predicting forgiveness and
blessings for those who participated in the exile, condemning
those who remained in the land. In Zechariah, the symbolic
visions express optimistic hopes for the restoration: the victory of Yahweh over Israel's enemies; theocracy; peace; purity;
and abundance. In Daniel, symbolic visions predict an end to
oppressive empires and the ultimate victory of the holy ones.
The theme of saved holy ones is further underlined in the post-
Biblical symbolic visions with which we have dealt. As in
Jeremiah 24, the message of hope for the worthy is counterbal-
anced with a prediction of doom for those who are not among the
worthy. Depending upon the specific symbols seen and the interpretation which is placed upon them, the form is limitless in
thematic expandability. Indeed in the visions of Daniel, 4
Ezra, and 2 Baruch, the authors' assumptions of a fiction of
the past allow them to review history for contemporaries even
within a form of future-telling.

2. The symbolic vision tradition reflects larger trends
in the history of Biblical literature. The study of stage II
of the form has been of special importance in this context. The

243

new syntheses of traditional material in post-exilic prophetic
forms, illustrated for example by Paul Hanson's analysis of the
salvation-judgment oracle, are paralleled by the increasingly
flexible, even eclectic, character of the symbolic vision form
in Zechariah. The rather tight demands of the form in stage I
have loosened and become freer. Similarly, the transcendent
view of God found in the theology of the Priestly Codifier and
of the Chronicler is reflected in Zechariah's use of intermediary interpreters instead of God, in the less sudden, past-tense
quality of the night visions, and in the more self-conscious,
literary quality of the visions. Finally the renaissance of
the ancient myths, exemplified by the prophecies of Deutero-
Isaiah, finds expression in Zechariah's use of divine warrior/
heavenly council imagery. In these ways, the symbolic vision
form falls into line with certain patterns in the growth of
Biblical tradition. Our findings reinforce those of scholars
who have worked with other strands of the Biblical corpus.

  3. On the level of a) language and b) content the form
evolves in a narrative direction.

  a) The simple visions of Amos and Jeremiah are characterized by a neat dialogue frame, structured by the repetition
of symbol language at key junctures in the vision. We refer to
this style as "economical-rhetorical" and have related the re-
use of symbol terms in metaphors or word-plays to the associative methodologies of dream interpretation.

  Amos' visions display a certain balance in line length,
though long lines and quite erratic patterns appear increasingly in Jeremiah 24, the latest example of the simple version
of the symbolic vision form. The rules of classical poetry -
balance, disenjambement, and parallelism - are not the chief
structural unifiers of the form even in stage I. Interesting,
however, is that the explanation motif which presents the
message of the Lord is often presented in a more poetic medium
(see Am 7:8, 9; 8:2, 3; Jer 24:6; Zech 1:16; 2:8, 9; and 5:3,
4).

  The visions of Zechariah are generally more prose-like.
Balance between lines diminishes (except in vision VIII, Zech
6:1-8), and instances of enjambement, evidenced by intertwining
grammatical constructions, increase. The introductory rubrics

of Zechariah vision V become quite elaborate, employing two
verbs and the longest possible references to the speakers. The
economical-rhetorical style is no more. In Zechariah vision VI
(5:1-4), the scroll symbol relates to its interpretation via
rhyme, a loose associative technique. In the remaining visions
of our form, all hint of divinatory technique or methodology is
gone. Relationships between symbol and meaning become more
complex and mysterious.

On the other hand, repetition is not abandoned altogether
as a literary device. In Zech 2:1-4, the repetition of the
horns symbol creates a marked emphasis if not an aesthetic balance for the passage. In Zech 6:1-8, the repetition of the
symbols in the explanation motif serves as a unifying device.

The use of repetition as a structural device becomes essential in the baroque prose visions of Daniel, 4 Ezra, and 2
Baruch as the symbolic descriptions become exceedingly lengthy
and complex. The author describes that which he sees from several angles; in Daniel 7 strings of synonyms are employed to
describe the same image. Daniel 7 and 8 are characterized by a
rhythmic prose style. Catchy, brief, and often self-contained
phrases fall one upon the next as the symbols and explanations
are revealed tense step by step.

In addition to the lengthened descriptions and explanations, 4 Ezra and 2 Baruch contain a lengthened question motif.
The request for interpretation has a prayerful hymnic quality
and emphasizes a didactic message about good and evil among
men. This lengthened question motif adds to the thematic
thrust of the late versions of our form and plays a literary
role, extending the telling of the vision experience and creating tension before the message is revealed. A similar use of
delays before the interpretation motif was noted in Zech 4:5,
13 and 1:9.

Finally, we observed that Daniel 7 includes a poetic interlude which appears to have been borrowed from another source.
The inclusion of what we consider to be borrowed material is
evidence of the author's anthological style of composition. In
line with such an anthological style is 4 Ezra 12:13 in which
the writer actually mentions the vision of Daniel and its relationship to his vision. One must conclude that, increasingly,

authors are borrowing ideas, formal models, and possibly more
specific excerpts from previous works. The use of language in
Daniel 8 reminiscent of certain phrases in the visions of Zechariah adds to the impression that the late authors in our tradition model themselves on or borrow from other works. Again
then one finds evidence of the literary, self-conscious quality
of the visions of stage III.

    b) The simple question/answer pattern of Amos and
Jeremiah is stretched and nuanced in Zechariah. Certain additions to the pattern are anticipated by the redactional layers
of Jeremiah 1 and 24. The date-line of Jer 24:1 is found in
Zech 1:7, Daniel 7:1 and 8:1, and in two of the four post-
biblical works. The charge motif found in Jer 1:17 is found in
Zech 1:14, Dan 8:26, and commonly in the post-Biblical examples
of the form. Of greater significance is the shift in the questioner in Zechariah vision V from God to the seer himself.
This change from stage I becomes the norm for the tradition as
it continues. Instead of God's rhetorical question to the
seer, "What do you see?," we find the seer's own request for an
interpretation of the symbolic image. The vision experience
becomes more like an act of dream interpretation as the seer
plays a seeking role. This narrative quality, which begins to
emerge in the visions of Zechariah, is enhanced by the delay
mechanisms discussed above which make the interpretation process lengthier and more dramatic.

    Also of narrative significance in the visions of Zechariah
is the motif, the observation of divine events. This motif is
tacked on to the end of the first and last visions of the cycle.
Such dramatic happenings, like brief narratives in themselves,
become more integrally related to the interpretation process in
the baroque visions of Daniel, 2 Baruch, and 4 Ezra, providing
the complex description motifs in each.

    The baroque visions include not only the observation of
dramatic happenings, date-line, and charge, but also additional
narrative touches which we have traced to the folktales about
wise interpreters of dreams in Genesis 41 and Daniel 2. The
seer expresses fear upon seeing the visionary image while
greater emphasis is placed on the dream-time aspect of the

vision. Features of setting and character thus become more
important.

4. The use of symbols in the developing formal tradition
is also characterized by a movement from the simple to the complex. While the symbols of Amos and Jeremiah are mundane
objects, those of the visions of Zechariah are drawn from the
rich fund of Near Eastern mythology and from the cult. Images
of the divine warrior and his heavenly court are prominent.
These complex symbols are not explained by word-play or simple
metaphor but are multi-vocal in meaning. In Daniel 7 and 8, we
observed a subtle transition in the use of symbols. While
strongly mythological, the images become suspiciously see-
through in meaning. We compared this imagery to a language
whose vocabulary is understood by the visionary and his audience. References to fallen kingdoms and current enemies are
thinly veiled in the visions of Daniel and in the post-Biblical
works which continue the tradition. Symbols have been consciously selected, adapted, and molded to fit the message.
Again, the planned, literary quality of the visions of stage
III is underlined.

5. Concepts of sympathetic magic and divination have been
important in our work. The very interpretation of symbols in
the visions of stage I has the power to bring about that which
is predicted. The associative technique found in these visions
smacks of divinatory technique. More basically, the question/
answer pattern of the form is rooted in the dream-vision interpretation situation. The dream interpretation process is much
more overt in the visions from Zechariah 4 on in which the seer
himself requests knowledge from an intermediary interpreter.
That divine revelation is received through a process of symbol
interpretation in these visions is of theological significance;
for a mysterious God is shown to communicate not directly but
through often complex symbolic imagery which must be explained
to the prophet.

*   *   *

Throughout this study an attempt has been made to avoid
superimposing an external concept of form on certain passages
and instead to describe the structure, content, and language

found in each vision. In the process has emerged a prophetic
tradition of considerable formal integrity, the symbolic vision
form. Yet this form has been adapted by the prophets in exciting, flexible, and creative ways to suit the changing needs of
Israelite history and to continue the process of divine revelation.

BIBLIOGRAPHY

Ackroyd, Peter R. *Exile and Restoration: A Study of Hebrew Thought of Sixth Century B.C.* Philadelphia: Westminster, 1968.

Albright, W. F. *Archaeology and the Religion of Israel.* Baltimore: Johns Hopkins, 1942.

————. "The Psalm of Habakkuk," in *Studies in Old Testament Prophecy*, ed. H. H. Rowley. Edinburgh: T. & T. Clark, 1946, pp. 1-18.

Allegro, J. "The Wiles of the Wicked Woman: A Sapiential Work from Qumran's Fourth Cave," *PEQ* 96 (1964), 53-55.

Andrewes, A. *The Greek Tyrants.* London: Hutchinson's University Library, 1956.

Baldwin, Joyce G. *Haggai, Zechariah, Malachi.* Downers Grove, Ill.: Inter-varsity, 1972.

Baumgartner, W. "Die Etymologie von hebräischem kelūb Korb," *Th. Z.* 7 (1951), 77-78.

Bentzen, A. *Daniel.* HAT 19. Tübingen: Mohr, 1937.

Beuken, W. A. M. *Haggai-Sacharja 1-8.* Assen: Van Gorcum & Co., 1967.

Bič, M. "Der Prophet Amos-Ein Haepatoskopos," *VT* 1 (1951), 293-296.

Boehmer, Julius. "Was bedeutet die goldene Leuchter Sach 4,2?" *BZ* 24 (1938), 360-364.

Brønno, Einar. *Studien über hebräische Morphologie und Vokalismus.*

Brunnet, G. "La vision de l'étain; réinterpretation d'Amos VII 7-9," *VT* 16 (1966), 387-395.

Bright, John. *A History of Israel.* Philadelphia: Westminster, 1976.

————. *Jeremiah.* Anchor Bible 21. Garden City: Doubleday, 1965.

Bryce, G. E. "Omen-Wisdom in Ancient Israel," *JBL* 94 (1975), 19-37.

Buzy, D. "Les Symbols de Zacharie," *RB* 15 (1918), 136-191.

Caquot, A. "Les Quatre Bêtes et le ≪Fils d'Homme≫ (Daniel 7)," *Semitica* 17 (1967), 37-71.

_____. "Sur les Quatre Bêtes de Daniel VII," *Semitica* 5 (1955), 5-13.

Ceriani, A. M. *Monumenta sacra et profana ex Codicibus praesertim Bibliothecae Ambrosianae Opera Collegii Doctorum ejusdem.* Vol. 5. Mediolani, 1868.

Charles, R. H. *Apocrypha and Pseudepigrapha of the Old Testament.* Oxford: Oxford University, 1913.

_____. *The Book of Daniel.* Oxford: Clarendon, 1929.

Chary, Th. *Aggée-Zacharie Malachie.* Paris: Gabalda, 1969.

Clapham, L. R. "Sanchuniathon: The First Two Cycles." Doctoral dissertation, Harvard University, 1969.

Clifford, R. *The Cosmic Mountain in Canaan and the Old Testament.* Cambridge: Harvard University, 1972.

Collins, Adela Yarbro. *The Combat Myth in the Book of Revelation.* Harvard Dissertations in Religion 9. Missoula: Scholars Press, 1976.

Collins, John J. *The Apocalyptic Vision of the Book of Daniel.* HSM 16. Missoula: Scholars Press, 1977.

_____. "The Court-Tales in Daniel and the Development of Apocalyptic," *JBL* 94 (1975), 218-234.

_____. "The Son of Man and the Saints of the Most High in The Book of Daniel," *JBL* 93 (1974), 50-66.

_____. *The Sybylline Oracles of Egyptian Judaism.* SBL Dissertation Series 13. Missoula: Scholars Press, 1974.

Coote, R. B. "Ripe Words for Preaching: Connotative Diction in Amos," *Pacific Theological Review* 8 (1976), 13-19.

Coppens, J. "La vision danielique du Fils d'Homme," *VT* 19 (1969), 171-182.

Cornill, C. H. *Das Buch Jeremia.* Leipzig: C. H. Tauchnitz, 1905.

Cripps, R. S. *A Critical and Exegetical Commentary on the Book of Amos.* Great Britain: SPCK, 1955.

Cross, Frank Moore. *Canaanite Myth and Hebrew Epic.* Cambridge: Harvard University, 1973.

_____. "The Olden Gods in Ancient Near Eastern Creation Myths," in *Magnalia Dei: The Mighty Acts of God, Essays on the Bible and Archaeology in Memory of G. Ernest Wright,* eds. F. M. Cross, W. E. Lemke, and P. D. Miller. New York: Doubleday, 1975, pp. 329-338.

_____. "Prose and Poetry in the Mythic and Epic Texts from Ugarit," *HTR* 67 (1974), 1-15.

_____. "A Reconstruction of the Judean Restoration," *JBL* 94 (1975), 4-18.

_____. "Ugaritic DB'AT and Hebrew Cognates," *VT* 2 (1952), 162-164.

Delcor, M. *Le Livre de Daniel*. Paris: Gabalda, 1971.

_____. "Les Sources de Chapitre VII de Daniel," *VT* 18 (1968), 290-312.

Dequeker, L. "Daniel VII et les Saintes du Très-Haut," *Eph. Theol. Lov.* 36 (1960), 353-392.

La Divination en Mésopotamie Ancienne et dans les Régions Voisines. (Travaux du Centre d'Études Supérieures Spécialisé d'Histoire des Religions de Strasbourg; XIVe Rencontre Assyriologique Internationale.) Paris: Presses Universitaires de France, 1966.

Dossin, G. "Sur le prophétisme à Mari," in *La Divination en Mésopotamie et dans les Régions Voisines*. Paris: Universitaires de France, 1966, pp. 77-86.

Douglas, Mary. *Purity and Danger*. New York: Praeger, 1966.

Driver, G. R. "Hebrew Notes on the 'Wisdom of Jesus Ben Sirach'," *JBL* 53 (1934), 273-290.

_____. "Linguistic and Textual Problems: Jeremiah," *JQR* 28 (1937), 97-129.

Driver, S. R. *The Book of Daniel*. Cambridge: Cambridge University, 1901.

_____. *The Books of Joel and Amos*. Cambridge: Cambridge University, 1934.

_____. *The Book of the Prophet Jeremiah*. London: Hodder and Stoughton, 1906.

Duhm, B. "Anmerkungen zu den zwölf Propheten VII. Buch Sacharja I. (Kapitel 1-8)," *ZAW* 31 (1911), 161-175.

Edghill, E. A. *The Book of Amos*. Westminster Commentary 27. London: Methuen and Co., 1914.

Ehlen, A. J. "The Poetic Structure of a Hodayah from Qumran: an analysis of grammatical, semantic, and auditory correspondence in 1 QH 3, 19-36." Doctoral dissertation, Harvard University, 1970.

Ehrlich, Ernst Ludwig. *Der Traum im Alten Testament*. Berlin: Töpelmann, 1953.

Eichrodt, W. "Von Symbol zum Typos," *Th. Z.* 13 (1957), 509-522.

Elliger, K. *Das Buch der zwölf kleinen Propheten*. ATD 25/2. Göttingen: Vandenhoeck and Ruprecht, 1964.

Emerton, J. A. "The Origin of the Son of Man Imagery," *JTS* N.S. 9 (1958), 225-242.

Falkenstein, A. "«Wahrsagung» in der sumerischen Überlieferung," in *La Divination en Mésopotamie et dans les Régions Voisines*. Paris: Universitaires de France, 1966, pp. 45-68.

Faron, Louis. "Symbolic Values and the Integration of Society among the Mapuche of Chile," in *Myth and Cosmos*, ed. John Middleton. New York: Natural History, 1967, pp. 167-183.

Finet, A. "La place du devin dans la société de Mari," in *La Divination en Mésopotamie et dans les Régions Voisines*. Paris: Universitaires de France, 1966, pp. 87-93.

Flaceliere, R. *Greek Oracles*, trans. D. Garman. London: Elek, 1965.

Gadd, C. J. "Some Babylonian divinatory methods and their inter-relations," in *La Divination en Mésopotamie et dans les Régions Voisines*. Paris: Universitaires de France, 1966, pp. 21-34.

Galling, K. *Biblisches Reallexikon*. Tübingen: Mohr, 1937.

Geissen, Angelo. *Der Septuaginta-Text des Buches Daniel*. Bonn: Rudolf Habelt, 1968.

Ginsberg, H. L. "The Composition of the Book of Daniel," *VT* 4 (1954), 246-275.

_____. "'King of kings' and 'lord of kingdoms,'" AJSL 57 (1940), 71-74.

_____. *Studies in Daniel*. New York: Jewish Theological Seminary, 1948.

Guillaume, A. *Prophecy and Divination among the Hebrews and Other Semites*. London: Hodder and Stoughton, 1938.

Gunkel, H. *Schöpfung und Chaos in Urzeit und Endzeit*. Göttingen: Vandenhoeck and Ruprecht, 1895.

Hammer, Raymond. *The Book of Daniel*. Cambridge: Cambridge University, 1976.

Hammershaimb, E. *The Book of Amos: A Commentary*. New York: Schocken, 1970.

Hanson, Paul D. *The Dawn of Apocalyptic*. Philadelphia: Fortress, 1975.

_____. "Rebellion in Heaven, Azazel, and Euhemeristic Heroes in 1 Enoch 6-11," *JBL* 96 (1977), 195-233.

_____. "Zechariah 9 and the Recapitulation of an Ancient Ritual Pattern," *JBL* 92 (1973), 37-59.

Haran, Menahem. *Temples and Temple-Service in Ancient Israel. An Inquiry into the Character of Cult Phenomena and the Historical Setting of the Priestly School*. Oxford: Clarendon, 1978.

Harper, William R. *A Critical and Exegetical Commentary on Amos and Hosea*. New York: Charles Scribner's Sons, 1905.

Hartman, Louis F. and Di Lella, Alexander A. *The Book of Daniel*. Anchor Bible 23. Garden City: Doubleday, 1978.

Haupt, Paul. "The Visions of Zechariah," *JBL* 32 (1913), 107-122.

Hayes, John H. (ed.). *Old Testament Form Criticism*. San Antonio: Trinity University, 1974.

Heaton, Eric W. *The Book of Daniel: Introduction and Commentary*. London: SCM, 1956.

Heidel, A. *The Babylonian Genesis*. Chicago: University of Chicago, 1951.

_____. *The Gilgamesh Epic and Old Testament Parallels*. Chicago: University of Chicago, 1963.

Hempel, J. "Jahwegleichnisse der Israelitische Propheten," *ZAW* 42 (1924), 74-104.

Hölscher, G. "Die Entstehung des Buches Daniel," *Th. St. und Kr.* 92 (1919), 113-138.

Horst, F. "Die Visionsschilderungen der altestamentlichen Propheten," *Ev. Th.* 20 (1960), 193-205.

_____. *Die zwölf kleinen Propheten, Nahum bis Maleachi*. HAT 14. Third Ed. Tübingen: Mohr, 1964.

Hurwitz, Avi. "The Date of the Prose-Tale of Job Linguistically Reconsidered," *HTR* 67 (1974), 17-34.

Janzen, J. Gerald. *Studies in the Text of Jeremiah*. HSM 6. Cambridge: Harvard University, 1973.

Jepsen, A. "Bemerkungen zum Danielbuch," *VT* 11 (1961), 386-391.

_____. "Kleine Beiträge zum Zwölfprophetenbuch III," *ZAW* 16
(1945-8), 95-114.

Jeremias, Christian. *Die Nachtgesichte des Sacharja.* Göttingen:
Vandenhoeck and Ruprecht, 1977.

Joüon, Paul. *Grammaire de l'Hébreu Biblique.* Rome: Pontifical
Biblical Institute, 1923.

Keel, Othmar. *Wirmächtige Siegezeichen im Alten Testament:
iconographische Studien zu Jos 8, 18-26, Ex 17, 8-13, 2
Kön 13, 14-19 und 1 Kön 22, 11.* Orbis biblicus et orien-
talis 5. Göttingen: Vandenhoeck and Ruprecht, 1974.

Köhler, A. *Der Weissagungen Sacharjas erste Hälfte Cap. 1-8.
Die nachexilischen Propheten 2.* Erlangen: Andreas Dei-
chert, 1861.

Kornfeld, Walter. "Der Symbolismus der Tempelsaulen," *ZAW* 74
(1962), 50-57.

Lambert, W. G. "The ⟪tamītu⟫ Texts," *La Divination en Mésopotamie et dans les Régions Voisines.* Paris: Universitaires
de France, 1966, pp. 119-123.

Lindblom, Johannes. *Prophecy in Ancient Israel.* Philadelphia:
Muhlenberg, 1962.

_____. "Wisdom in the Old Testament Prophets," in *Wisdom in
Israel and in the Ancient Near East,* eds. M. Noth and D.
Winton Thomas. Leiden: Brill, 1955, pp. 192-204.

Loewenstamm, S. A. כלוב קיץ לטיפולוגיה של חזרן נבואה, *Tarbiz*
34 (1964/65), 319-322.

Long, Burke O. "The Effect of Divination upon Israelite Literature," *JBL* 92 (1973), 489-497.

_____. "Reports of Visions Among the Prophets," *JBL* 95
(1976), 353-365.

_____. "Two Question and Answer Schemata in the Prophets,"
JBL 90 (1971), 129-139.

Lord, A. B. *The Singer of Tales.* New York: Atheneum, 1968.

Loud, Gordon. *The Megiddo Ivories.* University of Chicago Oriental Institute Publication 52. Chicago: University of
Chicago, 1939.

Luckenbill, D. D. *Ancient Records of Assyria and Babylonia.*
2 vols. Chicago: University of Chicago, 1927.

McKeating, Henry. *The Books of Amos, Hosea, and Micah.* Cambridge: Cambridge University, 1971.

Marti, K. *Das Dodekapropheton erklärt*. Kurzer Hand-Kommentar
zum A. T. 13. Tübingen: Mohr, 1904.

May, H. G. "A Key to the Interpretation of Zechariah's Visions,"
JBL 57 (1938), 173-184.

Meyers, Carol L. *The Tabernacle Menorah: A Synthetic Study of
a Symbol from the Biblical Cult*. ASOR Dissertation Series
2. Missoula: Scholars Press, 1976.

Milik, J. T. *The Books of Enoch*. Oxford: Clarendon, 1976.

_____. "Problèmes de la Littérature Hénochique à la Lumière
des Fragments Araméens de Qumran," *HTR* 64 (1971), 333-378.

Miller, P. "Animal Names as Designations in Ugaritic and
Hebrew," in *Ugarit-Forschungen* 2. Neukirchen-Vluyn:
Butzon and Bercker Kevelaer, 1970, pp. 177-186.

Mitchell, H. G. *A Commentary on Haggai and Zechariah*. Inter-
national Critical Commentary 25. Edinburgh: T. & T.
Clark, 1951.

Möhlenbrink, Kurt. "Der Leuchter im fünften Nachtgesicht des
Propheten Sacharja. Eine archäologische Untersuchung,"
ZDPV 52 (1929), 257-286.

Montgomery, James A. *Aramaic Incantation Texts from Nippur*.
Philadelphia: University Museum, 1923.

_____. *The Book of Daniel*. New York: Charles Scribner's
Sons, 1927.

Morgenstern, J. "The 'Son of Man' of Daniel 7 13f. A New Interpretation," *JBL* 80 (1961), 65-77.

Mowinckel, S. "Psalms and Wisdom," in *Wisdom in Israel and in
the Ancient Near East*, eds. M. Noth and D. Winton Thomas.
Leiden: Brill, 1955, pp. 205-224.

Newsome, J. D. "Toward a New Understanding of the Chronicler
and his Purpose," *JBL* 94 (1975), 201-217.

Niditch, S. and Doran, R. "The Success Story of the Wise Courtier: A Formal Approach," *JBL* 96 (1977), 179-193.

North, Robert. "Prophecy to Apocalyptic via Zechariah," *VT*
Sup. 22 (1972), 47-71.

_____. "Zechariah's Seven-Spout Lampstand," *Biblica* 51
(1970), 183-206.

Noth, M. "Die Heiligen des Höchsten," in *Gesammelte Studien
zum Alten Testament*. München: Kaiser, 1966, pp. 274-290.

_____. "Zur Komposition des Buches Daniel," *Th. St. und Kr.*
98/99 (1926), 143-163.

Nowack, W. *Die kleinen Propheten übersetzt und erklärt.* Göttingen: Vangenhoeck and Ruprecht, 1922.

Oppenheim, A. Leo. "The Eyes of the Lord," in *Essays in Memory
of E. A. Speiser,* ed. William W. Hallo. *JAOS* 88/1. New
Haven: American Oriental Society, 1968, pp. 173-180.

_____. *The Interpretation of Dreams in the Ancient Near
East.* TAPA 46/3 (1956).

_____. "Perspectives on Mesopotamian Divination," in *La
Divination en Mésopotamie et dans les Régions Voisines.*
Paris: Universitaires de France, 1966, pp. 35-43.

Petitjean, A. *Les Oracles du Proto-Zacharie: Un programme de
restauration pour la communauté juive après l'exil.* Paris:
Gabalda, 1969.

Porteous, John. *Coins.* London: Octopus Books, 1973.

Porteous, Norman W. *Daniel: A Commentary.* London: SCM, 1965.

Procksch, O. "Der Menschensohn als Gottessohn," *Christentum
und Wissenschaft* 3 (1927), 425-443.

Rahtjen, B. D. "A Critical Note on Amos 8:1-2," *JBL* 83 (1964),
416-417.

Richter, W. "Traum und Traumdeutung im Alten Testament," *BZ* 7
(1963), 202-220.

Rignell, L. B. *Die Nachtgesichte des Sacharja.* Lund: C W K
Gleerup, 1950.

Robinson, T. H. *Die zwölf kleinen Propheten, Hosea bis Micha.*
HAT 14. Third Ed. Tübingen: Mohr, 1964.

Rose, H. J. *A Handbook of Greek Mythology.* New York: Dutton,
1959.

Rost, L. "Bemerkungen zu Sacharja 4," *ZAW* 63 (1951), 216-221.

_____. "Zur Deutung des Menschensohnes in Daniel 7," in
Gott und die Götter (Festschrift für E. Fascher). Berlin:
Evangelische Verlagsanstalt, 1958, pp. 41-43.

Rothstein, D. J. W. *Die Nachtgesichte des Sacharja.* Beiträge
zur Wissenschaft vom Alten Testament 8. Leipzig: J. C.
Hinrich, 1910.

Rowley, H. H. "The Composition of the Book of Daniel," *VT* 5
(1955), 272-276.

_____. *Darius the Mede.* Cardiff: University of Wales, 1959.

_____. "The Unity of the Book of Daniel," in *The Servant of the Lord and Other Essays*. Oxford: Blackwell, 1965, pp. 249-280.

Rudolph, W. *Jeremiah*. HAT 12. Tübingen: Mohr, 1968.

Sellin, D. E. *Das Zwölfprophetenbuch*. KAT 12. Leipzig: Scholl, 1929.

Seybold, Klaus. *Bilder zum Tempelbau*. Stuttgart: KBW, 1974.

Sister, Moses. "Die Typen der prophetischen Visionen in der Bibel," *MGWJ* 78 (1934), 399-340.

Smith, Morton. *Palestinian Parties and Politics that Shaped the Old Testament*. New York: Columbia University, 1971.

Streane, A. W. *The Double Text of Jeremiah*. Cambridge: D. Bell and Co., 1896.

Talmon, S. "'Wisdom' in the Book of Esther," *VT* 13 (1963), 419-455.

Thomas, D. Winton. "A Note on מועדים in Jeremiah 24, 1," *JTS* 3 (1952), 55.

Torrey, C. C. "The Messiah Son of Ephraim," *JBL* 66 (1947), 253-277.

_____. "Poetic Passages of Daniel 1-6," *CBQ* 31 (1969), 317-326.

Turner, Victor. *The Ritual Process*. Chicago: Aldine, 1969.

Vermes, Geza. "The Present State of the 'Son of Man' Debate," *JJS* 29 (1978), 123-134.

Violet, Bruno. *Die Esra-Apokalypse (IV Esra)*. Leipzig: J. C. Hinrich, 1910.

Van Buren, E. Douglas. "Concerning the Horned Cap of the Mesopotamian Gods," *Or* 12 (1943), 318-327.

Volten, A. *Demotische Traumdeutung (Pap. Carlsberg XIII and XIV)*. Analecta Aegyptiaca 3. Kopenhagen: Munksgaard, 1942.

Volz, Paul. *Der Prophet Jeremia*. KAT 10. Leipzig: Scholl, 1928.

Weinfeld, M. "Ancient Near Eastern Patterns in Prophetic Literature," *VT* 27 (1977), 178-195.

Weiser, Artur. *Das Buch des Propheten Jeremia*. ATD 20. Göttingen: Vandenhoeck and Ruprecht, 1952.

_____. *Die Prophetie des Amos*. ZAW 53. Giessen: Töpelmann, 1929.

Wellhausen, Julius. *Die kleinen Propheten übersetzt und erk-
       lärt*. Berlin: Reimer, 1898.

Westermann, C. "Die Rolle de Klage in der Theologie des Alten
       Testament," *Gesammelte Studien II*. München: Kaiser, 1974,
       pp. 250-268.

Wilson, Robert R. "Early Israelite Prophecy," *Interpretation*
       32 (1978), 3-16.

Wolff, H. W. *Dodekapropheten, Amos*. BKAT 14. Neukirchen-
       Vluyn: Neukirchener, 1969.

Wright, G. Ernest. "The Lawsuit of God: A Form-Critical Study
       of Deuteronomy 32," in *Israel's Prophetic Heritage*, eds.
       B. W. Anderson and W. Harrelson. New York: Harper, 1962,
       pp. 26-67.

_____, *et al*. "The Significance of the Temple in the
       Ancient Near East," *BA* 7 (1944), 41-88.

Zevit, Z. "The Structure and Individual Elements of Daniel 7,"
       ZAW 80 (1968), 385-396.

Ziegler, J. *Septuaginta: Vetus Testamentum Graecum*. Göttingen:
       Vandenhoeck and Ruprecht, 1943-.

Zimmerli, Walther. *Ezekiel*. BKAT 13/1. Neukirchener-Vluyn:
       Neukirchener, 1969.